Islam in Black America

Islam in Black America

Identity, Liberation, and Difference
in African-American Islamic Thought

Edward E. Curtis IV

State University of New York Press

Published by
State University of New York Press, Albany

For information, address State University of New York Press, 90 State Street, Suite 700, Albany, NY   12207

Production by Michael Haggett
Marketing by Fran Keneston

Library of Congress Cataloging-in-Publication Data

Curtis, Edward E., IV, 1970–
   Islam in Black America: identity, liberation, and difference in
      African-American Islamic thought / Edward E. Curtis IV.
         p. cm.
   Includes bibliographical references and index.
   ISBN 0-7914-5369-3 (alk. paper)—ISBN 0-7914-5370-7
(pbk.: alk. paper)
      1. African American Muslims—History. 2. Black Muslims—History.
3. African Americans—Religion—History. 4. African Americans—
Ethnic identity. I. Title.

BP221.C87 2002
297.8′7—dc21   2002017746

         10   9   8   7   6   5   4   3   2   1

To *Walter Ray Elliston*

Contents

Acknowledgments

This book began as a doctoral dissertation, entitled "Toward an Historical Islam: Universalism and Particularism in African-American Islamic Thought," completed at the University of South Africa in the Department of Religious Studies. Its completion was—truly—a pleasurable experience due to the able guidance of my joint supervisors, Professor G. J. A. Lubbe, of the University of South Africa, and Professor Ahmet Karamustafa, director of the Religious Studies program at Washington University in St. Louis. Because of their gentle and supportive approach to the advising process, I never felt alone during the writing of this work. Professor Lubbe was always able to challenge and reassure me at the same time; and I consider myself especially fortunate to have worked with a man whose intellectual and personal contributions to the anti-apartheid movement were so courageous and unique. Shaikh Ahmet has been my teacher and adviser for many years now, and though I suspect he knows how much I respect and like him, he cannot know how much his example both as an intellectual and as a human being has inspired me. I can never repay either of my advisers for their generosity.

It is also a pleasure to thank those people who have influenced my interest in and approach to the study of religion, history, and the humanities in general. At Washington University, where I received my master's degree in history, they include Engin Akarli (now at Brown), Iver Bernstein, Howard Brick, the late Nancy Grant, and Peter Heath (now Provost of the American University of Beirut). At Kenyon College, my alma mater, they include Michael Brint, Leonard Gordon, George McCarthy, Royal Rhodes, and Vernon Schubel, who first nurtured my interest in Islam. Some other especially important teachers have been Cassie Samaha Caffery, James Caffery, Ann Garrett, the late Dexter Porter, and Donald Dow.

For reading and commenting on work related to this project, I am also grateful to Steve Angell, Henry Berger, Molly Bidwell, Alexandra Cornelius, Gerald Early, Amy Elefante, Tim Fox, Yvonne Haddad, Sylvester Johnson, Mark Kornbluh, Larry Mamiya, Sandy Martin, Maria Papacostaki, Sarah Pinnock, Mary Sawyer, Barbara von Schlegel, Ann Taves, Richard Walter, Judith Weisenfeld, and Mary Wiltenburg.

I also feel lucky to have revised this manuscript in the supportive intellectual community created by my colleagues at Trinity University's Department of Religion in San Antonio. They include Mackenzie Brown, Frank Garcia, Kris Lindbeck, Margaret Miksch, Randy Nadeau, Sarah Pinnock, Jeremy Rehwaldt-Alexander, Mary Ellen Ross, and Bill Walker.

I also want to thank those persons in the St. Louis Muslim community who first inspired me to dig more deeply into the history of African-American Islamic thought, including Imam Muhammad Nur Abdallah, Imam Samuel Ansari, Ahmed Ghani, Lorene Ghani, Khadijah Mahdi, Abdul Shabazz, Kareem Shabazz, and Abdul Shakir.

Finally, I acknowledge my parents, Ed Earl III and Susie Saffa, and my sister, Cassie, for their support and love. And I thank my adopted family for the same, especially Regan, Gordon, and Steve. I dedicate this book with love and respect to Dr. Walt, who has been my steadfast friend since seventh grade.

Usage

Following the *Chicago Manual of Style,* I have avoided, as much as possible, using diacritical markings in my transliteration of Arabic terms. In general, I have italicized any Arabic word when first introduced and thereafter reproduced it in normal print. I have also added an English translation of the word or concept in order to aid the reader. Finally, I have tried to preserve the sometimes differing transliterations of Arabic terms offered by the subjects of this study, while making it clear exactly what he or she meant by its use. In this, I have followed the precedent that, given the lack of any truly correct method of reproducing Islamic terms into English, scholars should be sensitive to the varying ways in which English-speaking Muslims themselves do so.

Chapter 1

Introduction

This book examines a tension common within the history of religions. The tension exists between the idea, on the one hand, that a religious tradition is *universally* applicable to the experience of all human beings and the idea, on the other hand, that a religious tradition is applicable to the experience of one *particular* group of human beings. The history of African-American Islam provides an especially useful vantage point from which to view this problem, since it has been so central to both African-American religion and American Islam. More specifically, this work seeks to explore the tension between universalism and particularism by analyzing the thought of five prominent black figures, including Edward W. Blyden, Noble Drew Ali, Elijah Muhammad, Malcolm X, and Wallace D. Muhammad. Understanding these thinkers in their respective historical contexts, which have been characterized by the struggle for black liberation and the continuous reconstruction of black identity, I explain when and how they came to understand Islam as a tradition for all human beings, a tradition for only black human beings, and sometimes, a combination of both.

This introductory chapter outlines the theoretical assumptions that underlie my argument and specifies how this study offers new ways of viewing African-American Islam. The first section argues against the static treatment of African-American Islam as "religion" in favor of a more dynamic definition of Islam as "tradition." Then, in order to develop a broader theoretical framework and show the relevance of this work to Islamic studies more generally, the second section examines the tension between universalism and particularism with reference to classical Islamic history. Finally, I discuss more fully the problem of studying universalism and particularism in African-American Islam and provide an outline of my argument.

DEFINING ISLAM AS TRADITION

In order to examine African-American Islam in new ways, one must note the lasting influence of C. Eric Lincoln's classic *The Black Muslims in America* on all scholarship related to Islam in black America. While more recent studies of African-American Islam add greatly to our knowledge of specific movements, historical events, and new sources for the study of African-American Islam, none has yet replaced Lincoln's work as the authoritative source on either the Nation of Islam or African-American Islam more generally.[1] Now in its third edition, the book still captures the most scholarly attention, despite the fact that it discounts the "religiosity" of the movement.[2] Viewing the Nation of Islam from a functionalist perspective, Lincoln argued that religious elements of the movement, including its Islamic "mystique," were incidental to its success. In his view, "religious values" had a "secondary importance." In fact, Lincoln said, "[t]hey are not part of the movement's basic appeal, except to the extent that they foster and strengthen the sense of group solidarity." Focusing on the various sociological factors that "pushed" disenfranchised blacks toward the Nation of Islam, Lincoln argued that the movement's success stemmed primarily from its ability to create an exclusionary sense of community among its members. For Lincoln, this was the essence of black nationalism.[3]

Lincoln's argument is especially important for this study since he seemed to distinguish "politics" from "religion" as if the two were diametrically opposed, as if politics were this-worldly and religion were otherworldly. Lincoln's definition of religion seemed to assume that "true" religion dealt mainly with issues of theology, salvation, and meaning, a definition seemingly shaped by Lincoln's own Protestant Christianity. His use of religion and politics as analytical categories ultimately obscured more than they revealed since he underemphasized the legitimately religious aspects of the movement's nationalistic activity. In reality, of course, the line between religion and politics was and is often more blurry than he indicated. Indeed, politics and religion were wedded in fascinating and problematical ways within the movement.

Lincoln, however, was not the only scholar of his generation to define religion in this way. Clifford Geertz's famous definition of religion was, in a similar fashion, highly reflective of "Enlightenment Christianity." As Talal Asad has shown, however, "religion" has not always been equated with belief or conscience as it has been in the modern age. In the European Middle Ages, for instance, religion often translated into intellectual and social discipline in submission to the authority of the Roman Catholic Church. The more contemporary definition emerged in early modern Europe. By the time of Immanuel Kant, religion came to be defined as a kind of belief that could withstand the criticism of reason and nature. "From being a concrete set of practical rules attached to specific processes of power and knowledge," Asad argued, "religion has come to be abstracted and universalized." Clifford Geertz's definition of religion reflected these modern biases, according to Asad, since Geertz viewed religion as a belief system designed ultimately to confront questions of meaning.[4] As Abdulkader Tayob summarizes, Geertz's approach meant that "[r]eligion as political practice or religion as social action could not constitute its core, essential characteristic. Any religious act that had a direct political intention was regarded as the political abuse of religion."[5] While this definition of "religion" as quest for meaning was not unreasonable in a modern context, said Asad, it should not be assumed to be true for all times and places.

Asad's analysis also raises an important question about whether the word "religion" in its modern usage adequately captures what the word "Islam" has meant to various Muslims throughout the past fourteen hundred years, including African-American Muslims. Etymologically speaking, *islam* most strictly refers to a spiritual state coterminous with the submission of all creatures to God. At the same time, Muslims have also referred to Islam as "religion" or *din,* a word that encompasses the obligations imposed by God upon human beings. But the word "Islam" has been used even more broadly to refer to social, political, and economic institutions, groups, and ideas—see, for example, "Islamic banking" or "the Islamic jihad." Modern Muslims, in particular, often speak of Islam not only as a personal creed or internal state of submission, but also as a social and political body of peoples, countries, and states. Some, like the Muslim Brothers of Egypt, have made famous the assertion that there is no separation in Islam between *din* and *dawla,* or religion and state. *Islam,* they argue, is both. Despite the fact that this definition ignores the historical split between *din* and *dawla* in Islamic history, it can be regarded as valid as any other definition of Islam.[6]

Given the theoretical problems and ambiguity involved in analyzing Islam as a "religion," I prefer to explore its history as that of a "tradition."

Admittedly, this change poses equally daunting methodological problems. But in making the semantic shift, I hope to emphasize the changing nature of Islamic tradition, its dynamism, and the provisional character of its elements. In so doing, I borrow in part from Alasdair MacIntyre's definition of a *living* tradition as "an historically extended, socially embodied argument, and an argument precisely in part about the goods which constitute that tradition."[7] For my purposes, tradition is not an historical product so much as an historical process in which human beings, interacting with each other in discrete social contexts, invent, embrace, and inherit *something* that they care about and argue over, whether explicitly or not. I say "something" because what it is that people create and pass along is never completely clear. While a tradition may seem to contain distinguishing characteristics and constitutive elements, including certain questions, ideas, rituals, and symbols, these "things" are always subject to alteration, reinterpretation, and abandonment.

This approach, however, begs the question of whether there are any limits or boundaries that define a tradition and set it apart from another— a question that continues to haunt Islamic studies or "Orientalism," which was founded partly on the premise that certain essential elements of the tradition are to be found in Islam's elite textual discourses. In his well-known essay about unity and variety in Islam, for example, Gustave von Grunebaum depicted Islam as a "universal culture whose essential tenets and values are, consciously at least, not to be compromised."[8] Von Grunebaum was a civilizationist who, according to Edmund Burke III, privileged the "high cultural artifacts of the major literary traditions." By examining them, he sought to discover the "timeless essences" of Islam that predetermined its fate from the "moment of [their] inception."[9] This approach often meant that once the Islamicist had been trained in these textual traditions, he or she could then track the spread of Islam by studying the degree to which "local" cultures adopted, corrupted, and/or rejected these "essential" elements. The central plot of Islamic studies thus became the clash between "Muslim civilization" and local cultures, between the universal and the provincial. While this type of Orientalism raised a number of problematic empirical issues, it also crossed an ethical line, since it placed scholars in the position of determining the essential, and by implication, the true Islam.

If one's goal is to avoid such essentialism in Islamic studies, there is not and cannot be any *one* normative definition of Islamic tradition or its boundaries and limits. But scholars can identify competing definitions of Islam by examining the historical interpretations of Muslims themselves.

As mentioned above, the most visible tradition in the Euro-American study of Islam, which is sometimes mistakenly seen to represent all of "Islam," has been the discourse in which the Qur'an and the Sunna are treasured as paramount sources of divine authority. For Islamicist Marshall Hodgson, the centrality of these texts and Muslim responses to them can be seen as the result of a threefold process of tradition-making. First, said Hodgson, came Muhammad's creative action, or "an occasion of fresh awareness of something ultimate in the relation between ourselves and the cosmos." Next, he argued, there was a group commitment to this creative action, so that Islam came to "be defined as commitment to the venture to which Muhammad's vision was leading: which meant, concretely, allegiance to Muhammad and his Book and then to the continuing community of Muhammad." Finally, there was "cumulative interaction, which eventually produces dispute." In fact, he said, "within the dialogue launched by the advent of Islam, almost from the start there came to be conflicting sets of presuppositions about what Islam should involve." These disputes, however, did not make impossible the unity of Muslims, which continued to be guaranteed by their commitment to "an initial point of departure." This commonality, according to Hodgson, led to the "integrality of dialogue that can provide an intelligible framework for the historical study" of Islam.[10] The history of Islam, then, is in part that of one "discursive tradition" that Muslims have constantly redefined and contested over time and in space through an "interaction with sacred texts and with the history of that interaction."[11] This definition of one, if not the most salient Islamic tradition also takes into account the historical reality that Muslims have supported competing and contrasting approaches to the most basic issues of authority and textual interpretation from the very beginning of their history in seventh-century Arabia.

Moreover, this definition of Islamic tradition does not establish any common norms, values, or beliefs, other than the centrality of the Qur'an and the Sunna—which is not to say that other commonalities have not existed in Islamic history. But it does suggest that any tradition which is truly universal, as the Qur'an nearly is to all self-identifying Muslims, is bound, in Ernesto Laclau's words, to have no "necessary body and no necessary content; different groups, instead, compete among themselves to temporarily give their particularisms a function of universal representation." In many cases, states Laclau, one group may attempt to exclude or subordinate another group by positioning itself as the only legitimate spokesperson for the "universal." Put another way, Laclau asserts that "[t]he universal . . . does not have a concrete content of its own (which would close it in itself) but is the always receding horizon resulting from the expansion of an indefinite chain of equivalent demands." These demands are the result of competition among people who attempt to define what the universal element of culture (here sacred texts) means in a given historical context; or as Laclau puts it, "[s]ociety generates a whole vocabulary of empty signifiers whose temporary signifieds are the result of political competition."[12]

The essential point is that any tradition, whether religious or not, is fashioned by human beings, who operate in historical time. "What people of faith share," Wilfred Cantwell Smith argued, "is not necessarily common definitions of what their religion means, but a common history." Hence, no person should be understood simply as a product of his or her tradition, but rather as a participant in that tradition. Faith is not "generated and sustained and shaped" by a religious tradition, according to Smith; rather, a person's faith is the result of his or her participation in "one historical phase" of an ongoing process. Moreover, these processes cannot be "reified" or "precisely delimited."[13] To take this reasoning to its logical conclusion, I would argue that the student of Islam should not even insist on using a person's identification with the Qur'an as a kind of minimal definition of what it means to be a Muslim. Instead, wherever and whenever a person calls himself or herself Muslim, scholars should include this person's voice in their understanding of what constitutes Islam. The mere fact that one has labeled oneself a Muslim indicates some sort of participation, however slight, in the process of Islamic history. That participation, in my view, is worthy of both scholarly attention, and in Hodgson's words, "human respect and recognition."[14]

In fact, the study of African-American Islam has been too consumed with dismissing certain Muslims as cultists, heretics, and sectarians.[15] All of these pejorative and unhelpful labels presume, by their comparison to "orthodox" Muslims, a normative Islam that in no time and in no place has ever existed. Rather, if we adopt W. C. Smith's approach, it is more useful to ask how African Americans have participated in the historical process of being a Muslim. What has Islam meant to them? What exactly is their connection to Islamic traditions in the Old World? Some scholars and many African Americans themselves understand their Islamic faith as being rooted in premodern African Islamic traditions. My own approach, which differs from those who see larger continuities between African Islam and African-American Islam, proceeds from the assumption that most African Americans have had little historical connection to any form of premodern Islam. Though many African slaves were Muslims and a number of them continued to practice Islam once in North America, African Muslim slaves never cohered into an American community of faith that passed on its traditions from one generation to the next.[16] The result is that when African Americans began to convert to Islam during this century, their connection to the ongoing discursive traditions in Islamic lands, including traditional sources of Islamic knowledge, was extremely tenuous and limited.

In turn, this fact made it easy for the first English-speaking black theorists of Islam, especially Noble Drew Ali and Elijah Muhammad, to define Islam without facing the criticism of most fellow Muslims. As more and more Muslim immigrants and missionaries made an impact on American and African-American Islam, however, their systems of thought came under increased scrutiny. It was at this point that Elijah Muhammad, in particular, attempted to utilize sacred texts in supporting his own system of thought. As this occurred, a larger debate about the place of difference within Islam ensued between Muhammad and his critics. But this type of debate was nothing new to the history of Islam. Indeed, a tension between universalism and particularism was present from the very beginning of Islamic history, a subject to which I now turn.

UNIVERSALISM AND PARTICULARISM IN CLASSICAL ISLAM

This tension between universalism and particularism in classical Islam can be observed in disputes over the meaning of egalitarianism and hierarchy within early Islamic society. Muslims debated whether the egalitarian tones of the Qur'an were meant to challenge the social hierarchies so prevalent within Islamdom. For the Qur'an proclaimed in 49:13 that God "made you into *shu'ub* (peoples) and *qaba'il* (tribes, ancestral groups) that you may know one another. The most noble among you in the sight of God is the most pious." While most commentators interpreted this verse to support an egalitarian ideal of "individual salvation," there was disagreement over whether "it also carried implications for social organisation in the here and now." In fact, while some interpreters used Qur'an 49:13 to champion this-worldly egalitarianism, the majority of commentators like Al-Tabari mentioned only its other-worldly implications, leaving particularistic social hierarchies unchallenged.[17]

This tension between the egalitarian and the hierarchical could be seen quite vividly in debates over the importance of tribal affiliation.

Because Islam began in the midst of strong tribal rivalries, much of the Prophet Muhammad's genius lay in trying to unite different Arab tribes under the banner of Islam, which was supratribal. Despite the Prophet's efforts, however, tribal conflict continued to characterize much of early Islamic history. Rivalries between Arab tribes often resulted in poetic forms of "boasting or deprecation," including forms of racial or ethnic prejudice. In addition to this tribalism, yet another manifestation of the tension between the egalitarian and the hierarchical was the friction between Arab and non-Arab Muslims in the nascent Muslim state. Because Islam also became "a badge of united Arabism, the code and discipline of a conquering elite," Arabs often claimed superior social status in the new Islamic order. This association of Islam with Arab culture had staying power and to a certain extent remained viable until the middle period, by which time other languages like Persian usurped the role of Arabic as the dominant language of political discourse. Throughout much of early Islamic history, including both the Umayyad and Abbasid caliphates, many claimed that "the Arabs were supreme among the nations." The reasons cited included the fact that the Prophet himself was an Arab; that the Qur'an was revealed in Arabic; and even that Bedouin culture surpassed all others in its hospitality and eloquence.[18]

That this arabocentrism conflicted with egalitarian views of many Muslims can be seen clearly in a story related by Louise Marlow about Bilal ibn Rabah, an Abyssinian freedman who became a companion of the Prophet and the first *muadhdhin,* or prayer-caller, of Islam. The story is that the caliph 'Umar invited Bilal into his presence before inviting Abu Sufyan, who was a member of the Quraysh, the tribe of the Prophet. When Abu Sufyan complained, an associate of the Caliph replied that "'you [Quraishis] should blame yourselves, not the Commander of the Faithful. [These] people were called [to Islam], and they responded, while you, who were also invited, rejected the summons. On the Day of Resurrection, they [will be] of greater degrees and more favour.'" To this, Abu Sufyan answered that "'[t]here is no good in a place where Bilal is [considered] noble (sharif).'" The general tenor of the story is transparent: ethnic and social status theoretically counted less than individual piety in the all-important issue of access to the center of political power. In this story, however, Abu Sufyan, a member of the Prophet's own tribe, dismissed this idea as he clung to notions of Arab superiority and privilege.[19]

One tangible political challenge to this ethnocentrism arose in the middle of the seventh century, when a group called the Kharijis protested against what they saw as the "reemergence of traditional Arab elements" in the selection of the leader of the faithful. That person, they said, should be the Muslim believer who is most pious, regardless of his (or, in some cases, her) social status. According to Hamid Dabashi, "[t]heir famous motto that anyone, even an Abyssinian slave, could become a caliph quite emphatically attested to, among other things, their total rejection of the traditional aristocratic criterion adopted by the Muslim majority." In justifying their arguments, Kharijis also drew on a report of the Prophet's farewell sermon, which quoted Muhammad as saying that "God has removed from you baseless pride of the period of ignorance and its glorying in ancestors. You are all from Adam and Adam was from the dust. The Arab has no superiority to the non-Arab except by virtue of righteousness." In fact, the Shabibiyah Kharijis took this egalitarian notion of Muslim leadership to include women in addition to men.[20]

On the whole, however, the Kharijis stressed that the question of leadership within the Islamic community should not be colored by issues of tribal affiliation or geographic origin. Khariji egalitarianism fueled much political revolt, especially in North Africa, where Kharijism was adopted to oppose Umayyad prejudice against the local Berbers. In A.D. 869, black slaves also revolted in Iraq under the leadership of a Khariji and established a state. Ironically, they tried to enslave their former slaveholders. This phenomenon raised the question of just how deeply many of these revolts were infused with the Khariji spirit of egalitarianism. In fact, some writers argued that most African and black Muslims adopted Kharijism merely as a rallying cry, without any knowledge of Khariji *fiqh*, or jurisprudence. As Al-Khirrit declared, "I have become Khariji, because they stand for *shura* [consultation between the ruler and the ruled] among men" and not presumably for any other reason.[21]

The radical egalitarianism of the Kharijis also had an ugly side, which was expressed in their moral absolutism. The great irony of the Kharijis is that while they insisted upon equality among believers with regard to rights of leadership, they rejected tolerance or even compassion as a virtue. Most believed that *jama'a*, or communal unity, must never come before *din*, or the obligations imposed on humans by God. In addition, most Kharijis often regarded *islam* and *iman* (faith) as one and the same, asserting that the "one who deviates from Iman, *ipso facto*, deviates from Islam and becomes an unbeliever." In practice, this view led to continual war against their own leaders and much of the Muslim community. Any Khariji leader who was found out as a sinner was to be rejected immediately. From the early days of the Kharijis, then, many Kharijis "began to brand everyone infidel . . . who did not accept their point of view."[22]

So, while the Kharijis battled tribal and Arab particularism, they also created their own form of moral absolutism, which was yet another form of particularism. While they invested this moral particularism with the "function of universalism," which in this case was the struggle for egalitarianism, its effect seemed to be more exclusionary and less humane than the emerging Sunni (majoritarian) Islamic order. Kharijis tried to define what was universal about Islam, like the idea that any righteous man or woman could become leader of the community, but did so in a way that refused to accept any alternate means for determining who should lead the Muslim community. While attractive to several groups, Kharijism ended up being—in political terms—a relatively unsuccessful series of movements. Too much internal conflict and unrealistic expectations of human goodness made it impossible for them to have more than a modest, if important impact against the more powerful forces of the early Muslim confederacy and the Umayyad and Abbasid dynasties. In the meantime, some of the very ideas against which they battled, especially the arabocentrism of the political elites, continued to dominate the formation of Muslim society.

Kharijism was not, however, the only response to this phenomenon. As the Abbasid dynasty grew to incorporate much of the Persian aristocracy of Khurasan into its new state apparatus, a new movement called the *shu'ubiyya* (roughly translated, the people's movement) arose to challenge the arabocentrism so central to the classic period. In fact, the Abbasid dynasty could be seen to be a result of the alliance between Arab "colonists" and Persian aristocracy. Some of these Persian elites utilized Sasanian court literature to denigrate and mock Arabs as a way of challenging Arab dominance. But these Shu'ubiyya had very little interest in a truly egalitarian Islam, often exalting the Persian literary traditions above all else. Using sarcasm to criticize Arab traditions, some poets and men of letters also reintroduced Manicheanism as a challenge to the Qur'an itself.[23]

Though embracing a title for their movement that would seem to indicate an interest in egalitararism, a belief in social hierarchy ran deep among the movement's ideologues. "[T]he Shu'ubi poets . . . are arguing, at most, for a parity of honor among the upper classes of two distinct peoples," claimed Roy Mottahedeh. While most Shu'ubi commentators argued that God viewed righteousness as the paramount criterion in establishing a human's worth, they also agreed that beneath this lay whole sets of social and political hierarchies to be viewed as "obvious" in determining one's place in worldly life. "Although the *shu'ubiyyah* has sometimes been loosely labeled an egalitarian movement . . . we have seen that the *shuʻubiyya* controversy soon reflected rival principles of social hierarchy." Humans may be equal before God, the argument went, but they are not equal before other humans, as Ibn ʻAbbas declared: "The nobility (*karam*) of this world is wealth (*ghina*) and of the next is righteousness (*taqwa*)."[24]

In this case, as with the Kharijis, a movement that arose to challenge certain prejudices within the new Islamic order ended up taking on the form of a particularism that was both exclusionary and hierarchical. This phenomenon also occurred much later in African-American Islam, which produced similarly particularistic calls for radical segregation and exclusion. One wonders, with Ernesto Laclau above, if such a phenomenon is not simply inevitable. If, as Laclau argues, the "universal" is usually an expression of one form of particularism that temporarily becomes dominant as a result of political competition, any brand of universalism in theory may remain a dream and in political reality may become a form of totalitarianism. Such an argument can be detected in the work of many students of imperialism, like Edward Said, who associates European hegemony with forms of "universalizing" scholarship.[25] But the prejudice of the Kharijis and the Shuʻubiyya depended not only on the assertion of their viewpoint as the most *universal*, but on other theoretical bases as well. In the case of the Kharijis, their total lack of any moral relativism translated into an absolutism that was devoid of compassion. The Shuʻubiyya refusal, on the other hand, to question their own notions of hierarchy meant that egalitarianism was a mere cover for their own particularistic interests.

It is, in fact, the ambiguity of the "universal" that provides various social actors with numerous strategic opportunities. For the oppressed, universalism can become a vehicle to articulate a more truly egalitarian social order. In African-American history, for example, leaders like Frederick Douglass and Martin Luther King, Jr., appropriated the universalism of American revolutionary ideals to fight for black liberation. Their actions show the power of employing an alternate "signified" or definition of the universal in challenging oppression and exclusion. Sometimes, the source of the "new" universalism may come from the very tradition that is seen as exclusionary. The Kharijis relied, for example, on Qurʼan and Sunnah, traditions that they both shared with their enemies and simultaneously used to oppose them. Other times, the source of the "new" universalism may be a critique that is made by using a foreign tradition, as was the case with the Persian literary challenge to arabocentrism in the Shuʻubiyyah movement.

Both of these patterns occur in the history of African-American Islamic thought, where alternate definitions of dominant universalisms (like Christianity and American revolutionary ideals) are combined with "foreign" forms of universalism (like Islam).

UNIVERSALISM AND PARTICULARISM IN AFRICAN-AMERICAN ISLAM

At first glance, it might be tempting to conclude that the tension between universalism and particularism in African-American Islamic thought is, by definition, a tension between *Islamic universalism* and *black particularism.* Such a formulation might posit that because Islam, by its very essence, is a universalistic creed, African-American Muslims were bound to face problems in creating any version of Islam that was both true to the "essence" of Islam and relevant to their particular experiences as African Americans. In reality, however, that formula is far too simplistic, because as has been shown in the previous sections, it utilizes an essentialist definition of Islam that ignores the historical debates among Muslims themselves regarding whether Islam is a universalistic tradition. Because Islam can signify whatever its confessors wish, it need not be identified with all of humankind as a group. In its classical period, for example, many Muslims felt it to be inseparable from Arab culture. Likewise, in more modern times, many African-American Muslims have viewed it as synonymous with being black. Hence, one can say for these Muslims that there was not any tension whatsoever between being part of a *particular* group of human beings and being Muslim; for them, it was one and the same.

However, when Islam has been embraced by Muslims as a universalistic tradition, questions about the meaning of diversity and difference have emerged with special urgency—in classical Islam as well as in African-American Islam. These questions have involved a number of different issues, including variation in ritual practice and belief as well as social justice and politics. In North America, as Haddad and Smith point out, contemporary Muslim debate often focuses on "how not to compromise the ideal of unity in Islam while still maintaining some degree of ethnic identity and cultural affiliation."[26] Many times, this debate becomes one over the question of what exactly constitutes "identity and culture" versus what constitutes proper Islamic belief and observance. But the root of the problem lies in the question of how much difference of any sort can be incorporated or tolerated within a tradition that is seen as universally applicable to all human beings, regardless of race, nation, ethnicity, or any other identifier. The same tension can be observed in African-American Christianity, which like African-American Islam has emerged in an historical context where race and racism have been central to the formation of nearly every aspect of the culture.[27]

It is this historical context of racism and racial difference that produced an unstable environment for the rise of a universalistic Islam within black America. Given this, it might seem unlikely that African-American Muslims would entertain any universalistic interpretations of Islam at all. And yet they have done so from the very beginning of their history as Muslim converts: African-American Islamic universalism has been a remarkably idealistic expression of the hope for human equality and dignity. It should not come as a great surprise, however, that the allure of particularistic interpretations of Islam has been stronger during certain moments in American history. Generally speaking, any fissure in human community, especially when involving a lack of equity, can lead easily to a challenge of universalism, whose ideals seem like unfulfilled promises or even propaganda to the oppressed. In this environment, a particularistic response that supports the humanity and solidarity of the oppressed can arise as an implicit challenge to the hollow universalism of the oppressors.

As mentioned above, C. Eric Lincoln understood the particularistic response advocated by the Nation of Islam as a form of black nationalism. He used that term rather broadly, emphasizing the elements of black nationalism that fostered a sense of group solidarity among African Americans in a hostile environment. In the latter 1960s and throughout the 1970s, some scholars of the black experience seemed to take Lincoln's definition of nationalism even further, equating black nationalism with nearly any "form of group behavior or expression of group sentiment." One scholar, for example, defined black nationalism as "the feeling on the part of black individuals that they are responsible for the welfare of other black individuals . . . because of a shared racial heritage and destiny." While this trend continued into the 1980s, more recent scholarship in black studies has problematized the use of nationalism as an intellectual category, paying more attention to the historically specific and contested meanings of "nation" to persons of African descent.[28] Likewise, this study attempts to employ ideas of nation and nationalism with the same historical precision.

But "nation" and "nationalism" are not the only problematic categories in the study of African-American Islam. Similarly, "race" and "racialism" can raise equally important methodological concerns. Most scholars no longer assume that race is a biological phenomenon. In fact, historians, sociologists, and other scholars of the American experience have asserted more and more that race is most properly understood as a social construction. Simply put, these scholars usually assert that "race is socially constructed insofar as selected physical characteristics [like the color of one's skin] have social meaning." Moreover, the social meaning of race is often tied to the structure of status and power among individuals and groups more generally. Of course, scholars still argue about how exactly race is related to issues of class, gender, and other sociological categories. But at the present moment, race is increasingly seen as the product of racialization, a social process which can affect nearly every aspect of one's life—where a person lives, the person whom one marries, and where one goes to school, among other factors. Like "nation," race is seen as a social construct whose most basic meanings can shift, depending on the historical contexts in which the term is being used.[29]

Rather than uncritically labeling certain varieties of African-American Islam as either nationalist or racialist, I have more generically labeled them particularistic. In my view, this term allows for the theoretical ambiguity necessary in describing the diverse and ultimately disputed meanings of blackness espoused by the subjects of this study. In employing this label, I mean to indicate only that these figures, like many other black persons in the modern world, have held in common a sense that they are part of a distinct group—they have shared, in others words, a sense of their own *particularity*. But what this particular identity actually means or signifies is never completely clear or stable, because the historical actors themselves constantly debate and contest the ideological bonds that hold them together. The category of particularism is methodologically useful because it can incorporate the various and ultimately ambiguous meanings of blackness that arise in this common historical universe.

These debates over the meaning of black identity have revolved around a large number of issues, including ongoing disputes about what name or label should be applied to African Americans as a group. In the past two hundred years, a number of candidates have vied for recognition, including Anglo-African, colored, free African, Black,' Negro, Afro-American, African-American, African American, and so on.[30] Moreover, for over two centuries African Americans have disagreed about other aspects of black identity, including the issue of whether the meaning of blackness is primarily biological, historical, and/or theological in nature. Being "black" has also been seen as invoking shared language, symbols, memories, myths, and lifeways. As will be shown in the following chapters, these contests over the meaning of black identity were central to the unfolding of African-American Islamic thought.

A second and related theme in the history of African-American Islamic thought is the struggle for black liberation.[31] All of the figures covered in this study, like many other modern black persons, have sought to liberate themselves and their fellows from some form of oppression. But their understandings of this oppression and their strategies for liberation from it have been incredibly diverse and complex. Here I refer not only to formal political involvement, but to all acts of liberation, including those that might be seen by some as apolitical. For example, I view the nineteenth-century African-American tradition of Ethiopianism as a form of black liberation. Founded upon the prophecy in Psalm 68:31 that "princes shall come out of Egypt, and Ethiopia shall soon stretch forth her hand unto God," Ethiopianism often focused on black suffering as a sign of divine favor. Its advocates also utilized biblical themes of exile and redemption to posit the imminent arrival of a personal savior or prophet and sometimes argued for a belief in the redemptive mission of the black race as a whole.[32]

By situating African-American Islamic thought amidst major historical themes of the modern black experience, this study proceeds along the assumption that any comprehensive understanding of the topic must analyze the relationships between the historical actors and the larger contexts in which they wrote and spoke. Moreover, my use of categories like universalism and particularism has emerged from an historical reading of the data. Put another way, the main methodological assumption of this book is that the tension between *various forms* of particularism and universalism in African-American Islamic thought is a historical phenomenon. It is a tension created, sustained, and sometimes dismissed by African Americans themselves. This is not to say that the historical actors explicitly refer to these terms. But as categories of analysis, universalism and particularism become real when subjected to historical scrutiny. In my view, phenomenological categories, if used at all, should always be tempered by such historical inquiry.

From the beginning of African-American Islam, I argue, there existed both universalistic and particularistic impulses, first expressed in the paradoxical and ambiguous thought of both Edward W. Blyden and Noble Drew Ali. Elijah Muhammad then attempted to rid African-American Islam of any paradox or ambiguity, eventually advancing an entirely par-

ticularistic interpretation of Islam. Malcolm X, however, rejected Elijah
Muhammad's absolutism, and in so doing, once again faced the tension
between universalism and particularism. But he was assassinated before he
could explore fully his own approach to these issues. In the 1970s, Wallace
D. Muhammad, the son of Elijah, sought to transform this intellectual
legacy by suggesting a new approach to the question of unity and diversity
within Islam. By viewing Islam through the lens of its various historical
contexts, Wallace Muhammad suggested a new model that incorporated
racial, ethnic, and national difference under an umbrella of Islamic unity.

It should be noted that my focus on five black thinkers—all obviously
male—has its limitations. While this work hopes to offer new directions
for the study of African-American Islam, it is by no means a comprehensive history of the various Islamic movements in black America. I have
focused on these figures both because of their crucial role in the formation
of African-American Islam and because of the irreplaceable quality and
originality of their thought. In addition, these men have produced the
primary source material necessary to any textual study. In fact, most have
been quite prolific, excepting Noble Drew Ali who left us only the *Holy
Koran of the Moorish Science Temple*. All others have published numerous
works, making it possible to explain how their thought both changed and
stayed the same usually over a period of decades. To reconstruct the contexts in which they wrote, spoke, and published, I have also relied on a
number of other sources, including African-American Muslim newspapers, FBI documents, mainstream press accounts, secondary sources, and
oral histories.

My study begins with an examination of Liberian nationalist Edward
Wilmot Blyden, a Caribbean émigré who became a leading intellectual
and political figure in the black Atlantic world of the late nineteenth century. Blyden, who never converted to Islam himself, was exposed to Islam
through his travels in the Middle East and his interaction with Muslim
"natives" in the West African interior. As a result, he appropriated Islam in
a largely polemical way both to criticize white Protestant missionaries and
to encourage the development of black nationalism. Blyden argued that
Islam, rather than Christianity, would lead to African self-determination,
racial equality, and black greatness. Sometimes, Blyden explained the salutary effects of Islam on blacks by arguing that blacks were by nature better
suited to Islam. Other times, however, he stressed the universalistic qualities of Islam, implying that Islam's message of human equality and justice
applied to black people as well as everyone else. The contradictions that
these definitions of Islam produced are explored in chapter 2.

While Blyden's promotion of Islam made him a rogue figure in the eyes of most black Christians, his use of Ethiopianism showed just how much he was part of the same modern black culture. In fact, across the Atlantic in black America, Ethiopianist themes had already become central to the theological discourse of the post-Reconstruction African-American Church, especially the Black Baptist and Methodist denominations. There, these ideas found a large audience not only among black intellectuals, but also among the literally millions of African Americans whose lives revolved around the Black Church during the nadir in race relations from 1880 to 1920. During this period, as Evelyn Brooks Higginbotham has demonstrated, the Black Church provided an alternate public sphere where black economic, political, and social life could find shelter from Jim Crow, disenfranchisement, and despair. In these years, the Black Church reigned as *the* popular cultural institution in black America.[33]

During the great migration of African Americans to the urban North between World War I and World War II, however, modern black advocates of Islam and others challenged the ubiquity of the Black Church by providing alternative discourses and social spaces. African-American Muslims reinterpreted many black Christian themes within a new Islamic matrix. Noble Drew Ali, the subject of chapter 3, was the first African American to appropriate Islam in such a way. Ali's religious system, however, owed nothing to the Islamic textual traditions of Qur'an and Sunnah. Rather, Ali combined themes from black messianism and Islamic symbols from the black Shriners with the teachings of several modern esoteric traditions, including both Theosophy and Rosicrucianism, to construct what he called "Moorish Science." Rejecting the existence of a specifically African racial heritage, he argued that African Americans were Moorish nationals who drew their biological lineage from a more generic Asiatic race. Though Moors possessed a unique national heritage, according to Noble Drew, they shared a common religion, Islam, with all nations of Asiatic descent. Drew Ali, too, was interested in world harmony, although his version of Islam also entertained particularistic notions that contradicted his universalism.

In studying Noble Drew Ali, I initially hoped to show some continuity between his thought and that of Edward Blyden. In this regard, I examined the role of Marcus Garvey's United Negro Improvement Association (UNIA) as a potential conduit in spreading Blyden's pro-Islamic polemic throughout black America during the 1920s. Alas, I could find little direct connection between Blyden and Ali. Furthermore, while the UNIA became one place where African Americans discussed Islam,

Garvey himself only adopted Blyden's ideas regarding race, even though he was intimately familiar with the African sage's advocacy of Islam. Indeed, there was much more than geographical distance that separated Drew Ali from Blyden. Blyden was a member of the elite black Atlantic intelligentsia of the latter half of the 1800s, whereas Drew Ali was a part of the urban black working class to have emerged during the Great Migration. Blyden had easy access to educational and cultural resources, including the Old World traditions of Islamic education, while Drew Ali seemed to have learned what he knew mostly from American popular culture. In part, Drew Ali's importance for this study is not that he disseminated traditional Islamic ideas in black America but that he launched "Islam" as a black particularistic tradition in the United States. At the same time, how he came to define Islam had reverberations throughout African-American Islamic history. For Ali, Islam was synonymous with the identity of people of color, who could ignore their "natural" religion only at their own peril. This became an important precedent that found a powerful spokesperson in Elijah Muhammad.

In fact, the expansion of Ali's black separatist Islamic tradition owes much to Muhammad, who led the most popular black Islamic movement in the history of African-American Islam. Chapter 4 explores the thought of this seminal figure by examining the development of his unique version of Islam within several historical contexts. I demonstrate, for example, how Muhammad combined the Christian dispensationalism of his youth with elements of Islam, a belief in "clean living," and even a post-World War II fascination with UFOs to create a new African-American Islamic tradition. I also show the pivotal role played by non-movement black converts to Islam, immigrant Muslims, and foreign Muslims in the genealogy of Muhammad's thought. In the late 1950s, these Muslims publicly questioned the Islamic legitimacy of Muhammad's teachings. They directed their criticism at the movement's claims of divinity for Nation of Islam (NOI) founder W. D. Fard, at Elijah Muhammad's own status as Messenger, and at the racist aspects of his Islamic thought, all of which they said contradicted the universal message of Islam. As a result, Muhammad's chief lieutenant, Malcolm X, sought to legitimate the movement's teachings by both questioning the motives and credentials of the critics and by mining proof texts from the Qur'an.

I argue that this latter act, the authentication of Muhammad and his movement through the use of Qur'anic scriptures, had monumental implications for the intellectual future of the movement. Once this occurred, it immediately elevated the status of traditional Sunni Islamic discourse, especially its sacred texts, within African-American Islamic thought more generally. Ironically, though English-speaking black thinkers had launched Islam as a tradition whose meaning would be determined exclusively within the black community, their vessel became more and more mired in the texts and traditions of Old World Sunni Islam. Moreover, the use of Islamic texts by Malcolm X ceded important methodological ground to Muhammad's critics, who were far better acquainted with the textual traditions of Islam than was he.

By 1964 Malcolm X, the subject of chapter 5, had publicly embraced the nonracial vision of Islam that was being actively advanced by Muhammad's Muslim critics, especially Muslim missionaries funded largely by petrodollars from Saudi Arabia. As a new convert, Malcolm faced an intellectual dilemma even more complex than that of Elijah Muhammad. After he separated from the NOI, Malcolm embraced a dual identity as both a Sunni Muslim missionary who stressed the need for transracial brotherhood and a pan-Africanist revolutionary who struggled for an explicitly black liberation. In so doing, however, Malcolm separated his "politics" from his "religion," creating a tension that remained unresolved before his assassination in 1965. Because Malcolm could not reconcile his race-less Islam to his racial struggle, he seemed unable to imagine a strategy of black liberation that would achieve his revolutionary ends through an Islamic means.

Wallace Muhammad, the subject of chapter 6, inherited Malcolm's dilemma after rising to the leadership of the Nation of Islam in 1975. During the first few years of his tenure, this son of Elijah Muhammad attempted to synthesize themes from the black consciousness movement with Islam in an effort to provide followers with an identity that was both "authentically" Muslim and African American. Certain immigrant and foreign Muslims closely aligned with Muhammad, however, asked him to abandon his attention toward blackness, which he initially agreed to do. But in the 1980s, Wallace Muhammad again took up his efforts to forge an approach to Islam that accounted both for the unity of humankind and the struggle for black liberation. In doing so, he stressed the historical contingency of any application of Islam. In creating his own program for black uplift, he hailed the value of the individual and personal responsibility in Islam while simultaneously calling on blacks to find a collective solution to the race problem in America. Whether he reconciled these collective and individualistic approaches to social change is a question for debate, although his approach in attempting to do so suggested new directions for African-American Islam.

Finally, in the conclusion, I explore the teachings of Louis Farrakhan, emphasizing how his thought is in many ways a recapitulation of earlier themes in African-American Islam. Though Farrakhan may have begun his career as an avowed Muslim particularist, he now celebrates Islamic universalism just as vociferously. In so doing, his thought recalls the paradoxical formulations of early African-American Islam. I then argue that Minister Farrakhan's thought is also indicative of the "essentialist style" in African-American Islamic thought—a style that has been challenged at least implicitly by the thought of Wallace Muhammad. In fact, I submit that in its historical understanding of Islam, Wallace Muhammad's methodology suggests that the tension between universalism and particularism might become a source for a dynamic interpretation of Islam that consciously balances views of the human community as one and many.

Chapter 2

Edward Wilmot Blyden (1832–1912)
and the Paradox of Islam

INTRODUCTION

Born on August 3, 1832, in the Dutch West Indies, Edward Wilmot Blyden became one of the more remarkable intellectual and political figures of the black English-speaking world during the nineteenth century. An immigrant to Liberia, Blyden was a largely self-taught Presbyterian missionary who went on to become a professor and President of Liberia College, two-time Ambassador to Great Britain, Liberian Secretary of State, Minister of the Interior, Director of Muslim Education in Sierra Leone, a Liberian presidential candidate, and one of the most noted black authors of his time. As a critic of missionary Christianity and an ardent Liberian nationalist, Blyden was also the first English-speaking black author to tout Islam as a more "natural" tradition for blacks than Christianity.

As I will show in this chapter, Blyden argued that Islam was a far better vehicle of black self-determination than Christianity. For in contrast to the Christian faith, he said, Islam encouraged African nationalism, the development of black civilization, and racial equality. But many of Blyden's arguments on Islam were inconsistent or at least ambiguous and prone to change, depending on what audience he was addressing and what his political motives were in so doing. When Blyden was seeking support from European or American Christian missionaries, for example, he might present Islam as a menacing adversary to Christianity, trying to spur his missionary audience to fund his education projects or other concerns of the young Liberian state, which he hailed as a Christian outpost in the infidel wilderness. When in Sierra Leone, however, he might actually call for better cooperation between Muslim "natives" and Christian immigrants. Later in life, his quest for international support of African nationalism led him to challenge the parochialism that he viewed as endemic among Christians, Jews, and Muslims everywhere. The point is that Blyden constantly shifted his rhetorical strategies in his life-long mission to build black nation-states in West Africa, which was the only truly consistent theme in his intellectual life.

As I will argue, however, Blyden's writings on Islam anticipated many themes that would figure prominently later in African-American Islam. His various constructions of Islam as a vehicle of black nationalism, civilizationism, and human equality have appeared in some form in the thought of nearly every African-American Muslim leader since the 1920s. In addition, Blyden's appropriations of Islam inaugurated the tension between universalism and particularism in black Islamic thought. On the one hand, Blyden assumed that Christianity was an essentially white tradition while Islam was essentially nonwhite. At the same time, he insisted on the universality of all monotheistic traditions, including Islam. How Blyden reconciled these particularistic and universalistic views of Islam remained unclear in his published works and letters. In fact, he used both interpretations of Islam sometimes in the very same speech, never discussing the theoretical problems suggested by his paradoxical views.

Moreover, Blyden became a fervent black messianist, supporting the view of Africa and Africans as potential messiahs in the redemption of the world. This belief further complicates our understanding of his thought regarding Islam, since it is also unclear exactly how Blyden conceived of Islam's role, if it was to play any, in the redemptive black mission. As mentioned in chapter 1, black messianism posited a special role for blacks in the salvation history of the world, often connecting the redemption of black people with the redemption of all humankind. This sense of being a chosen people was sometimes developed into a form of black Christian particularism that linked Christianity to biological blackness, black nationalism, and black messianism. Though Blyden came close to constructing Islam in this way, especially in associating Islam so closely with black nationalism, he never articulated specifically messianist or biological interpretations of Islam.

I will also assert that the irony of Blyden's thought was that in his mind these forms of particularism, including black messianism, black nationalism, and the defense of biological blackness, would lead to harmony between the three major monotheistic faiths. According to Blyden, if

Africans could build nation-states with the assistance rather than tyrannical control of the colonial powers, then Africans could make their essential and redemptive contribution to the world, and in so doing, usher in some sort of global harmony between Jews, Christians, and Muslims. This harmony, Blyden said, was merely a reflection of the truly universal message that formed the essence of each faith. But in espousing both black messianism and an Abrahamic universalism, Blyden seemed to believe in a particularistic means to a universalistic end. The tension between these positions remained beneath the surface of his thought as another paradoxical formulation that I develop further below.

BLACK NATIONALISM AND AFRICAN COLONIZATION IN BLYDEN'S EARLY THOUGHT

Blyden's story, like that of many other black intellectuals during the nineteenth century, was shaped largely by the circumstances of racial discrimination in which he grew up. As a talented student in St. Thomas, Blyden had very few career choices open to him. In 1845, however, he met the Reverend John P. Knox, a white American who had come to St. Thomas as pastor of a Dutch Reformed Church. Knox furthered Blyden's education and encouraged him to become a minister. In 1850, Blyden traveled to the United States in an attempt to enroll in Rutgers' Theological College, Knox's alma mater, but was denied admission on account of his color. He also tried to gain admission to two other divinity schools, but was unsuccessful.[1]

Blyden had come to the United States at the worst possible political moment. That year, President Millard Fillmore signed into law the Fugitive Slave Act, which required the cooperation of law enforcement officials in the capture and reenslavement of "fugitive" slaves in the north. This law threatened the security of all blacks, not just escaped slaves, and was a major blow to the abolitionist cause. As a result, more and more prominent African-American intellectuals, including the Harvard-trained physician Martin Delany, began to advocate black emigration from the United States. While Delany promoted Latin America and the Caribbean as potential sites for black settlement, Edward Blyden spoke early on in favor of Africa. Moreover, Blyden made a point of criticizing both New York Senator Garret Smith, who followed the lead of many abolitionists in opposing emigration, and Delany, who had challenged the motives of the American Colonization Society (ACS).[2]

During his visit to the United States, Blyden developed associations with several white Presbyterian colonizationists, including John B. Pinney, Walter Lowrie, and William Coppinger of the ACS. These three, in addition to Knox, encouraged Blyden to begin his life's work in the American colony of Liberia, which they argued was a territory full of potential for any ambitious young black man. Blyden accepted the offer, writing to Pinney in December 1850, that he might help to "bring those barbarous tribes under civilized and enlightened influences."[3] Blyden's chauvinist attitude toward the "natives" reflected a more widespread belief held by most black intellectuals in what Wilson J. Moses has called "civilizationism." As Moses defines it, African civilizationism "embodied a sense of obligation to aid in the uplifting, not only of the continent itself, but of black people everywhere, and argued that if the internal life of the continent could be improved, black folk in England and America would experience a corresponding elevation of status."[4] For Blyden, however, the "uplift" of the natives seemed important not so much because it would elevate the status of all blacks, but rather because he believed it would help to build a successful black nation in Africa.

After his arrival in Liberia during 1851, Blyden enrolled in Monrovia's Alexander High School, where he came under the tutelage of D. A. Wilson, a Princeton Theological Seminary graduate. In addition, he began an independent study of Hebrew, aided by Isidor Kalisch, an American Judaist who sent Blyden a Hebrew grammar and commentaries on Genesis and Exodus. After Blyden gained ordination as a Presbyterian minister in 1858, he served as principal of his old high school and as a Christian missionary throughout the latter part of the 1850s. In 1861, however, the ambitious Blyden entered politics, being posted as Liberian Educational Commissioner to Britain and the United States and then in 1862, as a Commissioner charged with the recruitment of black American emigrants.[5]

His recruitment tour throughout the United States during 1862 only added to Blyden's nationalist fervor. Blyden faced humiliation at nearly every turn, including the House of Representatives, where he was banned from making a visit. In *Liberia's Offering*, published that same year, he argued that separation of the races into separate nations was essential to racial equality. "We shall never receive," he wrote, "the respect of other races until we establish a powerful nationality." Moreover, Blyden said, "the heart of every true Negro yearns after a distinct and separate nationality," a yearning that he understood as an "ordinance of nature."[6] In fact, he wrote in a letter to the *Liberia Herald* reproduced in an 1862 *New York Colonization Journal:* "I would rather go naked and wander among the natives of the interior than occupy the position of some of the 'respectable colored people'" in the U.S., "[f]or then I should feel that I was in a country of my own."[7]

But this rhetoric, designed to evoke nationalist sentiment, partially obscured Blyden's civilizationist agenda in the building of Liberia. New World blacks, he said, should also secure Africa for "Christian law, liberty, and civilization." In establishing modern black states in Africa, he continued, blacks must focus on institution building, especially on the law, education, religion, the press, and government. With the exception of his changing views towards Christianity, Blyden continued to support this basic model of African statehood throughout his life:

> We must build up Negro states; we must establish and maintain the institutions; we must make and administer laws, erect and preserve churches, and support the worship of God; we must have governments; we must have legislation of our own; we must build ships and navigate them; we must ply the trades, instruct the schools, control the press, and thus aid in shaping and guiding the destinies of mankind.[8]

When Blyden returned from the United States later in 1862, he chose to focus his own nation-building efforts on the establishment of sound educational institutions and received an appointment as Professor of Classics at the new Liberia College, having learned both Greek and Latin on his own. Soon after, however, Blyden would once again become entangled in the politics of his new nation.

BLYDEN'S APPROPRIATION OF ISLAM AS A VEHICLE OF BLACK NATIONALISM

By the time Blyden had arrived in West Africa, the region had undergone a remarkable period of religious and political change. While Islam had been present in the western Sudan from at least the eleventh century, it was mainly the religion of ruling elites, merchants, and missionaries. From the seventeenth until the nineteenth century, however, a number of reformers emerged who were committed to sponsoring *jihads* that would make their Islamic vision the guiding force in people's lives. Most famous among these leaders was Uthman dan Fodio, whose Sokoto jihad of 1804 created the largest Islamic empire of its time in the central Sudan. The power of Uthman's political and social reforms, which were based on certain Islamic traditions of law, mysticism, and saint worship, reverberated throughout the entire region. By the late nineteenth century, at the dawn of Europe's imperialist scramble for the region, "Islam had come to be the almost universal language of political ambition and moral reform" in West Africa.[9]

Blyden became aware of the importance of the Muslim presence soon after his appointment by Liberian President Daniel Warner as Secretary of State in 1864.[10] While Blyden continued to press for Liberia's rights in diplomatic circles, especially with regard to its border disputes with Sierra Leone, one of his main goals came to be the development of better relations with the indigenous populations of the West African interior. Even before 1864, however, Blyden had come to oppose the struggle to subdue the "natives," instead hoping to cooperate with them, especially in the effort to educate and convert them to Christianity.[11] In 1853, Blyden had joined other American Liberians in an expedition against King Boombo of the Vai, a native tribe of the region. Blyden was quickly impressed with the fortifications of Vai villages and with the "inventive nature of the natives." Thereafter, he espoused the idea that these populations should be incorporated into, rather than shunned from the republic. He also reaffirmed this idea in an 1860 letter to the Reverend John Wilson of the Board of Foreign Missions of the Presbyterian Church.[12]

Because of the burgeoning strength of Islam in the region, Blyden also believed that the Arabic language could become an important medium of communication with the interior tribes. Writing to Secretary of the Presbyterian Board of Foreign Missions Walter Lowrie, Blyden said that Arabic would be of "great importance to us as our settlements extend into the interior."[13] Moreover, Blyden hoped to gain enough proficiency in the language to one day teach it at Liberia College. Thus, Professor Blyden set out in May 1866 for Beirut, then part of Ottoman Syria, to study Arabic at the Syrian Protestant College (now the American University of Beirut). He later published recollections of the trip in one of his first major works, a travel memoir entitled *From West Africa to Palestine* (1873).

This first work showed that Blyden's earliest attitudes toward Islam were clearly filtered through the eyes of Euro-American Orientalism. Orientalism, as Edward Said famously defined it, was not merely the academic study of "the Orient" or the imaginative realm where the Euro-American exotic imagination could wander, but was also a "Western style for dominating, restructuring, and having authority over the Orient."

Orientalism, in Said's terms, was a discourse of power, a "corporate institution for dealing with the Orient—dealing with it by making statements about it, authorizing views of it, describing it, by teaching it, settling it, [and] ruling over it."[14] Said's arguments about the nature of power in the West's "dealing with the Orient" clearly applied to Blyden, who over time fashioned himself as a spokesperson for Islam.

In fact, Blyden's early understanding of Islam derived almost exclusively from what other westerners had written on the topic. On the leg of his journey that took him from the Gambia river to Teneriffe, one of his first *compagnons de voyage,* as he put it, was a graduate of Cambridge (unnamed) who noticed Blyden reading Palgrave's *Arabia.* The Englishman was something of an Arabic scholar and tried to assist Blyden in the translation of some West African manuscripts that Blyden had in his possession. When neither of them could figure the text out, Blyden entrusted it to the mysterious gentleman, who eventually returned it with an annotated translation. During Blyden's stay in Lebanon from July through August 1866, his social and intellectual intercourse was almost entirely with Europeans and Americans like Dr. Daniel Bliss, president of the Syrian Protestant College. In describing his travels through the Holy Land in August, Blyden relied mainly on the words of white travelers like Edward Robinson, Walter Keating Kelly, the Reverend W. M. Thomson, Henry Osborne, J. L. Porter, and Norman Macleod to illustrate the attractions of that sacred place. Moreover, he seemed not to have had one conversation with a native Palestinian—Muslim, Christian, or Jew. In Jerusalem, Blyden recorded encountering some pilgrims from Senegambia, but did not actually approach them for a conversation.[15]

Blyden also thought the Christian sects of Lebanon and Palestine to be superstitious and sleepy. On the whole, he seemed to believe, the Holy Land was a religious backwater. Moreover, he found local cultural practices to be quite bizarre or silly at times, especially veiling, ululation, and the several-day wedding ceremonies that he was invited to attend. During his stop in Cairo en route to Beirut, Blyden also saw "nothing to admire" in the subtly beautiful Sultan Hassan mosque—the claims of natives notwithstanding—compared to the larger Ottoman-style Muhammad Ali mosque. Overall, Blyden communicated an attitude of condescension toward the "natives" and their "quaint" culture that his English readers might find amusing.[16]

But Blyden's writing quickly moved from the satirical to the elegiac in describing his visit to the Pyramids, which he viewed as a great black

African historical accomplishment. While "standing in the central hall of the pyramid [of Cheops]," Blyden had an epiphany of sorts. Remembering the words of Liberian poet Hilary Teage, Blyden explained that he

> felt I had a peculiar 'heritage in the Great Pyramid.' . . . The blood seemed to flow faster through my veins. I seemed to hear the echo of those illustrious Africans. . . . I felt lifted out of the commonplace grandeur of modern times; and, could my voice have reached every African in the world, I would have earnestly addressed him in the language of Hilary Teage—Retake your fame![17]

To make the link between the Pyramids and his own Liberian nationalism perfectly transparent, Blyden then engraved the word, "LIBERIA," with his name and the date, 11 July 1866, on the entrance to the ancient wonder. In so doing, Blyden revealed the nationalist purpose of his trip. Unlike many of the Euro-American pilgrims and travelers whom he quoted in his book, Blyden did not travel to the Middle East to find some mysterious and exotic backdrop for the struggles of his own soul. He was not particularly moved by Islamicate culture, either. Rather, the purpose of his trip was to learn Arabic so that he could expand links with the interior populations at home and so build a new nation.

It made sense, then, that Blyden's views of Islam only changed after he made contact with the Muslims of West Africa, for it was with them that he had desired social intercourse in the first place. After returning to West Africa, Blyden conducted a series of expeditions first into the Liberian interior, then into Sierra Leone, confirming his beliefs about the importance the Arabic language in West African culture. His report to the governor of Sierra Leone regarding his 1873 expedition to Timbo, located in the hinterland of Sierra Leone, revealed a man who was especially impressed with the degree of literacy present there, as he made clear to the governor: "Nearly every man and woman can at least read Arabic. Children begin very early to learn to read. I often saw little boys and girls, four or five years old, with their boards upon which are written easy passages from the Koran, gathered morning and evening around a fire, repeating their lessons after the teacher." While most of this learning was rote, Blyden said, some students later became quite advanced in Maliki law, one of the four major Sunni Islamic law schools; in al-Hariri's *Assemblies*, an Arabic classic from the Middle Ages; and in Qur'an. "[M]any," he concluded, "have become skilled in the use of Arabic, reading, writing and speaking with great fluency; and these can sometimes improvise Arabic verses with remarkable facility."[18]

What Blyden saw as a high degree of literacy among West African societies changed his mind about Islam itself, which he began to view as the source of this great learning. For Blyden, what the "natives" had created was true black civilization, forged outside of the oppression of slavery and colonialism. "[I]t was . . . refreshing," Blyden wrote to the governor of Sierra Leone in 1873, "to turn from the unsatisfactory daguerreotypes of civilization presented in the Europeanized Negroes on the coast to the genuineness and reality of the self-governing and self-respecting Negroes of the interior." In fact, Blyden said, the "so-called civilized Negro" had suffered a great loss in his becoming civilized in a white manner. The natives, according to Blyden, were "natural and genuine" and, in contrast to Euro-American blacks, had experienced "a more reliable basis of true and permanent progress than a cramped and ill-proportioned straining after a foreign and incompatible ideal." Articulating an argument that would later be repeated by numerous African-American Muslims, Blyden stressed that Islam created an authentically black civilization, which encouraged a type of progress that also created dignity and self-respect.[19]

But Blyden was not exactly consistent in his analysis of Islam, willing to change his interpretations depending on his audience and his goals. During the 1870s, he was still an agent of both the Presbyterian Church and several related colonization groups, upon whom he and his family relied for financial sustenance. When he was communicating with these groups, rather than with the leader of Sierra Leone, he presented Islam in a different light. Speaking as a Christian missionary, Blyden used the strength of Islam to encourage the contribution of more human and financial resources to Christian-dominated educational and cultural institutions in the region. For instance, in the January 1871 edition of *Methodist Quarterly Review*, he published an article on Liberia that included an analysis of Islam's "salutary character." Islam, he argued, had come to West Africa by the pen, not the sword; it encouraged temperance; it was the "sole preservative" against the onslaught of the slave trade; and it encouraged learning, social unity, and industry. Blyden assured his Christian readership, however, that despite the strong presence and positive societal contributions of Islamic civilization, West Africa could still be turned toward the Gospel of Christ. "Mohammedanism," Blyden wrote, "could easily be displaced by Christian influence, if Christian organizations would enter with vigour into this field."[20] In fact, he offered himself as someone with the necessary expertise to accomplish this task. In 1873, for example, he urged the Presbyterian Board of Foreign Missions to establish an institution of higher learning in the interior, where he might be able to work towards this goal. Instead, they reassigned him to Alexander High School, which he had left to join Liberia College in 1862.[21]

But Blyden continued to fight for support of his own educational initiatives, soon focusing on a British audience. Clearly relishing his background as an Orientalist, a self-trained classicist, and a West African ethnographer, Blyden published several articles in *Fraser's Magazine,* a British periodical, criticizing Christian missionary activities in Africa, while praising Islam as an alternative religious tradition more respectful of African culture. Though it remained submerged in Blyden's articles, the Victorian context of his arguments was important. During the latter half of the nineteenth century, a debate raged in British politics over the future of the British Empire. While most Tories upheld the duties of the "white man's burden" and its imperial aspirations as an absolute good, liberals were split over the dilemma of whether to "civilize the natives" or leave them to their natural state. The famous sociologist Herbert Spencer, whose sociological classifications of "Negrotic" peoples appeared in 1874, was avowedly anti-imperialist, stressing a kind of social Darwinism that supported a "natural" state of social evolution.[22] Blyden's findings regarding the level of civilization in the West African interior challenged Spencer's views on the abilities of black persons. At the same time, Blyden clearly did not support a typically Tory view of imperialism. Unlike Spencer, Blyden used his "menacing" descriptions of Islam rather than any appeal to reason to solicit support for his brand of imperial intervention. In so doing, his approach paralleled that of his great hero, Liberal party leader W. E. Gladstone, who appropriated religious rhetoric to gain mass appeal among a growing voting public during the 1870s.

In criticizing Christianity and simultaneously promoting Islam, Blyden hoped to convince his white audience that all Africans, both immigrant and indigenous, should be allowed to develop their own authentic civilization. For instance, in "Mohammedanism and the Negro race," published in November 1875, Blyden praised R. Bosworth Smith's claims that Islam provided a sense of dignity to its adherents that Christian converts did not possess. Blyden magnified Smith's comments, asserting that "whenever the Negro is found in Christian lands, his leading trait is not docility, as has been often alleged, but servility." Devoid of self-reliance and true independence, countries like Haiti existed only by the whims of white power, according to Blyden. "On the other hand," Blyden continued, "there are numerous Negro Mohammedan communities and states in Africa which are self-reliant, productive, independent and dominant," including Sierra Leone, for example. Whereas missionary Christianity's arrival in Africa was associated with colonialism and slavery, Islam had spread, Blyden argued, by "choice" and "conviction," finding Africa in the midst of its "manhood." Christianity, on the other hand, "subdued," "soothed," and inspired sympathy even for the enslavers—so much so, in fact, that black "ideas and aspirations could be expressed only in conformity with the views and tastes of those who held rule over them." Conversely, Islam managed to inspire spiritual feelings "to which they [African pagans] had before been utter strangers," while simultaneously strengthening and hastening "certain tendencies to independence and self-reliance which were already at work."[23]

Blyden amplified this view in "Christianity and the Negro Race," an article published in 1876 in which he turned the common European notion of black inferiority on its head, implying that it was European culture rather than the African "jungle" that had transformed blacks into apes. "From the lessons he everyday receives," Blyden protested, "the Negro unconsciously imbibes the conviction that to be a great man he must be like the white man." Blacks, according to Blyden, were not taught to be the companions, equals, or comrades of whites, but the "imitator, his ape, his parasite. . . . To be like the white man as much as possible—to copy his outward appearance, his peculiarities, his manners, the arrangement of his toilet." Worse yet, Blyden argued in "Christian Missions in West Africa," European and American missionaries often measured their success by how much the "natives" had become imitators of white culture. They mistook the "thin varnish of European civilization" left with the native as a genuine "metamorphosis." The result was that the convert's "Christianity, instead of being pure is superstitious, instead of being genuine is only nominal, instead of being deep is utterly superficial."[24]

In full view of his white audience, Blyden had begun to question more fundamentally the entire missionary enterprise and Christianity itself. In "Islam and Race Distinctions," published in 1876, Blyden focused not only on the ill effects of European Christianity on blacks, but also on its complicity in the advancement of a secular Western culture. Why, Blyden demanded, has "the grand Semitic idea of the conversion to Divine truth of all the races of mankind, and their incorporation into one spiritual family" made such slow progress under the direction of Europeans? The answer, he offered, was that Christianity had been subsumed under the more general Western tendency to divide and conquer the world as a material possession. The West, he remarked, was anthropocentric, power-hungry, and materialistic. Even "religion is . . . cherished as a means of subserving temporal and material purposes." In the Middle Ages, Blyden argued, Roman Catholicism advanced this obsession with material things through its emphasis on the "visible" rather than the "unseen and spiritual," while Protestantism, through the actions of the Puritans, Presbyterians, and Episcopalians, focused on "material aggrandisement at any cost," including the enslavement of Africans and the wholesale murder of Indians. But if the absence of a true spirituality in Christian Europe made slavery and genocide possible there, Islamic spirituality had the opposite effect in Islamdom. Because the Muslim has a deeper trust in God and reliance in God's revelation in the Qur'an, Blyden said, Islam "extinguishes all distinctions founded upon race, colour, or nationality. . . . [T]hroughout the history of Islam, in all countries, race or 'previous condition' has been no barrier to elevation." A true faith, Blyden implied in this article, led to true brotherhood.[25]

Bernard Lewis has criticized Blyden's views regarding race and racism in Islam, grouping Blyden with a number of European Orientalists like Snouck Hurgronje and Alfred von Kremer who perpetuated what Lewis calls the "myth of Islamic racial innocence." In fact, Lewis argues that it "is significant that one of the most influential proponents of the myth was Edward W. Blyden. . . . His writings, with their stress on Christian guilt and on a somewhat romanticized Muslim tolerance, were widely read. Writers of this school usually make the illogical assumption that the reprobation of prejudice in a society proves its absence."[26] In one sense, Lewis' grouping of Blyden with Hurgronje and von Kremer is fair: Blyden did draw heavily on the work of European Orientalists to derive his historical and theological picture of Islam. Furthermore, his description of the utter absence of racism in Islamdom was certainly an exaggeration.

But in another respect, there is a critical difference between Blyden and European Orientalists. Unlike his European counterparts, Blyden appropriated Islam as part of a polemic designed to solicit support for his own educational and cultural projects and more political autonomy for Liberia and Sierra Leone. Moreover, contrary to what Lewis claims, Blyden was not ignorant, intentionally or otherwise, regarding the existence of racism within Islamic societies. In 1890, for example, he referred to "the destructive influence of wicked Arabs in their slave-trading in the Sudan" in a speech delivered throughout the United States.[27] For Blyden, the presence of racism in Arab society did not reflect poorly on Islam, since he regularly observed sub-Saharan Muslims mounting effective challenges to this racism based on Islamic traditions themselves. Educated Sudanese Muslims, Blyden said, knew the difference between what Arabs do and what Islam says to do. In fact, he had often heard them quoting Sura 9:97 (which he mistakenly identified as verse 98): "The Arabs are most stout in unbelief and hypocrisy, and are more likely not to know the bounds which God has sent down to His Apostle" [Blyden's translation]. According to Blyden, "this passage has protected the Soudanic Muslims against undue reverence for the Arab and armed him against imposition from the wiles of the unscrupulous among the countrymen of the Prophet." The point is that, despite the shortcomings of Muhammad's countrymen, that is, Arabs, Blyden still believed that Islam was an historically positive force in African life, helping to preserve black dignity and support African self-determination and civilization. Islam, Blyden said in the same article, is the African's "greatest solace and the greatest defense" against the on-slaught of European civilization. Over and over again, Blyden remarked on the respect shown to Muslims by foreigners. Moreover, argued Blyden, Islam had never been the kind of vehicle for terror and genocide that Christianity had been. "With Islam," he reiterated, "Africa is at least safe from physical destruction; with popular Christianity it might share the fate of the North American Indians, Sandwich Islanders, New Zealanders, & c."[28]

BLACK MESSIANISM AND UNIVERSALISM IN BLYDEN'S LATER THOUGHT

The above section makes clear that Blyden viewed Islam as capable of serv-ing a very particularistic purpose, namely, as a tradition that could foster African nationalism and help to develop African civilization. But Blyden's particularistic use of Islam did not mean that he viewed Islam as an exclu-sively black tradition. In fact, he also saw Islam, Judaism, and Christianity as universalistic traditions that advocated the same essential theological message among all human beings. Ironically, however, Blyden also be-lieved in a theological formulation of black messianism that posit-ed a special role for blacks as the chosen people in creating this more harmonious world. During the 1880s, he developed his own version of black messianism, which seemingly became the particularistic means to a universalistic end.

Blyden's black messianism grew in part out of his belief in what George Fredrickson has dubbed romantic racialism, which "held that each 'race' or 'nation' had its own inherent peculiarities of mind and temperament and would develop according to its own special 'genius' rather than follow some model based on the experience of peoples with different inherited or inbred characteristics." Races, said Blyden, had been created by the Almighty to do particular kinds of work in the universe. Thus, Blyden argued, the various races should be valued for their diversity and be preserved against miscegenation: "As in every form of the inorganic universe we see some noble variation of God's thought and beauty, so in each separate man, in each separate race, something of the absolute is incarnated. The whole of mankind is a vast representation of the Deity. Therefore we cannot extinguish any race either by conflict or amalgamation without serious responsibility." By the 1870s, Fredrickson argues, Blyden had combined these ideas of romantic racialism with "some of the doctrines of nineteenth-century scientific racism."[29]

The latter found expression in Blyden's beliefs in the biological nature of blackness and the inferiority of mixed race persons. In fact, Blyden sometimes made these opinions public to his own detriment. In 1871, for example, he was nearly lynched after being accused of committing adultery with the Liberian president's wife, whom he had praised as having "pure Negro" blood. Blyden's comment infuriated the largely "mulatto" Americo-Liberian ruling class, who, according to Blyden, incited a small mob to drag him around the streets with his neck in a rope. Fearing for his life, Blyden then sought exile in Sierra Leone. But rather than making him question his views on racial purity, this incident only heightened Blyden's hatred of "mulattos." Throughout the 1870s, he pleaded with William Coppinger of the American Colonization Society to send only "pure Negroes" to West Africa. When Blyden actually met some rather prominent men of mixed heritage, including Frederick Douglass, Senator Blanche Bruce, and other African-American leaders at the 1880 Republican Convention in Chicago, only Douglass impressed him. The rest of the "mongrel tribe," as Blyden called them, struck him as typical mulattos, "as light and empty as the men professing to lead a race could well be." He viewed Douglass as an exception, however, due to his "strong Negro instincts."[30]

In other words, Blyden believed that what made a person "black" was his or her biological descent. Moreover, Blyden argued that the preservation of the black "race" was especially important since black traits were much needed in the development of world civilization. By 1880, Blyden had developed this particularistic vision into his own version of black messianism. Recently chosen as president of Liberia College, Blyden delivered an address entitled "Ethiopia stretching out her hands unto God; or, Africa's Service to the World" to the ACS in May of that year. In crafting his speech, Blyden appropriated one of the most quoted biblical verses in African-American religious history, namely, the prophecy in Psalm 68:31 that "princes shall come out of Egypt; Ethiopia shall at once stretch forth her wings unto God." Blyden used this "Ethiopianist" prophecy to explain the contributions that black persons had already made to the historical development of humankind. According to Blyden, these contributions included (1) African involvement with the advent of the earliest religious sensibilities; (2) the helper role Africa played in the rise of both Judaism and Christianity; and (3) the labor blacks provided in the making of the modern world, most specifically in the United States. While he had often criticized the lack of self-determination brought about by white oppression, in this speech Blyden argued that it was through submission, service, and suffering that Africa had fulfilled her special mission.[31]

Even more, he defined black messianism to include a special role not only for Africans, but also for the African continent itself as a "spiritual conservatory" where all peoples could "recover some of the simple elements of faith" in the midst of a materialistic world. Blyden developed this theme further when he returned to the United States for an anniversary of the ACS in 1883. Invoking Nazareth and Bethlehem, the towns where Jesus was annunciated and born, Blyden prophesied the appearance of such places in Africa and then, perhaps for the first time, spoke of himself publicly as a prophet of black messianism:

> In the solitudes of the African forests, where the din of Western civilization has never been heard, I have realized the saying of the poet that the 'Groves were God's first temples'. I have felt that I stood in the presence of the Almighty; and the trees and the birds and the sky and the air have whispered to me of the great work yet to be achieved on that continent. I trod lightly through these forests, for I felt there was a 'spirit in the woods'. And I could understand how it came to pass that the prophets of a race—the great reformers who have organized states and elevated peoples, received their inspiration on mountains, in caves, in grottoes.

In this passage, Blyden linked the redemption of humankind not only to the development of Africa as a spiritual conservatory but also to black nationalism itself. The founding of black nation-states in Africa, he implied, would produce men who would not be suffering servants, but political leaders and prophets. Their leadership, he implied, would be inspired by numinous experiences on top of "mountains" and in "caves," much like those of Moses and Muhammad. But their contributions to the world, he said, would be shaped above all by their blackness. For the African, Blyden exclaimed, will "bring as his contribution the softer aspects of human nature. The harsh and stern figure of the Caucasian races needs this milder element. The African is the feminine; and we must not suppose that this is of the least importance in the ultimate development of humanity."[32]

What is so confusing about Blyden's intellectual development is that once he had articulated this black messianist vision, he did not integrate it in any way with his advocacy of Islam. In 1884, he delivered "Sierra Leone and Liberia: Their Origin, Work, and Destiny" in front of a West African audience. In this address, Blyden did the usual recounting of the advances in civilization due to colonization and launched into a critique of Christianity, this time praising Roman Catholicism and dismissing Protestantism as the inferior religious alternative for persons of African descent. According to Blyden, Catholic missionaries, who came in significant numbers in 1864, possessed several superior traits: (1) they engaged in an uncompromising war against evolution, agnosticism, and positivism; (2) they opposed socialism; (3) they opposed divorce, preserving the integrity of the family; and (4) they respected racial diversity, often incorporating black saints into their celebrations and encouraging the achievements of blacks in countries like Brazil, Venezuela, Cuba, and Peru.[33]

Blyden also praised Islam in the same way that he had in his publications during the 1870s. He reminded his audience that Christian missionaries would inevitably confront the "irrepressible," "aggressive" fact of Islam's presence among the populations of the interior, mentioning Islam's importance to the educational and commercial life of Africa. And like his African-American Muslim heirs, he also stressed the historic achievements of blacks in Arabia and under the umbrella of Islam, speaking of the "warrior and poet Antarrah," a pre-Islamic figure, and of Bilal ibn Rabah, one of the Prophet Muhammad's companions. Quoting Sir William Muir's *The Life of Mahomet* (London, 1858), yet another work of European Orientalism, Blyden recounted Bilal's important role as an early convert to Islam, as a confidant of the Prophet, and as the first *muadhdhin,* or prayer-caller, in Islam. In a later article, Blyden also mentioned the black hero Wahshi, who killed Hamzah, the Prophet's uncle and one of Islam's bitterest enemies, at the Battle of Uhud in 625 A.D. In addition, Blyden noted that an entire chapter of the Qur'an was named after Luqman, whom, he noted, Arabic poetry had identified as "black as night." Chapter

31, said Blyden, proved "the high degree of respect entertained for *Loqman* in Arabia." Moreover, he argued, Luqman's presence in the holy book indicated that Muhammad "did not believe that any slur would be cast upon the new religion by connecting the Koran with the name of that remarkable slave."[34] Luqman's inclusion meant that "no Muslim, whether Arab, Turk, or Indian, can read the 31st chapter of the Koran . . . and separate the Negro from participation in the privileges of God's elect." Finally, Blyden again linked Islam's success among blacks to its ability to create national unity. Africans, he said, "gather under the beams of the Crescent not only for religion, but for patriotic reasons; till they are not only swayed with one idea, but act as one individual. The faith becomes a part of their nationality."[35]

But what role Islam would play, if any, in his new vision of black messianism and Abrahamic harmony was unclear. Blyden only suggested that Africa might someday be the site of reconciliation between Islam and Christianity and began to develop a new theology in which Africans—and Jews, as shown below—would play a chosen role. The amalgamation of Islam and Christianity would not only rid Africa of its darkness, he believed, but would have the potential to erase the religious differences between all Christian, Muslims, and by implication, Jews, too. Blyden prophesied that "Japheth [i.e. Europe] introducing Isaac [Christianity], and Shem [i.e. Semites] bringing Ishmael [i.e. Islam], Ham [i.e. Africa] will receive both," adding that "[w]here the light from the Cross ceases to stream upon the gloom, there the beams of the Crescent will give illumination; and as the glorious orb of Christianity rises, the twilight of Islam will be lost in the greater light of the Sun [and not Son, he wrote!] of Righteousness. Then Isaac and Ishmael will be united, and rejoice together in the faith of their common progenitor—*Abrahim Khalil Allah*—Abraham, the Friend of God."[36]

The following year, in 1887, Blyden published this speech in a collection entitled *Christianity, Islam, and the Negro Race*. He also included two fresh pieces, an introduction by West African barrister Samuel Lewis and a preface that both reiterated and reworked a number of the themes outlined above. Once again, Blyden asserted the complementary nature of Islam and Christianity, when blacks themselves acted as spokespersons for the two traditions. Whereas Islam, by its "respect for order," mitigated against religious fervor, European libertinism, and ignorance, Christianity promised to bring a vital and spontaneous spirituality to the "formalism of the Muslims."[37] According to Hollis Lynch, the book had its detractors and its fans, but by any account it was a huge hit, ensuring Blyden's international celebrity. The first five hundred copies sold out quickly, prompting a second printing. Reviews appeared throughout the English and American press. *Notes and Queries* wondered whether Blyden was a "full-blooded Negro," implying that such a tour de force must be touched in some way by European blood. Blyden's friend, R. Bosworth Smith praised the book in the *Nineteenth Century,* calling it "one of the most remarkable books I have ever met." The Reverend J. Stephen Barras agreed, writing in *The Times* of London that it "may yet prove the greatest contribution of the age on the gigantic subject of Christian missions." The *Church Missionary Intelligencer,* on the other hand, savaged the opus, noting that its positive remarks regarding Islam and Roman Catholicism were just too much to stomach. Across the Atlantic, the *AME Church Review* praised Blyden as the "one Negro of standing in the English world of recognized scholarship," while the *Southern Recorder* pronounced the "work not only the most learned production that ever emanated from a black man, but one of the most learned in the English language." A slightly more sober review in the *Nation* noted that Blyden was "not deficient in the rarer qualities of thorough and patient study." His scholarship, proclaimed the weekly, showed "broad reading, minute investigation, [and] a surprising mental alertness." Moreover, discussion of Blyden's book spilled into more general public discourse when Canon Isaac Taylor endorsed Blyden's viewpoint towards Islam at an Anglican Church Conference held at Wolverhampton in November 1887, and after Blyden visited North America in 1888.[38]

That year, William Coppinger, secretary of the American Colonization Society, summoned Blyden, his movement's brightest star, to promote South Carolina Senator Matthew Butler's proposal for the United States federal government to fund black emigration. On January 19, 1890, Blyden addressed the ACS, this time in Washington, D.C., on the occasion of their seventy-third anniversary. Quoting Thomas Jefferson, Blyden argued that "nothing is more clearly written in the Book of Destiny than the emancipation of the blacks" but that "it is equally certain that the two races will never live in a state of equal freedom under the same Government." Blyden inaccurately described the growing acceptance of Jefferson's views among African Americans, who, he argued, were also advancing in education and culture, and thus in "love and pride of race." Such people were now ready, he said, for the "regeneration of the African fatherland." Blyden had sympathy for the sentiment that African Americans had earned their right to full citizenship because of their sacrifices in building the country, but asserted that emigration is not "a question of reason. It is a question also of instinct." According to Blyden, the romantic racialist destiny of blacks could only be fulfilled in Africa. "The work to be done beyond the seas," he said, "is not to be a reproduction of what we see in this country. It requires, therefore, distinct race perception and entire race devotion. It is not to be the healing up of an old race, but the unfolding of a new bud, an evolution; the development of a new side of God's character and a new phase of humanity."[39]

Unlike his previous visits in 1880 and 1883, this one also featured much discussion about Islam. On March 3, 1890, for instance, Blyden read a paper entitled "The Koran in Africa" before the Presbyterial Ministerial Association in Philadelphia. In another address entitled "Problems before the Christian Church," delivered at various locations throughout the United States, Blyden also chastised missionaries for arrogantly ignoring any cultural and social contributions that "Mohammedan" and "pagan" societies might have to offer. Even so, throughout his stay during 1889 and 1890, Blyden did not tout the vision of religious synthesis so prominent in his famous work. Rather, he warned that the only way to prevent the spread of Islam and the decline of Christianity was the foundation of an indigenous African Church. When Islam ceased to be the only tradition protecting Africans from "self-deprecation in the presence of Arabs or Europeans," Blyden told his Philadelphia audience, only then might Christianity have the chance for growth.[40]

Still, his pro-Islamic polemic fueled rancor among Blyden's detractors and rivals, including former U.S. Minister to Liberia Charles H. J. Taylor, who published a letter in the *Atlanta Constitution* accusing Blyden of being "a Muslim, a fetish-worshipper, and a hypocrite." Most African Americans, however, admired Blyden for his intellectual accomplishments, as his warm reception in both the South and North indicated, while tending to reject his emigrationist rhetoric. Blyden also faced the negative impact of having his name mentioned so frequently alongside that of Senator Butler, whose emigration plan inspired overwhelming opposition in both the black and white press. Senator Butler, not surprisingly, was simply delighted by Blyden's support and quoted a long passage of Blyden's book during debate over his bill in the Senate.[41]

In addition to his continued appropriation of the "Islamic menace" to garner American support for the peopling of Africa with black Christians, Blyden also reiterated his romantic view of Africa as the site where the great monotheistic faiths would become universalized and unified. But Blyden never made explicit the theological relationship, if any existed, between his nationalist appropriations of Islam and his beliefs in

Abrahamic universalism. With regard to the latter, however, he continued to develop this notion late into his life. In 1898, for example, Blyden published a small tract on the "Jewish question" that advanced his views on universalism, argued for a special Jewish role in this process, and solicited Jewish support for West African nationalism. The timing of the tract's publication pointed to its strong nationalistic overtones, as it appeared on the heels of the 1897 resolution of the first Zionist Congress to create a home in Palestine for the Jewish people. He dedicated the treatise to Louis Solomon, a Jewish resident of Liverpool, with whom, Blyden said, he had enjoyed many conversations about the topic. The purpose, Blyden proclaimed, was to make known the views of an African on "the work and destiny of a people with whom his [Blyden's] own race is closely allied, both by Divine declaration and by a history almost identical of sorrow and oppression." His hope, he continued, was to spur a deeper sympathy between the two groups.[42]

Blyden believed that Jews, like blacks, had a special role to play in realizing his vision of a universal monotheism. "Whenever the Jews . . . move together on any question of religion," he said, "the whole world is affected." The "spiritual life," he argued, was connected to their particularly "special work and destiny." For this reason, Blyden submitted, Jews had "a far higher and nobler work to accomplish for humanity than establishing a political power in one corner of the earth." The redemption of the world, Blyden posited, did not lay in the gathering of the Jews in Israel, as some biblicists would have it, but in Jews' continued intermingling with less spiritually inclined peoples. Jews, he said, had been "entrusted [with] the spiritual hegemony of mankind." It would be the Jewish people, Blyden asserted, who would "bring about the practical brotherhood of humanity by establishing, or, rather, propagating, the international religion in whose cult men of all races, climes, and countries will call upon the Lord under one Name."[43]

Launching into an exegesis of the Bible, Blyden explained that the meaning of God's refusal to give Moses any more specific name than "I am who I am" was to set forth the universality of Judaism. God, Blyden speculated, seemed to be saying that "if I give you a specific designation, it must be in Hebrew, and you will be tempted, such is human nature, to identify me with the Hebrews, and call me the Hebrews' God." To make his point perfectly unambiguous, Blyden reiterated that "God could not define Himself . . . [because] Jehovah is a universal sovereign, adapting Himself to all races, and answering to any name by which, in sincerity and truth, they call upon Him."[44]

Blyden also applied this universalistic interpretation of Judaism to Islam in an article written while he was serving as director of Mohammedan Education in Sierra Leone from 1901 to 1906. Lest any Muslims believe that true Islam was any different in nature than any other Semitic tradition, Blyden argued that "Islam is monotheism, not only as contrasted with polytheism, but also as expressing the idea of a universal, unapproachable, incomparable, and solitary supremacy." But, Blyden lamented, some believers of every faith insisted on asserting a parochial view of their faith, including Muslims. "[T]here are Mohammedans," he claimed, "as there are Christians and Jews and Buddhists, who, inferior to the true teachings of their creed, cannot believe that God is where He is not reached by such paths as those they have been taught are the only paths that lead to Him." It was especially important, he believed, that Jews refuse the temptations of this particularistic orientation. Fortunately, Blyden said, many Jews had begun to realize the ecumenism of their creed. Quoting Jewish thinkers Herman Adler, Felix Adler, and Israel Abrahams, Blyden applauded what he believed to be the growing consciousness among Jews themselves of the universality of Judaism. Such a development was critical, Blyden thought, since the world was "immersed in materialism," and science and philosophy had become the gods that humans worshipped. Of course, he said, the Europeans could offer no way out of the darkness. Christianity, rather than practicing the Semitic traditions of Jesus, had become too European in character. For example, Blyden claimed that whereas Jews and Muslims in Semitic countries were drawn to the synagogue and the mosque both by training and "racial and religious instinct," Europeans and Americans had to be attracted to worship by "expedients" such as contests that ranked the best sermons. Only Jews, Blyden said, could carry out the "'ideals of Zion.'" "Imperial races," he concluded, "cannot do the work of spiritual races."[45]

But, Blyden argued, Jews had only begun to realize the true meaning of being a chosen people; they continued, he said, to overlook potent areas for missionizing, especially West Africa. "Have the Jews no witness to bear in inter-tropical Africa?" Blyden asked. "Have they no word of comfort or of help for millions of the descendants of Ham in that land?" Interestingly, the comfort advocated by Blyden seemed to be more than spiritual in nature. In fact, Blyden called on Jews to aid their spiritual cousins with their knowledge of science and "other culture." Quoting the prophecy made in Zephaniah 3:10, Blyden implied that such help was divinely commanded: "From beyond the rivers of Ethiopia, my suppliants, even the daughters of my dispersed, shall bring mine offering."[46] This was a telling argument, showing how much the development of African nationalism was consistently at the center of Blyden's thought, linked inextricably to nearly every other moral and philosophical issue.

CONCLUSION: ISLAM AS PARADOX

In soliciting Jewish support on behalf of African nation-building, Blyden invoked a universalistic interpretation of Judaism, calling on Jews to work for more than just Jewish concerns. He asked Muslims and Christians to do the same. But Blyden preserved a high degree of particularism in his eschatology by positing a special role for blacks in the creation of Abrahamic harmony. Moreover, Blyden's version of black messianism required the establishment of black nation-states in Africa. What remained ambiguous was how Islam figured into Blyden's Ethiopianist vision of world salvation. By associating Islam so closely with black nationalism (which he often justified in terms of black messianism), Blyden came one small step away from creating a form of black Islamic particularism that would link the redemption of the world with the growth and development of Islam among blacks. In addition, Blyden seemed not to notice—or perhaps be bothered by the fact—that he promoted Islam as the tradition best suited to advancing African nationalism, while also describing it as an essentially universalistic tradition. He seemed to accept as paradoxical the idea that Islam could serve a particularistic purpose without questioning whether this particularistic construction threatened its universalism. Islam, his thought implied (though he never said), was both a tradition specifically suited for black people and a tradition generally suited for all people.

Towards the end of his life, Blyden rejected this paradox, instead embracing a stark form of particularism that had nothing to do with Islam. Broke, sick, and politically powerless, this former champion of civilizationism published a series of articles in the *Sierra Leone Weekly News* that advanced a cultural relativist approach to the understanding of African societies. This series, which became *African Life and Customs,* once again drew from the work of European scholars, including Mary Kingsley, Lady Lugard, J. E. Dennett, Major Leonard, and Dudley Kidd, among others, to reiterate the British liberal position that the "native" way of life should be left undisturbed. Blyden criticized his life-long civilizationist agenda, defending an African social order which was, he claimed, agrarian, patriarchal, communistic, polygamous, and religious in character. Anticipating contemporary Afrocentrism, he praised the collectivist mentality of the

"African," savoring the irony that communism and socialism, essentially African norms to him, were gaining ascendancy in a Europe overrun by individual acquisitiveness. He again criticized missionaries, albeit this time for their shallow understanding of pantheism, which he deemed to be a holistic and thus highly laudable form of religion. Interestingly, he made no mention of Islam or of his vision of a world religion. Blyden had become conservative in the most classic sense, hoping against all odds that the "native" cultures of West Africa might be preserved against the onslaught of modernity.[47]

But Blyden's legacy with regard to Islam was anything but conservative, for his innovative thinking about Islam foreshadowed most of the central themes of African-American Islamic thought in the twentieth century. Like many of his African-American heirs, Blyden indicted white Christianity on the grounds that it stunted the development of black self-determination. Instead, he promoted Islam as a tradition more in tune with the political, social, and cultural aspirations of blacks. Specifically, he believed that Islam had contributed to black nation-building, the development of the black racial "essence," and historic black achievements, especially in the area of black civilization. Suggesting an even stronger link between various forms of black communalism and Islam, his thought also implied that some sort of synthesis of black messianism, nationalism, and Islam might be possible. But Blyden never answered the question of whether Islam would become explicitly associated with this kind of particularism. And the tension implied by such an association—that is, whether Islam would be a tradition for all or just for blacks—also lay unexplored. Ultimately, Blyden left it to others to make the hard theoretical choices about how black Muslims should perceive themselves in relation to other blacks, other Muslims, and the rest of humanity. Left unresolved, then, was also a more complete explanation of what the central message of Islam would be within the story of black liberation.

Chapter 3

Noble Drew Ali (1886–1929) and the Establishment of Black Particularistic Islam

INTRODUCTION

Over a decade after Blyden's death, Timothy Drew founded the Moorish Science Temple (MST) in Chicago. Though Drew incorporated Islamic symbols into this original tradition, his use of them apparently owed very little to the Islamic traditions of the Old World. Instead, Drew seemingly appropriated Islamic symbols from Freemasonry, which itself had a long history of adopting Oriental themes into its esoteric culture. In particular, as Peter Lamborn Wilson has suggested, Drew borrowed elements from one of Freemasonry's brother organizations, the Shriners. Founded in the 1870s by Scottish Rite Masons from New York, the Ancient Arabic Order Nobles of the Mystic Shrine claimed lineage to the "Grand Shaykh" of Mecca, Sultan Selim III, the Bavarian Illuminati, and the Bektashi Sufis. Using the title "Noble," they donned fezzes, established lodges with Arab-Islamic names, and appropriated the Islamic crescent and star in the organization's jewelry. At Chicago's World's Fair in 1893, African Americans formed their own version of the Shriners. Claiming the consent of visiting Muslim dignitaries, these Masons called their organization the Ancient Egyptian Arabic Order of Nobles of the Shrine. It was almost certainly from this group that Noble Drew Ali, as he became known, adopted his movement's few Islamic symbols, including his own title of "Noble" and his fez.[1]

Yet while Drew Ali had virtually no direct connection to the traditions of Old World Islam, he was a seminal figure in the history of African-American Islam. For Drew Ali not only fostered the introduction of

45

"Oriental" symbols and language into African-American vernacular, he also produced a number of ideas that were perpetuated by later African-American Islamic thinkers. Like Edward Blyden, Drew Ali linked black liberation to both national and moral renewal. But, I will argue, Drew Ali differed from his predecessor by attempting to recast black identity strictly in terms of nation and creed. Refusing to be called black, colored, or Negro, Drew Ali hoped to separate himself from the legacy of nineteenth-century racialism. African Americans, he argued, were Moors, a nation that emerged out of a more general group of Asiatic peoples. While Moors possessed a unique national heritage, according to Drew Ali, they shared a common religion, Islam, with all nations of Asiatic descent. For Drew Ali, unlike Blyden, there was little ambiguity in the question of whether Islam was a universalistic or particularistic tradition. Islam was not a tradition for all humans, Drew Ali implied, but the unique heritage of Asiatic peoples. Moreover, he suggested that only Muslims, who were by definition nonwhite, would be divinely saved.

But while clearly defining Islam in a particularistic manner, Drew Ali's thought also contained important elements of universalism. Drew Ali developed the ethics of his particularistic Moorish Science by borrowing liberally from universalistic teachings of theosophy and Rosicrucianism. Secondly, he adopted the Blydenian notion that the establishment of self-determination for all people might lead to a more harmonious world. This belief at least raised the question of whether Drew Ali, like Blyden, saw Islam as a particularistic means to a universalistic end or whether, as indicated above, he viewed Islam as a particularistic eschatology that promised the ultimate demise of whites. While there is no definitive answer to this question, I focus below on the historical development of these ideas in the context of Garveyism and the growth of nationalism during the 1920s. Drew Ali seemed to have very different aims than Marcus Garvey, who used Islam, like Christianity, as a means mainly to promote his brand of African nationalism. In some ways, Drew Ali's thought shared much more in common with the general tenor of white American nationalism during the decade. Using the same logic that informed certain pieces of U.S. immigration legislation, Drew Ali attempted to filter biological forms of racial identity into containers of cultural and national identity. But like much of the immigration legislation, these new constructions belied a continuing commitment to more old-fashioned biological notions of group identity and racial purity. By redefining black identity in these terms, Drew Ali appropriated Islam as a particularistic tradition supporting racialism and separatism.

Despite this, Drew Ali's ethics encouraged peace, justice, and brotherhood among all peoples. In the final section of the chapter, I show how these teachings emerged from Drew Ali's use of various "occult" texts in his *Holy Koran*. I also explain how his use of them reflected a larger fascination among African Americans with modern esotericism and I outline how he synthesized these universalistic traditions into his own particularistic tradition.

THE PROPHET'S HAGIOGRAPHY AND THE MYTHICAL ORIGINS OF MOORISH SCIENCE

There are few reliable sources with which to construct an accurate biography of Noble Drew and the origins of the Moorish Science Temple. What do exist, however, are colorful hagiographies of Noble Drew's life that at least illuminate the beliefs of his followers regarding the nature of his prophetic mission. According to reports catalogued by Wilson, Timothy Drew was born January 8, 1886, in North Carolina to a Cherokee mother and "Moorish" father. At age sixteen, Drew Ali joined the merchant marine, which enabled him to travel to Egypt. Once there, he met the "last priest of an ancient cult of High Magic who took him to the Pyramid of Cheops, led him in blindfolded, and abandoned him." When Drew found his own way out, the priest offered him initiation in the cult. Henceforth, he would be called Noble Drew Ali. When Drew Ali returned to America, he established the "Canaanite Temple" in Newark, New Jersey, around 1913. At this time, Noble Drew also wrote President Woodrow Wilson, requesting that the Moorish flag, which he believed to be hidden in Independence Hall since 1776, be given back to him and his people. Legend has it that Wilson complied with Noble Drew's request.[2]

Importantly, none of these reports can be confirmed by sources external to the movement—a fact that leads one to question nearly every aspect of these stories, including the date for the founding of the Moorish Science Temple. Every scholarly source of which I am aware lists the date of the founding of the MST as 1913, though none of these sources produces any evidence for this date except references to other secondary sources or oral history interviews with movement members themselves.[3] Curiously, there are also no reports about the activities of the MST during and immediately after World War I. Official Moorish history, which supposedly began in the 1910s in New Jersey, does not recommence until 1925 in Chicago, where Noble Drew is said to have moved. This, and not the

1910s, is the period during which the FBI believed the MST to have been founded.[4] Moreover, a number of external sources, including newspaper articles and pictures, exist to document this chapter in Noble Drew's history. It was also during this period that Noble Drew published the *Holy Koran of the Moorish Science Temple*, often called the *"Circle Seven Koran,"* because of an encircled number "7" on its cover.[5] Because this sacred text borrowed so much from other books published in the 1920s, it stands as the most reliable historical source with which to understand Noble Drew's Moorish Science during this period.

In 1928, the Moorish Science Temple was officially incorporated. That year, the Moors in Chicago used Unity Hall, located on 3140 Indiana Avenue, as their headquarters. The movement apparently attracted enough interest to warrant coverage by the *Chicago Defender.* But the favorable impressions did not last long. In the first half of 1929, Noble Drew's business manager, Claude D. Greene, was brutally murdered. The Chicago police responded by arresting forty MST members, including the Prophet himself. While Noble Drew maintained his innocence, he was arraigned, released on bond, and then killed—either by movement rivals or the police. He died on July 20, 1929. Despite his death, Moorish Science continued to spread throughout black America, including the Deep South. Judging by FBI records, it may not have achieved its greatest numerical success until the late 1930s and early 1940s, when the Bureau found Moors in obscure places like Mounds City, Illinois (a tiny village located near the city of Cairo).[6]

THE ROLE OF GARVEYISM
IN THE CREATION OF NOBLE DREW'S ISLAM

Because seminal studies of African-American Islam, including Lincoln's and Essien-Udom's, stressed the nationalistic aspects of the Nation of Islam (NOI), these works often viewed black nationalist Marcus Garvey as a key precedent to the formation of Islamic movements among blacks, including the Moorish Science Temple and the NOI. Richard Brent Turner's more recent study perpetuates this notion, but goes further in claiming that Garvey's movement was a conduit for Blyden's ideas regarding Islam.[7] While some evidence exists for all of these claims, the role of Garveyism in helping to create African-American Islam has been greatly exaggerated. This section introduces the Garvey movement, explores the use of theology and ritual within it, and develops the hypothesis that Garveyism played a rather modest role in the creation of Noble Drew Ali's thought.

Born in 1887, Marcus Garvey grew up in St. Ann's Bay, Jamaica, where he imbibed what Robert Hill has called the "social consciousness and drive for self-governance of the Caribbean peasantry and Afro-American traditions." After study and work in London during the early 1910s, Garvey left his native country for Harlem in 1916. Once in New York, Garvey popularized the Universal Negro Improvement Association (UNIA) through his extraordinary abilities as a propagandist and organizer. Garvey's goals, as Beryl Satter summarizes, were "to arouse a unified race consciousness in all peoples of African descent . . . to strengthen this united black race by organizing black-owned . . . business enterprises . . . and finally, to create a black-governed nation in Africa that would host the creation of a renewed black civilization and stand up for the rights of black people everywhere." In 1919, he launched the Black Star Steamship Line, which sought to carry goods and persons between the New World and Africa. By 1920, according to George Fredrickson, "the organization had developed all the trappings and auxiliaries of an African empire-in-exile, with its own uniformed paramilitary units, titles of nobility, and patriotic rituals." But three years later, Garvey was charged with and convicted of mail fraud. He was imprisoned in 1925 and pardoned by President Coolidge in 1927. By this time, Garvey's movement was a mere shadow of its former self, despite the fact that at the time it had represented the most successful black nationalist organization to date among people of African descent.[8]

Ritual and theology were important aspects of Garveyism, although they were not central to Garvey's mission. Garvey espoused beliefs in the "God of Ethiopia," divine retribution against whites, and black chosenness. In addition, he oversaw the creation of the African Orthodox Church under the leadership of Bishop George Alexander McGuire. But Garvey also rejected the typically romantic view of black messianism, instead arguing for what Randall Burkett has dubbed a social Darwinist perspective. Burkett also points out that Garvey believed that God was "no respecter of persons. He has nothing to with the affairs of men. . . . Otherwise he would be an unfair God." If blacks desired salvation, Garvey argued, they should be self-reliant and amass earthly power.[9] When Garvey did appropriate Ethiopianist themes, it was often to legitimate and justify his program of social, political, and economic uplift. He repeatedly referred to "Ethiopia" and "Ethiopians," words laden with theological meaning, in discussions of strictly secular matters.[10] Echoing Garvey's sentiments, McGuire, the general chaplain of the UNIA, interpreted Psalm 68:31, the foundational verse of black messianism, as a call for practical national development rather than the promise of direct divine intervention into human affairs, as it was usually seen. He included this interpretation in the Universal Negro Catechism written for movement members:

> Q. What prediction made in the 68th Psalm and the 31st verse is now being fulfilled?
> A. "Princes shall come out of Egypt, Ethiopia shall soon stretch out her hands unto God."
>
> Q. What does this verse prove?
> A. That Negroes will set up their own government in Africa, with rulers of their own race.[11]

Like Blyden, McGuire linked black messianist prophecy to African nationalism and black self-determination.

Likewise, Garvey and other UNIA members used Islamic references to support their nationalist agenda. The *Negro World*, for example, praised pan-Islamic efforts to overthrow European power. Arnold Ford, the musical director of the UNIA, used allusions to "Allah" in some of his original songs. Garvey even compared himself to the Prophet Muhammad, though he was careful to contrast his own "political" aspirations with what he (inaccurately) characterized as the exclusively "religious" accomplishments of the Prophet.[12] But despite this use of these Islamic allusions, Garvey never developed any kind of Islamic approach to the black nationalist struggle. Moreover, it seems safe to assume that this was a choice, either conscious or unconscious, on Garvey's part, since he had had extensive exposure to Islam through his reading of Blyden. While in London in 1913, for example, he had studied Blyden's works in the reading room of the British Museum. Then, in a 1914 pamphlet, Garvey explicitly cited Blyden as an example of black achievement and reproduced a large excerpt from *Christianity, Islam, and the Negro Race*. In fact, Blyden was such an influential symbol of black success that McGuire included him in the movement's catechism:

> Q. Who was Edward Wilmot Blyden?
> A. The most learned Negro of modern times; born in the Danish West Indies in 1831 but was identified with Africa for fifty years;

he was a distinguished statesman, philosopher, linguis[t] and Arabic scholar; the author of several works on Negro history and sociology.

But as the catechism and Garvey's writings showed, Blyden was appropriated in the context of the UNIA as a secular figure. Furthermore, Blyden's advocacy of Islam never became a core component of Garvey's program or thought.[13]

Despite Garvey's intentions, however, Garveyism became a more traditional form of black messianism for many UNIA members and admirers. Robert Hill speculates that the UNIA rank and file experienced "Garvey's teachings on two distinct levels, the one mundane, the other mystical." These followers rejected Garvey's social Darwinist perspective, usually reaffirming the nineteenth-century romantic ideals of black messianism. Moreover, while still embracing the more political aspects of Garveyism, some viewed Garvey himself as a prophetic figure. For instance, in a 1924 book entitled *The Holy Piby,* Robert Athlyi Rogers depicted Garvey as a leading player in the "redemption of Ethiopia and her suffering posterities." Ignore Garvey's personal sins, Rogers said; God had sent Garvey "to prepare the minds of Ethiopia's generations." Similarly, the movement's incorporation of Arabic words and Islamic figures into its lexicon increased consciousness of and ideological support for the practice of Islam. For example, journalist John Bruce, a prominent columnist in the *Negro World,* openly espoused Blyden's arguments regarding Islam's lack of racial prejudice in front of a Boston meeting of the UNIA during 1923. Perhaps such ideas reached the ears of Drew Ali. But whether or not this was true, the influence could hardly be seen by the middle 1920s. Drew Ali's appropriation of Islam within Moorish Science was completely different from Blyden's descriptions of Islam—that is, from the one to which some UNIA members had been introduced.[14]

In fact, Noble Drew's most direct connection with Garveyism seemed to come through his appropriation of Garvey as the harbinger of his own message of salvation. "In the modern days there came a forerunner," Drew Ali wrote in chapter 48 of the *Holy Koran,* "who was divinely prepared by the great God-Allah and his name is Marcus Garvey, who did teach and warn the nations of the earth to prepare to meet the coming Prophet [i.e., Noble Drew Ali]."[15] Garvey was no black Moses, the Prophet implied; he was John the Baptist, preparing the people for the coming of a new Christ. Noble Drew indicated that he had a different message from Garvey and that Garvey had only been the warm-up act.

DREW ALI'S MOORISH SCIENCE
IN THE CONTEXT OF 1920s RACIAL DISCOURSE

Drew Ali's new dispensation included a rather unique approach to black nationalism that can best be viewed in the more general context of the 1920s, when racism and xenophobia played a powerful role in the discourse of American national identity. The legislative history of the period, for example, revealed a desire among many to redefine the descent-based aspects of American identity in terms of nation and culture. In 1924, Congress passed the National Origins Act, which severely limited immigration from all "non-Nordic" countries. Based on a quota system, the Act required that 85 percent of all new immigrants come from northern and western Europe. One Kansas congressman who voted in support of the act explained its necessity by outlining the potential threats of further immigration from the non-Nordic countries; the difference, he said, was between "beer, bolshevism . . . and perhaps many flags" and "constitutional government; one flag, stars and stripes." The American way of life, the argument went, was under siege, and America, as one grand dragon from the KKK put it, must be made safe for Americans. For the Kansas congressman, being an American meant allegiance to the Constitution in addition to the eschewing of certain political ideologies and drinking habits—in short, it meant being a part of a particular culture.[16]

But lurking behind much of this "cultural" nationalism was the traditional specter of racialism, or at the least, a xenophobia that assumed racialist forms. For example, Senator Albert Johnson of Washington, the National Origins Act's chief supporter, viewed "homogeneity" as a necessary component in the preservation of American institutions. President Coolidge, who signed the bill into law, shared Johnson's view. When he was Vice President, President Coolidge had published an article entitled "Whose Country Is This?" in which he supported notions of Nordic supremacy and argued that intermarriage produced weak children. The National Origins Act itself was equally racist. Through a convoluted set of provisions, the effect of the act was to ban almost all Asians from immigrating. Ironically, racism also figured into efforts to create the Indian Citizenship Act, which Congress passed that same year. The act declared that all Native Americans were henceforth citizens of the United States, at first glance a seemingly tolerant gesture toward the inclusion of nonwhite persons into the American family. When viewing the act in light of the immigration bill, however, a logic of racial exclusion can be seen to have inspired both bills. "They were both designed to keep people from *becoming* citizens," argues Walter Benn Michaels. While the immigration bill sought to prevent aliens from immigrating, the Citizenship Act "guaranteed that Indians would not become citizens by declaring that they were already citizens." The effect of both bills, in other words, was to change the meaning of being an American from "a status that could be achieved through one's own actions (immigrating, becoming 'civilized,' getting 'naturalized,') to a status that could better be understood as inherited." The largely symbolic Indian Citizenship Act said, in effect, that being an American is not something *you do,* it is something that *you are.*[17]

In sum, the repackaging of nineteenth-century racialism in nationalist and "culturalist" terms figured prominently throughout the legislative history of the 1920s. Interestingly, Drew Ali constructed Moorish Science in similar ways. Whereas Marcus Garvey had reaffirmed the Blydenian idea that a "nation" was the only natural container for a biologically based racial group, Noble Drew denied the existence of biological blackness on both essentialist and historical grounds. For example, Drew Ali refused to call himself Negro, black, or colored. "According to all true and divine records of the human race," he said, "there is no negro, black, or colored race attached to the human family, because all the inhabitants of Africa were and are of the human race" (47:9). In case his readers did not understand his point, he reiterated it in the very next chapter, stating bluntly that "you are not negroes." But Drew Ali's comments that all blacks were simply human beings did not mean that he wanted to rid the world of diversity and difference. He believed rather that all humans should separate themselves according to their respective national groups. For Drew Ali, a "nation" signified a common history, creed, and value system—in short, a whole culture.[18] In this, his ideas were exactly parallel to those invoked during the discussion of the National Origins Act.

But Drew Ali, no matter how hard he tried to reconfigure biological ideas of race into new cultural and nationalist forms, continued to use racial, rather than national identity as the primary determinant of what it meant to be black. Drew Ali's discussion of miscegenation, for example, provides a revealing peek behind the veil of nationalism in his thought. Like Garvey, Drew Ali denounced interracial relationships, arguing implicitly that racial purity was necessary to black redemption: "We, as a clean and pure nation [read: race] descended from the inhabitants of Africa, do not desire to amalgamate or marry into the families of the pale skin nations of Europe" (48:6). Moreover, as the *Holy Koran* made clear, Drew Ali nowhere articulated a desire for the trappings of a modern nation-state. The *Holy Koran* did not possess a constitution and its body of laws referred mostly to moral rather than political matters. In other words, Drew Ali was not really an advocate of any form of black nationalism, as were both Blyden and Garvey. Instead, he tried to conceal familiar nineteenth-century forms of black particularism, including a biological definition of blackness, behind popular conceptions of nation and culture.

His attempts to redefine black particularism in terms that avoided an explicitly black nomenclature also camouflaged an intense desire to escape the derogatory attitudes associated with blackness in the United States. In place of this specifically "racial" understanding of black identity, Drew Ali offered a complex genealogy that viewed Moors in light of a glorious, but fallen past of historical achievements. According to the Prophet, the "Moslems of northwest and southwest Africa are actually the Moabites, Hamathites, and Canaanites, all of whom were driven out of Canaan by Joshua. Having received permission from the Pharaohs to settle in Africa, these Muslims formed the modern-day kingdoms of Morocco, Algiers, Tunis, Tripoli, etc." Other Asiatic peoples, including the Egyptians, the Arabians, the Japanese and Chinese, the "Hindoos," the Turks, the South Americans, and even the "Mexicans in North America," settled the rest of the non-European world (45:1–7; 47:1–8). Synthesizing and rewriting various parts of ancient history, Noble Drew explained that African Americans were the Moorish descendants of an ancient Asiatic race; their creed was Islam.[19]

For Drew Ali, it was not enough that blacks should be true to their nation; they should also be true to their particular creed. Specifically, he said, Moors should not "serve the gods of their [whites'] religion, because our forefathers are the true and divine founders of the first religious creed, for the redemption and salvation of mankind on earth" (48:6). Drew Ali, in other words, believed that being a good Moor meant keeping both foreign blood and foreign creeds out of the "nation." In constructing his particularistic Islamic tradition along lines of blood and geographic origins, Drew Ali also reinterpreted the meaning of Christ, arguing that Jesus was the Moors' genealogical ancestor. "Jesus himself was of the true blood of the ancient Cannanites and Moabites and the inhabitants of Africa" (46:2). He had come to redeem "His people . . . from the pale skin nations of Europe" but "Rome crucified Him" (46:2–3). Drew Ali saw Jesus as a pan-Asiatic prophet whose teachings had been betrayed by the Church. Christianity, founded by the Romans, had little to do with the message of Jesus, Drew Ali said. "The holy teaching of Jesus," he wrote, "was to the common people, to redeem them from under the great pressure of the hands of the unjust. That the rulers and the rich would not oppress the poor" (46:5). But Rome, according to Drew Ali, had essentially rejected these principles, which explained in part why white Christians had not acted in a Christian-like manner towards nonwhites.[20]

The "pale skins," however, were not the only ones to blame for the degradation of the Moors, according to Noble Drew. In fact, the Prophet blamed the enslavement of blacks on moral and national decline among the Moors themselves. Because "they honored not the principles of their mother and father, and strayed after the gods of Europe," they had been stripped of their nationality and had been called "negro, black, and colored" (47:16–17). By not being true to their heritage and its obligations, said Drew Ali, blacks had suffered the worst of fates: they did not know who they were and instead accepted the labels of their oppressors. "Through sin and disobedience," Noble Drew wrote, "every nation suffered slavery, due to the fact that they honored not the creed and principles of their forefathers" (47:17). Redemption, he taught, would come not from the acts of a single black messiah but through the collective actions of a whole nation—uplifting "fallen humanity," he insisted, must include linking oneself with the "families of nations" (48:11). Asiatics still held the "key to civilization," he continued, if they would only embrace their God-Allah and seek national renewal. What this really meant for Drew Ali was not that blacks should return to Africa and establish nation-states, but that they should separate along racial lines from their oppressors. "Every nation shall and must worship under their own vine and fig tree, and return to their own and be one with their Father God-Allah" (48:3). Drew Ali also argued that only by returning to "their own kind" could humans hope to live in harmony: "All nations of the earth in these modern days are seeking peace, but there is but one true and divine way that peace may be obtained in these days and it is through Love, Truth, Peace, Freedom and Justice being taught universally to all nations, in all lands" (46:9). Peace among human beings would be possible, said Noble Drew, but only if every group would "learn of your forefathers' ancient and divine Creed. That you will learn to love instead of hate" (48:10). Drew Ali seemed to assert that while there may be universal values linking all human beings, one could learn them only by adhering to the original creed of one's national group. Like Blyden, Drew Ali believed that the separation of races might yet lead to harmony among all humans.[21]

At the same time, however, Drew Ali seemed to support notions of Asiatic superiority and chosenness. The Asiatics were of a "Divine origin," he said, failing to mention what he thought about the origins of whites. He also asserted that the Church and Christianity might provide the Europeans with *earthly* salvation, but that Islam would grace Asiatics with earthly and *divine* salvation (48:7–8). These verses contradicted the universal spirit of his comments above and seemed to situate Islam as a form of particularism that dashed any hope for the divine salvation of whites. But how strongly Drew Ali believed in this idea is never made clear in the *Holy Koran,* which does not devote much space to the issue. In fact, very little of the text's contents were the original ideas of Drew Ali, as the next section explains.[22]

MODERN ESOTERICISM IN DREW ALI'S *MOORISH SCIENCE*

In creating his particularistic Moorish Science, Noble Drew plagiarized from a number of texts published by "esotericist" groups during the 1920s. Esotericism, as defined by Wouter Hanegraaff, is an umbrella word used to describe premodern traditions like cabalism, alchemy, hermeticism, neoplatonism, astrology, and magic. Each of these premodern traditions, which had ancient roots but were developed significantly during the Renaissance, "formed a counter-force against a mechanistic worldview and against science based on wholly secular principles." Refusing to view the heavens as separate from Earth, esotericism sought an "organic worldview and a science based on religious assumptions." Ultimately, "esoteric" traditions fostered the hope that human beings could broach the spiritual realm through some gnosis and/or practice, and in so doing, affect their state of being for the better. In the modern era, argues Ahtoine Faivre, esotericism has come to include four essential characteristics: (1) the belief that there are symbolic and/or real correspondences between all parts of the visible or invisible universe; (2) the idea that nature is alive; (3) the notion that meditation and imagination are necessary to connect to this enchanted universe; and (4) the possibility of the real and symbolic transmutation of one thing into another. Furthermore, many of the esoteric traditions have been made to conform to secular assumptions—that is, they have been remade upon foundations of modern science while trying to preserve the experience of the sacred. It is these traditions that scholars have often called the "occult." In the modern religious history of the United States and Europe, according to Hanegraaff, esotericism has been manifested in a number of traditions, including Rosicrucianism, Mesmerism, Spiritualism, New Thought, Theosophy, New Age, and nineteenth-century Mormonism.[23]

During the 1920s, these traditions were also prominent in African-American popular culture. Black women, in particular, were often associated with special "occult" powers. Princess Mysteria, for example, was an "East Indian mentalist" who wrote a weekly column for the *Chicago Defender,* one of black America's most prominent newspapers. Draped in Asian robes, a headband, and loads of beaded necklaces, the princess could also be found on stage and on WJKS, a Gary, Indiana, radio station where she demonstrated her abilities as a "human radio." Occult powers were also marketed as consumer culture. In one advertisement, Madame Annette, graduate astrologer, offered to "interpret your star of destiny" for twenty-five cents. Annette, who also appeared on radio, could be reached at her Madison Avenue address in New York, where she promised to "amaze" the "unhappy, discouraged, lonely, [and] unsuccessful in love or business" with her astrological readings. Like the Princess Mysteria, Annette wore "orientalist" garb, including a *khitab,* or face veil. Both women also incorporated "Oriental" signs and symbols into their teachings.[24]

Drew Ali seemed to participate in this popular culture, as well. For example, a 1927 flyer presented Noble Drew as a kind of magician. "Don't miss the Great Moorish Drama!" the flyer exclaimed. The poster promised theatrical excitement, national renewal, healings (no charge), and a magic act: "The Prophet Noble Drew Ali will be bound with several yards of rope, as Jesus was bound in the the [*sic*] temple at Jerusalem."[25] In using magic, the MST was just one of the many groups to appropriate this kind of esotericism. For example, according to Hans Baer, spiritualist churches also emphasized "the manipulation of one's present condition through magico-religious rituals and esoteric knowledge. In contrast to the common but probably exaggerated view that black religion is 'other-worldly,' spiritual people are concerned primarily with discovering solutions to their difficulties in the here and now." One of the most remarkable spiritual churches was Father George Hurley's Universal Hagar's Spiritual Church, which was founded in Detroit in 1923. George Willie Hurley (b. 1884), a native of Reynolds, Georgia, had originally trained for the Baptist ministry during his time at Tuskegee. But after migrating north to Detroit, he had converted to the Holiness Church in 1919. After this, the ferment of the spiritualism among African Americans quickly attracted Hurley's attention. In 1922, blacks formed their own parent organization, the National Colored Spiritualist Association. Hurley then split from the Spiritualists to launch his own movement. The Universal Hagar's Spiritual Church was a highly syncretistic group in which themes of black redemption and

Hurley's own messianic aspirations were mixed with séances and other forms of communication with spirits. Hurley also utilized astrological timetables, and in 1924, launched the School of Mediumship and Psychology. He thus combined modern science and psychology with spirit mediums, séances, and astrology into one syncretistic esoteric tradition.[26]

While there seem to be no direct links between Hurley and Noble Drew Ali, both shared a belief in the esoteric sciences, and even more importantly, a fascination with Levi Dowling's theosophical text, *The Aquarian Gospel of Jesus the Christ.* Hurley frequently treated the text as sacred scripture, using it in his religious services. Noble Drew, on the other hand, attempted to claim it as his own. Chapters 1 through 19 of the *Holy Koran,* nearly half of the sixty-four-page text, are copied in exact form from the *Aquarian Gospel,* which was written in 1908. Dowling, who early on followed in his father's footsteps as a Christian minister, later became interested in comparative religion and theosophy. His version of the Gospels, like other modern theosophical texts, incorporated beliefs in the universality of all religions, the mystical nature of the East, and the possibility of spiritual mastery of the "higher worlds." These themes, in addition to some information from the apocryphal Gospel of James, are apparent throughout Dowling's text. Dowling also borrowed from *La Vie Inconnue de Jesus Christ* (1894) by Nicolas Notovich, who may have also influenced Ahmadiya founder Ghulam Ahmad, author of *Jesus in India* (1899).[27]

Dowling himself explained the *Aquarian Gospel* as the product of his ability to "read" or sense the "Akashic Records," which existed in the highest realm of consciousness called the "Supreme Intelligence" or the "Universal Wisdom." According to Dowling, the Akashic Records were not physical things, but a spiritual substance that reverberated throughout the universe. "When the mind of man," he wrote, "is in exact accord with the Universal Mind, man enters into a conscious recognition of these Akashic impressions, and may collect them and translate them into any language of the earth." Using this process, Dowling claimed to have reproduced the gospel. His *Aquarian Gospel* posited that time was broken into dispensations determined by the rotation of the solar system around the center of the universe. Each age, he taught, was 2,100 years long. As the world entered the twentieth century, a transition from the Piscean Age, or the Christian dispensation, to the Aquarian Age had begun. Dowling, reflecting theosophical influences, implicitly criticized the Christian age and the dominance of the Church, claiming that the New Age, unlike the old, would be one of spirituality. Like other esotericists, Dowling believed in the possibility of mastering higher spiritual powers. In each human, he taught, there was a higher self, which was "human spirit clothed in soul," and a lower self, which was carnal and illusory. The soul, he said, was a divine thought planted in the human body, where it must undergo trials and tribulations before it could become pure soul again. These premises, the most fundamental in Dowling's creed, are highlighted in the first three chapters of the *Holy Koran.*[28]

Noble Drew's text also included Dowling's Christology. Christ, he taught, was no particular person, but a force, or *logos,* that might manifest itself in any human if that human were so anointed. Like many theosophists, Dowling posited that belief in Christ's divinity must be understood symbolically rather than literally, lest humans mistake heaven as a reward for moral behavior. In Dowling's text, Jesus teaches that heaven is present to and abiding in the "conscious" soul. Drew Ali excerpted this lesson in chapters 11 and 12 of the *Holy Koran.* In addition, Dowling believed that Christ was a universal religious figure who had traveled throughout the entire ancient lettered world to spread his good news. During these travels, Dowling depicted Christ meeting with a representative of every world religion. Of these, Drew Ali selected Jesus' meetings with a Buddhist priest, some Brahmins in India, and a Jewish scholar for inclusion in the *Holy Koran.*[29] Finally, Drew Ali chose the stories of Elizabeth, John the Baptist, Jesus' Egyptian journeys, the Crucifixion, the Resurrection, and Jesus' "full materialization" (i.e. "transmutation of flesh into spirit-flesh") in different sites throughout the world to proclaim his resurrection.[30] In total, Drew Ali selected 19 of the 182 chapters and part of the introduction to Dowling's text for inclusion in his *Holy Koran.*

Chapters 20 through 44 of the *Holy Koran,* on the other hand, were copied from either *Unto Thee I Grant* or *The Infinite Wisdom,* which were completely identical texts. First published in Chicago in 1923 by the de Laurence Company, this work purported to be a translation of an ancient manuscript "found in the Grand Temple of Thibet" by a "Dr. Cao-Tsou, Prime Minister of China." The book's introductory sections included a letter supposedly written by the Chinese Emperor to the Tibetan Grand Lama asking for permission on behalf of the Prime Minister to read and examine ancient Tibetan writings. Also included in these sections was a letter dated May 12, 1749, addressed to an anonymous English Earl from the English translator of Cao-Tsou's Chinese translation of the original manuscript. This letter, which explained that the style of translation was intentionally biblical, also contained descriptions of Lhassa, the Potala, the Grand Lama, an account of Cao-Tsou's journey, and the text's Brahmin, Confuscist, and Taoist origins.[31]

In 1925, the Ancient and Mystical Order Rosae Crucis (AMORC), the largest Rosicrucian group in the United States, published an almost exact replica of the text. These Rosicrucians were another modern esoteric group that traced their roots to early modern history, specifically to the Reformation and Counter Reformation. Founded by the mythical Christian Rosencreutz, the Order of the Rose-Cross was as much an intellectual current as a real secret society. Like other esotericists, Rosicrucians believed that the heavenly realm of reality could be broached through the use of esoteric sciences. John Dee, one of the better-known Rosicrucian philosophers, developed a "bold . . . supercelestial mathematical magic . . . [an] angel-conjuring magic," as Frances Yates put it. But their larger social goals by the 1900s were to use this knowledge in the reform of ethical behavior and education. In publishing *The Infinite Wisdom*, the Order said that its first goal was to encourage "health, happiness, and peace in the earthly lives of men." Their second goal was "to enable men and women to live clean, normal, natural lives." In fact, the crux of the text espoused rather Victorian moral ideals that could have been mistaken for the basic uplift values of the Black Church.[32]

Noble Drew Ali selected a large portion of these for inclusion in the *Holy Koran*, including a number of passages regarding the duties of men, women, and children toward each other. Women were to be submissive, industrious, nurturing, and modest. Men were to select mates prudently and treat their wives with kindness. Children were to honor their parents. Masters were to be good to their servants, and servants were to be "patient" under the reproof of their master. All people, the text instructed, should be good citizens by avoiding envy, vanity, deception, oppression, inconstancy, weakness, and ignorance. Those who practiced the "infinite wisdom" would be thankful, sincere, truthful, consistent, and faithful. The pinnacle of wisdom, however, would be to accept life as it was, neither inherently good nor bad, but only what one makes of it. Only with work, the text urged, could humans avoid the miseries of life and lift themselves into a realm of pleasure and joy known only to the Universal Soul.[33]

All of these esoteric texts offered the idea that human beings, through effort, might liberate themselves from their various forms of slavery, especially to a negative state of mind itself. Salvation was defined not as the other-worldly resting place of good souls, but as a this-worldly state of being. Drew Ali seemed to be saying, though not explicitly, that blacks could achieve true liberation in the here and now rather than in the after-life. The path towards this liberation, as articulated in Drew Ali's text, can be summarized in the following way: blacks must separate from whites, reclaim their original group identity, understand their own divine origins, meditate upon the true spiritual nature of all being, and follow a strict moral code.

DREW ALI'S AMBIGUOUS PARTICULARISM

Noble Drew's incorporation of modern esoteric texts into his *Holy Koran* represented an important moment in the history of African-American Islamic thought, especially since Drew Ali was the first to popularize certain Islamic symbols in African-American culture. It is ironic that the Prophet drew from works like *Unto Thee I Grant* and the *Aquarian Gospel* to concoct his Moorish Science, since these texts so clearly aimed to create a modern nonsectarian and universalistic tradition. While invoking "Oriental" wisdom or the Spiritual Orient itself, modern esotericism usually did so to show the universality, rather than the particularity of its beliefs. Drew Ali did precisely the opposite, claiming the traditions of the Orient as his people's rightful heritage and thus launching this version of Islam as a black separatist tradition.

At the same time, however, like Blyden, Drew Ali viewed national and "religious" pluralism as necessary to world harmony. If all peoples would gather under "their own vine and tree" and be true to their respective ethical and theological traditions, he asserted, world peace and justice might become a reality. Moreover, while Drew Ali claimed a unique national heritage for blacks through his use of a Moorish legend, he also argued that blacks were part of a shared Asiatic Islamic culture. But he never articulated exactly how he conceived of the relationship between "Moors" and their fellow Muslim Asiatics; the idea of pan-Islamic unity could be inferred from his thought, but he did not mention it explicitly.

Overall, he seemed little concerned by such thoughts. More important to Drew Ali was the development of a tradition that would facilitate moral renewal and self-determination among black Americans. In constructing such a tradition, Drew Ali defined black identity—or in his words, Moorish identity—in terms of biological descent, national origin, and creed. Going even further, he claimed divine origins and salvation for the Moors, while casting doubts on the beginning and end of whites. Drew Ali's famous heir, Elijah Muhammad, would later take that idea and place it at the center of his understanding of Islam. In fact, Elijah Muhammad would adopt Drew Ali's entire particularistic formula for understanding Islam and turn it into the most well-known tradition in the history of African-American Islam. But unlike Muhammad, Drew Ali seemed to express a large degree of ambiguity with regard not to the particularistic identity of Islam, but to its goals. For Drew Ali, like Blyden, seemed to desire a world in which all nations and peoples would be separate, but equal and free. With the creation of Elijah Muhammad's Nation of Islam, however, even that dream would be abandoned.

Chapter 4

Elijah Muhammad (1897–1975) and the Absolutism of Black Particularistic Islam

INTRODUCTION

Like Blyden and Drew Ali, Nation of Islam (NOI) leader Elijah Muhammad viewed Islam as a religious alternative to Christianity that fostered a positive sense of black pride and advanced the fight for black liberation. Muhammad, who led the NOI from the 1930s until his death in 1975, also saw Islam as the "natural" religion of blacks. In fact, as I argue below, he did not distinguish between being black and being Muslim: for Muhammad, these identities were identical. Muhammad's particularistic vision, however, was far darker than that of Blyden or Drew Ali. Unlike his predecessors, he did not share the hope for a rapprochement between blacks and whites. Instead, Elijah Muhammad embraced an absolutist particularism, espousing a fire-and-brimstone approach to race relations. Whites were the devil, Muhammad taught, and both they and their civilization would perish in the coming Apocalypse. Muhammad based these millennialist beliefs on the teachings of W. D. Fard, who appeared to him in early 1930s Detroit. Fard, Muhammad believed, was God in the flesh; Muhammad understood himself to be His Messenger. He believed that Fard had chosen him to "mentally resurrect" the "black man" through the propagation of Islam. Muhammad's mission of Islamic renewal, however, encompassed more than the mere reconversion of African Americans to their "original" faith. Being a Muslim, Muhammad taught, also meant exhibiting a high moral character, industriousness, and independence. Hence, Muhammad advocated a strict code of ethical behavior, an economic program of self-help, and the rejection of white American national identity.

Unlike Drew Ali, Muhammad was familiar with many Old World Islamic traditions and texts, and synthesized them with his own prophetic vision. But as the Nation of Islam gained more national prominence during the 1950s, his synthetic vision came under fire from a number of Muslims outside of the movement. When these attacks on Muhammad's Islamic authenticity became more frequent in the late 1950s and 1960s, he faced an important choice between abandoning parts of his particularistic vision or risking his Islamic legitimacy among non-movement Muslims. He chose the latter, entrenching himself even more deeply in his own prophetic authority.

This chapter begins with the emergence of Muhammad's thought by placing him within the general context of African-American Christianity and more specifically within the history of millennial dispensationalism so central to the black Protestantism of his youth. After outlining the experiences that led to Muhammad's conversion to W. D. Fard's Nation of Islam during the Great Depression, I depict the immigrant Muslim milieu in which Muhammad may have gained much of his knowledge about Islam. The following section then shows how Muhammad combined these Islamic influences in the postwar era with the dispensationalism of his youth, a fascination with UFOs, and other elements to form a unique body of African-American Islamic thought. Finally, I discuss Muhammad's decision in the 1960s to dismiss the criticism of non-movement Muslims, and in effect, to rid his own version of Islam of any universalism whatsoever.

THE BLACK CHRISTIANITY OF ELIJAH'S YOUTH AND THE DISPENSATIONALIST IDEA

Born in 1897 in Sandersville, Georgia, Elijah actually grew up in Cordele, a town whose race relations were governed by the system of Jim Crow segregation that arose in the post-Reconstruction South. Elijah had come into the world just one year after the Supreme Court ruled in the famous *Plessy v. Ferguson* case that segregation in public accommodation could be "separate, but equal." *Plessy* codified what had already been happening in the South since the presidential election of 1876, after which blacks were systematically denied the right to the ballot, to equal opportunity, and to due process. Lynchings were not uncommon. In the midst of this depressing scene, African Americans still struggled to support themselves and to find meaning and dignity in their lives. The Black Church, dominated by the Baptists and Methodists, played the most vital role in the survival process. Young Elijah knew the Church's importance firsthand, since his father, William, was a Baptist preacher. According to Muhammad, his father's sermons, like others of the period, were often apocalyptic in nature, although his son constantly questioned his religious beliefs, including his scriptural interpretations.[1]

Given Elijah's later teachings, it seems likely that the brand of apocalypticism to which he was exposed as a youth was Christian dispensationalism, then en vogue among many black preachers. Deeply rooted in Christian history, dispensationalism was the belief that God had dealt with human beings in epochs or dispensations. For many Christians, the dispensation of ultimate concern was the Day of Judgment and the Second Coming of Christ, a subject whose timing was vigorously debated. "Premillennialists" posited that a great battle between God and Satan would occur *before* Christ's triumphal reign of a thousand years. "Postmillennialists," on the other hand, countered that Armageddon would occur *after* Christ's triumphal return. Further, postmillennialists tended to believe that human effort might encourage the coming of the millennium, whereas premillennialists generally posited that only God could initiate the superhuman events of the eschaton. One of the most prominent advocates of premillennial dispensationalism was John Darby (1800–1882), a former official of the Church of Ireland, who visited the United States during six tours conducted between 1859 and 1877. Dozens of influential pastors, including Dwight L. Moody and St. Louis' James Brookes in addition to institutions like Chicago's Moody Bible Institute, the Bible Institute of Los Angeles, and William Bell Riley's Northwestern Bible and Missionary Training School in Minneapolis shared and disseminated Darby's views.[2]

Several key black ministers also espoused his brand of dispensationalism. These preachers often combined black messianist themes of black chosenness and the redemption of Africa with the darker vision offered by premillennial dispensationalism. James Theodore Holly (1829–1911), the first African-American Episcopalian bishop and a staunch emigrationist, emerged as one of dispensationalism's most articulate advocates. History, Holly wrote in the *African Methodist Episcopal Church Review* in 1884, was divided into three dispensations: the Mosaic, in which the Semitic race received God's revelation; the Gospel, in which the Japhetic race, that is, whites, spread the word; and the millennial, during which the sons of Ham, that is, blacks, by virtue of their Christ-like suffering for four thousand years, would finally realize the Gospel's promise. Observe the Crucifixion, Holly argued: Semites (Jews) had denied Christ; the Japhetic race, in the person of the Romans, had crucified Him; only blacks, represented by Simon the Cyrene who had carried the cross, were morally capable of replacing Japhetic (white) control of ecclesiastical and social institutions. How ironic, Holly thought, that "warlike and predatory nations" were "at the same time very busily engaged in publishing and circulating the Bible." They would be punished, he said, for their hypocrisy. "The apostolic phase of the Christian dispensation," Holly cried, "is to terminate in a deluge of blood, shed by those warlike nations in fratricidal combat, at Armageddon in the great battle of God Almighty when He shall declare war and assemble the bloodthirsty nations for slaughter."[3]

Theophilus Gould Steward (1843–1924), another premillennialist, shared Holly's vision of eschatology. An AME pastor, Steward served as chaplain to the U.S. Colored Infantry in the Philippines in addition to teaching at Wilberforce University. Like Holly, Steward prophesied that the end of the world would be coterminous with the halt of Anglo-Saxon supremacy. As outlined in his 1888 work *The End of the World; or, Clearing the Way for the Fullness of the Gentiles,* Steward believed that anarchy would result from challenges posed to modern industrial capitalism in Europe. He argued that law and order would be threatened there, encouraging waves of immigration to the United States. America, he said, would become a searing cauldron, whose only hope would be to embrace the black prophets of a bigotry-free Christianity. According to Steward, signs of the Apocalypse would include the Jews' return to Israel and the rise of world leaders from Asia and Africa. Invoking the violent prophecy of the four beasts in Daniel 7, Steward further predicted that militaristic and clannish whites would receive God's divine judgment as the "Church of Abyssinia" led "Africa's millions" into an age of peace.[4]

But the dispensationalism of Steward and Holly was only one form of black liberation theology then circulating in the Black Church. AME Bishop Henry McNeal Turner, for example, had been a hopeful believer in the promise of postwar Reconstruction to create social justice for persons of African descent. With its failure, however, he became a downright pessimist and an advocate of emigration. Turner also became famous for popularizing the idea that the Almighty was black. At an 1895 Baptist convention, Turner said that African Americans had "as much right biblically and otherwise to believe that God is a Negro, as you buckra or white people have to believe that God is a fine-looking, symmetrical, and ornamented white man. For the bulk of you and all the fool Negroes of the country believe that God is white-skinned, blue-eyed, straight-haired, projecting nosed, compressed lipped and finely robed *white* gentleman, sitting upon a throne somewhere in the heavens." As Turner made clear later, his point was ironical. He merely hoped to illustrate how racism had warped the American view of God among both blacks and whites. But others actually took Turner's statement literally and images of the black Jesus were not uncommon in several black churches.[5] Later, Elijah Muhammad would structure his interpretation of Islam around the idea that God was a black man.

Whether Elijah Muhammad knew anything about Steward, Holly, or Turner cannot be known for certain. But their influence is discernible enough in his later writings. Muhammad emerged out of a cultural context in which black Christianity was replete with ideas that he would later include in his own Islamic vision.

MUHAMMAD'S GREAT MIGRATION TO ISLAM

After marrying Clara Evans in 1919, Muhammad decided in 1923 to join the Great Migration to the North, landing in Detroit, where decreased foreign immigration (due to new anti-immigration laws, as explained in chapter 3) created a need for unskilled labor. Elijah's arrival preceded what Richard Thomas has described as a major wave of immigration throughout 1924 and 1925 that helped to increase Detroit's black population 194 percent during the 1920s. What had started out as a tiny northern black community of 5,741 in 1910 grew to 40,838 in 1920 and finally to 120,066 in 1930, when African Americans would account for 7.6 percent of the Motor City's total inhabitants. Like other working-class residents of Detroit, Muhammad viewed the northern city as both a refuge from Jim Crow and a place for potential economic advancement. Like many, Muhammad sought employment in the automobile industry. From 1923 to 1925, according to information that the Messenger gave to the FBI in a 1942 interview, he worked at the American Nut Company, the American Copper and Brass Company, and Chevrolet Axle.[6]

After this time, Muhammad seemed unable to hold steady work, an occurrence not uncommon among black migrants. The harsh working conditions for blacks, who still faced discrimination in the workplace, often prompted them to use constant shuffling between jobs as one technique to preserve their own humanity. Other challenges faced black migrants, as well. Because Detroit was segregated and little housing was available to the city's new residents, blacks lived in horribly overcrowded conditions and were charged excessively high rents in the city's burgeoning ghetto. Moreover, migrants experienced discrimination in health care, education, and nearly every other aspect of life. Detroit's Salvation Army even refused to give many Christmas baskets. While most migrants reported that they never wanted to return home, their living conditions prompted them to find a variety of coping and protest strategies. For some, the self-help strategies of churches like Second Baptist and Bethel AME, two of black Detroit's most popular institutions, proved effective. Others helped to build their local chapter of the United Negro Improvement Association, established in 1920, into one of the most colorful in the nation. Still others turned to the Detroit underworld, where African Americans found recreation and escape in vice, including prostitution and the numbers rackets.[7]

But as challenging as African-American life in Detroit was during the 1920s, the Great Depression made matters much worse. In addition to exacerbating the problems mentioned above, the Depression saw the failure of several black banks and an inability among black institutions to cope with the enormity of the crisis. A lack of professionalization and the sheer depth of the Depression also hindered the efforts of volunteer organizations like the Black Church. In fact, as Drake and Cayton found in their massive study of black Chicago, there was widespread dissatisfaction with the mainstream black denominations. Criticisms of the Black Church, which Elijah Muhammad would repeat throughout his lifetime, included the accusation that the Church was a "racket"; it was too emotional; it offered no real religion; preachers were hypocritical and failed to condemn sin; and blacks were too "religious." In a sense, the Black Church had become the victim of its own success. As the most popular grassroots institution in the black community, it was bound to be the target of vigorous criticism as well.[8]

During these years, according to one of his sons, Muhammad himself had succumbed to despair, relying on his wife, Clara, to literally pick him up off the streets of Detroit after repeated spells of drunkenness. The Church, he felt, had failed him too. But in 1931, Muhammad's life changed dramatically when he met W. D. Fard. Muhammad understood Fard to be an Arab peddler, although no scholarly consensus has yet emerged as to the true identity of the mysterious stranger. The standard histories of the Nation of Islam, nearly all of which are based on interviews with movement members or a seminal article by sociologist Erdmann Beynon, posit the following: when Muhammad met Fard, Muhammad felt himself to be in the midst of a divine presence and asked Fard whether he was "that one we read in the Bible that he would come in the last day under the name Jesus." Fard indicated that he was, but that Muhammad should keep it a secret. Muhammad later claimed that Fard was an immigrant from Mecca, Saudi Arabia, who came in 1930 to "mentally resurrect" the so-called Negro from his deceptive views of self. Muhammad became Fard's best pupil and left for Chicago later that year to spread the stranger's teachings. By 1934, Fard had disappeared, apparently without a trace, leaving Muhammad in charge of the Lost-Found Nation of Islam.[9]

The search for Fard's identity, which might help us speculate about the forms of Islam with which he was familiar, reveals the difficulty of conducting research on the Nation of Islam. The scholar's only sources originate either with movement members themselves or with the surveillance and counterintelligence operations of the FBI. Beynon's article, on the other hand, was written four key years after the disappearance of Fard, after which his actual story may have become hagiographic in nature. Furthermore, FBI memos suggest that the Bureau actively tried to discredit the movement's founder through a disinformation campaign throughout the 1950s and 1960s. The result is that the historical record offers a number of different possibilities for Fard's identity. According to the Bureau, Fard was born either of British, Hawaiian, or Polynesian parents, became a criminal, and eventually served out his time in San Quentin. Other accounts identify him as a Palestinian, a Syrian Druze, a black Jamaican whose father was a Syrian Muslim, a Turkish-born Nazi, and/or some sort of Turko-Persian.[10]

There is, however, another way to view the problem of Fard's identity. Rather than trying to ascertain Fard's true place of origin, we can explore the larger immigrant milieu of Detroit in which he lived and worked. In so doing, we can also understand the link between the emergence of the NOI and the rise of Islam in the United States more generally.

POSSIBLE SOURCES OF MUHAMMAD'S BLACK ISLAM

Detroit itself teemed with thousands of Muslim immigrants from Lebanon, Syria, Turkey, Albania, and India during the 1920s and 1930s.

According to Kemal Karpat, as many as 1.2 million emigrants from the Ottoman Empire, including both Christians and Muslims, came to North and South America from 1860 through the founding of the Turkish Republic. Approximately half of them were Arabic-speaking. The Motor City attracted anywhere from two to ten thousand Muslim immigrants for the same reasons that it "pulled" in African-American migrants: that is, the economic opportunities offered by the growing automobile industry. In 1907, for example, several young Turkish men were employed in the Ford Plant at Highland Park. By 1920, over a thousand Turkish Muslims, hailing both from Anatolia and the Balkans, formed a Detroit chapter of the Red Crescent and purchased three thousand grave plots to bury the dead according to Islamic law. Syrians, including Christians and Muslims, also found employment in the automobile industry. In 1916, the Ford sociological department listed 555 Arab men as factory workers. While no direct connection between these populations and Elijah Muhammad has been found, it is worth speculating that the factory became the place where Muhammad first gained exposure to Muslims and perhaps Islam.[11]

Still, his main influence seemed to be W. D. Fard, who spread his message not as a factory worker, but as a peddler. Immigrant Arabs, especially around the turn of the century, often made their mark economically as peddlers. Willing to construct themselves as exotic Orientals, they frequently sold their wares, including clothing and sweets 'among other items, by promoting their goods and themselves as products of the "Holy Land"—even though most of these Syrian immigrants had never even been to Ottoman Palestine before. In the midst of the Depression, unemployed Turks, like many other Americans, also took up peddling, hawking anything from cigarettes to watermelon. Whether or not Fard was an immigrant himself, he probably emerged out of this significant subculture in American life. Like immigrant peddlers, he presented himself as a mysterious Easterner from the Holy Land. Moreover, Fard disseminated his message in a city where Islamic practice was both diverse and abundant. Lebanese immigrant Muhammad Karoub built the first mosque in the area in 1919, where his brother, Husain, served as *imam,* or prayer-leader. Shi'is, Bektashis (mostly Albanians), and mevlavis, the so-called whirling dervishes, all actively practiced their particular forms of Islamic life in immigrant Detroit from the 1920s onward. In addition, the Ahmadiya had a presence there and even more so in nearby Chicago.[12]

The Ahmadiya are particularly important to the development of African-American Islamic thought, since, like the Moorish Science Temple, their theological orientation may have been one of the sources from which Elijah Muhammad fashioned his black Islamic thought. Begun in the Punjab, part of British India, in 1889 by Mirza Ghulam Ahmad, the Ahmadiya were a messianist movement that revolved around Ahmad's claim to be *mujaddid,* or a renewer of religion, the Christian Messiah, and the Islamic Mahdi. Ahmad's prophetic claims garnered fierce opposition from most Muslims, who have historically understood the Prophet Muhammad to be the "seal" and thus the final prophet in world history. Nevertheless, the Ahmadiya became effective missionaries for their movement and Islam, in general. In particular, their mass distribution of English translations of the Qur'an was the first such effort among Muslims in the modern world. Importantly, it was an Ahmadi Qur'an that Elijah Muhammad would frequently cite in his religious teachings.[13]

The Ahmadiya were also quick to focus on urban African Americans as a group ripe for conversion. In 1920, the Qadiani faction sent Mufti Muhammad Sadiq as a missionary to North America. Though Sadiq began to teach in New York, he quickly moved from there to Chicago, then to Highland Park in the greater metropolitan Detroit area, and finally back to the Windy City, where he established his headquarters on the Southside's Wabash Avenue. While the Ahmadiya both preached and practiced racial cooperation and equality, Sadiq did not hesitate to use racialist arguments to promote Islam among blacks. Through his speeches and the *Moslem Sunrise,* Sadiq also associated white Christianity with slavery, which he argued destroyed the African's original language, Arabic, and his religion, Islam. In 1923, after giving five lectures at UNIA meetings in Detroit, Sadiq claimed to have converted forty Garveyites to Islam. Later, Sadiq's successor, Sufi Bengalee, also promoted Islam (à la Blyden) as the inspiration behind historical black achievements, including, for example, the accomplishments of former slaves Bilal ibn Rabah and Zayd ibn Muhammad under the banner of Islam.[14]

This early immigrant missionary activity suggests that Muhammad may have been influenced by plenty of other sources besides W. D. Fard— or at the least that these sources may have influenced Fard himself. In light of these facts and the lack of contemporaneous accounts of the relationship between Fard and Muhammad, the claim made by Muhammad's biographer that Muhammad repeated Fard's teachings with remarkable "consistency" throughout his life seems problematic.[15] My goal in the following section will be to understand less what Fard taught Muhammad and more how Muhammad translated Fard's theories into a unique body of thought that synthesized a number of American traditions.

MUHAMMAD'S
BLACK ISLAMIC DISPENSATIONALISM
IN POSTWAR AMERICAN CULTURE

Whether the details of Muhammad's religious system were actually in place by the end of the 1930s or whether they changed throughout that decade is difficult to tell, especially since Muhammad himself seemed to be a wanderer for much of the period. During 1934, according to movement accounts, internal dissension within the NOI forced Muhammad to flee both Detroit and Chicago, where he had established the second Temple of Islam. After a stay in Milwaukee, Muhammad left the Midwest for the nation's capital. For the following four years, Muhammad traveled up and down the eastern seaboard until he established Temple No. 4 in Washington in 1939. Still a relative unknown, he was arrested in 1942 on the charge that he had failed to register for the Selective Service Act. He was then released on bond and later apprehended in Chicago, where he was charged with sedition.[16]

Ernest Allen argues that Muhammad's arrest was linked to the FBI's sweep of pro-Japanese African-American organizations during that year and early 1943. The NOI may have had connections to Satokata Takahashi's Development of Our Own organization, which disseminated pro-Japanese literature in the United States during the 1930s. In connecting anti-Western struggles to the rise of the Japanese Empire, Takahashi garnered support among a number of African-American groups, including the Pacific Movement of the Eastern World and the Original Independent Benevolent Afro-Pacific Movement of the World. While the NOI may have been yet another black organization linked to the Japanese cause, it is important to note that the federal government never convicted Elijah Muhammad of sedition. In fact, according to an internal FBI memorandum, the charge was dismissed and Muhammad was forced to serve out a conviction on the less serious charge of draft evasion. In 1943, he entered the Federal Correctional Institution in Milan, Michigan, where he stayed until released in 1946.[17]

After his release, Muhammad created the Nation of Islam so firmly etched in American memory—the organization known for disciplined corps of bow-tied men hawking bean pies, salvation, and copies of his books; the "supportive" white-robed women who attended "Muslim Girls Training"; and most important of all, an articulate, good-looking young minister named Malcolm X. By the late 1950s, the NOI had grown to include dozens of temples in twenty-eight cities and thousands of card-carrying members. To some observers, especially C. Eric Lincoln, the NOI seemed far more like a political organization than a religious one, as I outlined in chapter 1. Indeed, the Nation of Islam had very explicit political overtones, especially in its opposition to the civil rights movement. During the 1950s, the struggle for civil rights took huge steps forward in both the judicial assault on segregation (most famously in the 1954 decision in *Brown v. Board of Education*) and in an African-American grassroots movement of marches and sit-ins that produced powerful black leadership, including Martin Luther King, Jr. Elijah Muhammad, of course, rejected King's vision of an equal and integrated America, arguing that King was trying to make blacks love the white devil, a self-defeating act that perpetuated the values of slavery. Even more, said Muhammad, King failed to understand the "scripture, for it surely teaches you that the world has been under the rule of Satan (the devil) for 6,000 years, and now separation must come between God's people and the devil so that the righteous can survive."[18]

Despite this opposition to King and his ideal of integration, however, Muhammad never became a terribly articulate spokesperson for black nationalism. His call for racial separatism, for example, did not translate into a concrete plan for the establishment of a modern nation-state or even for support of emigration. While the Nation of Islam contained many of the trappings of a nationalist organization, including its own flag and paramilitary group, Muhammad's plan for his "Nation" only sometimes mentioned the designation of a small number of black-belt states for the use of African Americans. In most lectures, Muhammad merely said that blacks should have some "land of our own." Even more, he did not usually associate this land with a geographic region (like Africa), a specific form of polity (democratic, authoritarian, etc.), or even with a particular sense of history, all of which usually constituted the imagined signs of the modern nation-state. Rather, Muhammad tended to focus on economic self-sufficiency within the American marketplace. Muhammad adapted the nineteenth-century yeoman ideal of agrarian independence into his own racialized worldview: he believed that true freedom could exist only outside the white-dominated market. This economic separatism included the call for the boycott of white businesses; the development of a black nation-wide bank, black hospitals, and black-owned factories; and the purchase of farmland from which blacks could extract necessary raw materials for their economic independence. These activities, and not agitation for the establishment of a black state, consumed the energies of many of the NOI's members.[19]

Elijah Muhammad himself, however, concentrated most of his intellectual efforts not on political or economic nationalism, but on his own particularistic interpretation of Islam. His views could be heard over the radio, in person, or read either in the *Pittsburgh Courier* or his numerous published works. In 1957, *The Supreme Wisdom* appeared. Then in 1965, he published his magnum opus, *Message to the Blackman in America.* The *Message* contained edited versions of *The Supreme Wisdom* and the *Prayer Service in Islam* in addition to articles and sermons published previously in the *Pittsburgh Courier* and *Muhammad Speaks,* which began weekly publication shortly after its inception in 1961. The content of these published works revealed Muhammad to be a man fascinated by biblical and Qur'anic scriptures, his own prophetic status, numerology, and myth. In fact, of the 341 pages in *Message,* less than one hundred were devoted to explicitly political and economic themes. The remainder revealed Muhammad's views on theology, mythology, eschatology, scriptural interpretation, and Islamic prayer, among other such topics.[20]

Like Blyden and Drew Ali, Muhammad defined Islam as a counter-tradition to Christianity. Christianity, said Muhammad, was a "slave religion," used by whites to keep the truth of blacks' divine nature from them. Islam, on the other hand, promoted black achievement, and according to Muhammad, forbade slavery: "No Muslim will enslave a[nother] Muslim." If slavery had been practiced by Arabs, he argued, then they were not true Muslims. Christianity, on the other hand, had been used, according to Muhammad, to decimate the black family in slavery, making "Uncle Toms" out of black men and "Jezebels" out of black women. Whereas Islam made blacks industrious and self-reliant, Muhammad argued, Christianity made blacks "lazy, careless, and dependent." Muhammad also indicted white Christians on account of their easy use of violence as a means to accomplish racist ends. Christianity, he said, was a religion of war. Taking the Gospels literally, Muhammad cited Jesus' own words as proof for his polemical stance: "Do not think that I have come to bring peace on earth; I have not come to bring peace, but a sword. For I have come to set a man against his father, and a daughter against her mother . . ." (Matt. 10:34–5). According to Muhammad, even "if Jesus was a peacemaker, then the Christians are not his followers" since "Christianity, as we see it in practice in America, certainly does not unite but rather divides the people against each other . . . its sword is never sheathed."[21]

All of these themes had been articulated previously by Blyden and Drew Ali. But where Muhammad differed significantly from his predecessors was in the propagation of a rather unique dispensationalist tradition called the "myth of Yacub." This alternate creation myth represented a radical and creative reconceptualization of black identity by trying to establish black superiority, explain how it was usurped, and describe the conditions necessary for its restoration. Altering a classic dispensationalist timeline, Muhammad claimed real Earth time began sixty-six trillion years ago, when an explosion separated the moon from the Earth, leaving only the great black tribe of Shabazz, the Earth's original inhabitants, intact. The original Nation spoke Arabic and practiced Islam. Twenty-four scientists, one of whom acted as Judge or God, ruled this paradise. But 6,600 years ago, the original Nation suffered a blow at the hands of a mad scientist named Yacub, who was hell bent on grafting a new race of devils, whites, out of the original man. After six hundred years, the mad scientist's followers succeeded in their horrible task, Muhammad explained, using Qur'an 49:15 and 76:2 as proof texts. For six thousand years, it was prophesied, the white devils would be allowed to exist on Earth.[22]

These six thousand years represented known world history for Muhammad. From 4000 to 2000 B.C., he believed, whites lived as barbarous and violent cavepeople in Europe. Sounding strikingly similar to the nineteenth-century black Presbyterian minister Henry Highland Garnet, Muhammad said that whites "wore animal skins for clothes . . . they became so savage that they lost all their sense of shame . . . they made their homes in the caves on hillsides . . . they lost all knowledge of civilization." Since whites were naturally brutish in Muhammad's view, only God could lift them up and permit them to conquer the world. Beginning in 2000 B.C., Allah, according to Elijah Muhammad, sent a number of prophets, including both Jesus and Muhammad, to disseminate Islam among the whites. But, Muhammad claimed, "the white race, by nature, can't be righteous. Islam was taught to them from Moses to Muhammad, but they were never able to live the life of a Muslim believer." Nevertheless, the Prophet Muhammad (of seventh-century Arabia), whom Elijah Muhammad viewed as an Arab and a member of the black nation, refused to give up on his mission to convert the white devils. Even though the omniscient twenty-four scientists governing world history informed the Prophet of the futility of his mission, Elijah Muhammad taught, his compassionate heart led him to continue, prompting the scientists to laugh at him.[23]

Though the Prophet's mission was unsuccessful, according to Muhammad, his "bottling up" of the savages in Europe did represent an important moment in history. For the success of Islam throughout the Old World, he said, prevented whites from spreading their evil ways, including their false religion, for at least one thousand years. This, Muhammad argued, was in fulfillment of the prophecy in Rev. 20:7: "And when the thousand years are ended, Satan will be loosed from his prison." From A.D. 570 to 1555, Muhammad wrote, the Prophet's successors had succeeded in preventing the "loosening" of Satan. But, in the fateful sixteenth century, "John Hawkins and others deceived our foreparents in Africa and brought them into slavery in America." This instituted another millennium in which the satanic race freely reigned over the world. Why was the "man of sin" permitted to do this by the all-powerful Black God, Muhammad asked. This, too, could be explained by biblical prophecy in 2 Thess. 2:9: "The coming of the lawless one by the activity of Satan will be with all power and with pretended signs and wonders." "The man of sin," Muhammad paraphrased, "had a work to do and God wouldn't interfere with this work." Ironically, however, in fulfilling their prophesied mission by enslaving blacks, the white devils committed moral suicide, insuring God's retribution in the end time.[24]

For Muhammad, the events leading to judgment began with the earthly appearance of W. D. Fard, God in person, among the blacks of Detroit. In Rev. 18:1, Muhammad wrote, "it says that the Revelator saw an angel come from Heaven (from the Holy Land) having great power and the earth (the so-called Negroes) was enlightened with His glory . . . this angel can be no other than Master W. F. Muhammad [W. D. Fard], the Great Mahdi, who came from the Holy City of Mecca, Arabia, in 1930."[25] For God, Muhammad emphasized, was no "spook in space"; he was a man, the Mahdi, the Messiah, the Christ, and the Son of Man all in one. Even more, despite Fard's light-skinned appearance in movement photographs, Muhammad considered him to be a black man. After Fard left, according to Muhammad, he would be permitted to carry his Message to the original Nation for an unspecified, but relatively short period of time before the Apocalypse. Signs of the coming doom, according to Muhammad, would include human corruption, drought, immorality, homosexuality, nudity, adultery, robbery, gambling, drunkenness, drugs, deception, and the decline of the dollar. Overall, Muhammad said, these elements would translate into the fall of the Christian West, which he said began in 1914 with the Great War (a belief also shared by the Jehovah's Witnesses). The American government, which represented the fourth beast of Rev. 18:4 in Muhammad's view, would also have a special role to play in this prelude due to its continued persecution of its former slave population.[26]

In the final hour, according to Muhammad, a "Mothership" or "Motherplane," a human-built planet measuring one-half mile by one-half mile "squared," which was invisible to all but Muhammad and his believers, would send horrible bombs on the Earth, destroying all major cities. To support his theory, Muhammad cited the prophecy of Ezek. 10:2. This verse depicted God instructing a scribe to gather burning coals from cherubim that would be hovering above "whirling wheels" in the sky. These coals would then be distributed over Jerusalem, which had become a city of sin. For further proof, Muhammad also offered that the "small circular-made planes called flying saucers, which are so much talked of being seen, could be from this Mother Plane."[27]

It is worth interrupting our narrative to explore Muhammad's appropriation of this belief in UFOs into his thought, since it serves as such a good indication of the postwar roots of many of his beliefs. Spaceships, of course, were nothing new to American popular culture by the 1950s. In 1938, for example, anywhere from four to twelve million Americans tuned in to hear the radio adaptation of H. G. Wells' novel, *War of the Worlds,* aired on the CBS radio network. The adaptation, written by Howard Koch and produced by a young Orson Welles, reported in news-like fashion the destruction of New Jersey by a cylindrical Martian spaceship. The participation of fictional, but realistic sounding officials, including a Princeton professor, military men, and the Secretary of the Interior, led 28 percent of those listening to mistake the play for real news, according to one poll. The resulting panic jammed phone lines, created traffic jams, and stirred apocalyptic thought. Some interviewed after the panic, for instance, reported thinking that the country was being punished for "our evil ways"; another tried to reconcile the events to the biblical prophecy that the first destruction was by flood, while the next would be by fire. In Harlem, according to the *New York Times,* some "evening prayer services became 'end of the world' prayer meetings."[28]

In the postwar period, however, the belief in UFOs took a slightly different form. In the 1940s, according to a Gallup poll, most Americans did not associate flying disks with extraterrestrial spaceships. But in 1947 farmer William Brazel found the remains of a weather balloon carrying radar reflection devices (used to detect the sound waves of atomic blasts) near Roswell, New Mexico. While the military remained silent about its Cold War hardware, a myth developed in the popular imagination that the government actually concealed the crash of a spaceship carrying extraterrestrials. Frank Scully codified this belief in his 1950 bestseller, *Behind the Flying Saucers.* The obsession with UFOs also spawned several feature films, including the 1956 *Earth vs. the Flying Saucers*. Even more, some groups incorporated the Roswell myth into their system of beliefs. One Midwestern group studied by Leon Festinger and Henry Riecken posited that Jesus, or "Sananda" as he was called in the group, commanded a spaceship that would initiate the Apocalypse, while also whisking true believers away to a heavenly planet.[29] Muhammad's dispensationalist Islam was clearly another tradition during this period to support the flying object as deus ex machina, indicating the crossracial appeal of this particular phenomenon in the popular imagination.

What is so noteworthy about Muhammad's use of the Mothership myth is that it did not translate into an escapism on the part of his believers. In fact, quite the opposite became true. Heaven, Muhammad taught, was a state on Earth achieved when blacks liberated themselves from the authority of the white devils and determined their own future. The mystical world, Muhammad explained, coexists with the material world. Reflecting one of the founding principles of modern esotericism, Muhammad rejected the dualistic thinking that depicted a division between two spheres of reality: the earthly, where human beings could exert some control, and the heavenly, where human beings were powerless. Muhammad characterized this belief as a self-defeating tradition from slave times. "We are in Islam what Christianity offers beyond the grave," Muhammad wrote. "Stop looking for anything after death—Heaven or Hell. These are in *this* life. Death settles it all." There was, said Muhammad, no sweet bye-and-bye where blacks could finally get their due: "No already physically dead person will be in the hereafter; that is slavery belief, taught to slaves to keep them under control. . . . The slave is made to believe his will came after death, and his master knows that death settles all, and that you can't return to tell him whether he lied or told the truth." Slavery, Muhammad taught, was not so much the bondage of a black person's body, but of his or her mind; in so much as blacks remained tied to what he defined as "white" ideas, including the traditional Christian belief in an unseen heaven, they remained enslaved. Muhammad's thought sought instead to place black destiny mostly in black hands. Returning to God involved no physical resurrection brought about by the Almighty, as most Muslims understood the Day of Judgment; it was, according to Muhammad, a mental resurrection that meant seizing control of one's own economic, political, and moral course. This, Muhammad insisted, was the meaning of Qur'anic verses like 89:27–30, which referred to paradise: "O soul that is at rest, return to Your Lord, well-pleased with Him, well-pleasing; So enter among My servants, and enter into My Paradise."[30]

Muhammad's thought, then, contained both this-worldly and other-worldly aspects. On the one hand, Muhammad's dispensationalist beliefs discouraged believers from joining any broad-based reform movements that aspired to change the status quo. After all, such efforts would be futile according to his prophecies. Muhammad believed that no true revolution would occur until the appointed hour, which the council of scientists had already designated. In this, Muhammad reflected a strict premillennialism: no matter what human beings did to make the world better or worse, they could not affect the timing of the Apocalypse. On the other hand, Muhammad also taught that believers need not wait until doomsday to realize some of God's promises for them. In fact, he said, if they embraced his program of black uplift, they would experience a heavenly life on Earth, which he defined as a state of freedom, self-determination, and economic well-being.

While Muhammad treated economic self-sufficiency as an important component of his code of ethics, he also stressed a need for "clean living" that usually focused on some aspect of the black body. For example, he sought to change the way people ate by banning many foods associated with slave culture, including pork and cabbage. He also prohibited certain styles of coiffure, like the straightening of one's hair, which he considered to be imitative of white style. In addition, he criticized the usual vices like gambling, drinking, and smoking. In place of these behaviors, he required believers to follow a complex set of rules regarding their personal appearance and behavior. Muhammad also instructed his followers to practice the Islamic prayer as another way of bringing these values to life. In the final section, I explore Muhammad's changing writings on prayer not only to show how he synthesized his own particularistic vision with certain Old World Islamic traditions, but also to demonstrate how he defended his authority in reaction to Sunni Muslim criticism of his movement.

SUNNI MUSLIM CRITICISM, ISLAMIC PRAYER, AND MUHAMMAD'S ENTRENCHMENT

For nearly all Muslims outside of the NOI, Muhammad's unique Islamic dispensationalism directly contradicted the most basic beliefs of any acceptable interpretation of Sunni or Shi'i Islam. But in the beginning, some movement allies argued that these differences were unimportant. One was Pakistani Abdul Basit Naeem, the Sunni Muslim publisher of *The Moslem World and the USA*, which included extensive coverage of the movement.

In 1957, Naeem was the guest of honor at the NOI's annual Savior's Day Convention in Chicago. Naeem admitted that "certain differences" existed between traditional Islam and Elijah Muhammad, but argued that this situation was by design. He also conceded that the movement "operates on racial lines," but maintained the "wisdom of such practices on" the part of Muhammad. Paraphrasing the Messenger, Naeem asserted that "my people must be dealt with on a special basis, because their background and circumstances are different from those prevailing elsewhere in the world. You cannot use the same medicine to treat altogether different diseases." It was hard to argue with success, Naeem continued, since "Mr. Muhammad's teachings . . . have enabled more Americans to form an acquaintance with Islam than the efforts of all other individuals seeking converts to Islam here put together."[31]

In 1959, however, Muhammad's movement gained national prominence when WNTA-TV in New York aired a five-part series on the NOI produced by Mike Wallace of CBS News. It was entitled *The Hate that Hate Produced*. Following this blistering bit of investigative journalism, articles about the movement appeared in *Reader's Digest, Time, U.S. News and World Report,* and the *New York Times*. These publications usually characterized the NOI as a black supremacist group or as anti-American. Many civil rights leaders, including the NAACP Executive Director Roy Wilkins and Martin Luther King, Jr., also denounced the NOI as a hate group. Wilkins faulted the lack of a strong civil rights bill and white racism in general as the causes of the NOI, claiming that the NOI only had a following because of the lack of equal opportunity for blacks. Following all of this bad press, more and more Muslims also publicly criticized Muhammad, hoping largely to distinguish themselves and the "true Islam" from Muhammad and his teachings. Writing to the *Pittsburgh Courier,* the newspaper in which Muhammad had published religious articles since 1956, one Muslim begged the paper's readers not to "confuse the sect of Muhammad with that of true Islam. Islam does not preach hate," he asserted, "it does not preach racism, it only calls for love, peace, and understanding." Yet another writer to the paper argued that Elijah Muhammad "twists the Koran around to fit his hate teachings." In Chicago, Talib Ahmad Dawud, an émigré from Antigua who had founded the Moslem Brotherhood of America in 1950, also joined the criticism of Muhammad. Dawud, who was the husband of jazz singer Dakota Stanton, shared Muhammad's anti-integrationist and anti-Christian views, but rejected his beliefs in Fard's divinity and his own prophetic status. In 1959, Dawud launched a campaign against Muhammad, accusing the movement of being an illegitimate Islamic sect. Dawud attacked Muhammad's "denial of a future, bodily resurrection, and his follower's failure to adhere to the proper Muslim prayer rituals." He also charged that Muhammad could not perform the pilgrimage to Mecca, because the Saudi Arabian government and its pilgrimage committee had banned him from Mecca. In addition, he published a picture of W. D. Fard, whom he claimed was white, with the caption, "White Man Is God for Cult Of Islam." Others joined Dawud in his anti-Muhammad crusade, including his wife, Dakota Stanton, and jazz pianist Ahmad Jamal. Jamil Diab, a Palestinian Arab who had taught formerly at the NOI's elementary and secondary school, also contributed a negative article that appeared on the front page of a December 5 edition of the *Chicago Defender,* one of black America's most popular dailies. Then, in 1962, Adib Nurud-din, a Chicago follower of Ahmadiya figure Nur al-Islam, accused Elijah Muhammad of being a "race-hating, scheming, cynical, and power hungry fanatic." His teachings, Nurud-din said, were full of "crude absurdities and trivial nonsense."[32]

The criticism from both the mainstream press and rival black Muslim leaders also influenced immigrant and foreign Muslim reaction to Muhammad. For example, the Islamic Center of Washington, D.C., which received support from various Arab governments, attempted to dispel the notion that Muhammad's NOI was a "sect" of Islam. And in 1963, the Federation of Islamic Associations in the United States and Canada, the largest umbrella organization of its time, declared the NOI illegitimate. That same year, Ahmad Kamal, an official of Jami'at al-Islam, published an article in the *Chicago Defender* that labeled Elijah Muhammad's doctrines as "satanic."[33]

In response, Muhammad joined his sons Herbert and Akbar in late 1959 and early 1960 for an *'umra,* or lesser pilgrimage to Mecca, in order to solidify his claims to Islamic authenticity. While articles in *Muhammad Speaks* wrote only glowing reports about the experience, his son Wallace later claimed in a 1996 address that Muhammad, who expected to see "streets of gold" in Mecca, had been disappointed by the trip. In fact, upon his return, Muhammad paid increasingly less attention to the questions raised by other Muslims about his legitimacy as an Islamic leader. He seemed to care even less whether his own prophecies and those of his teacher, W. D. Fard, adhered to what other Muslims considered to be the "real Islam."[34]

This entrenchment into his own prophetic authority can be seen clearly in the changing nature of his writings on Islamic prayer. In the late 1950s, Muhammad instructed believers to pray in a traditionally Sunni manner, although there is no evidence to suggest that a significant number ever actually did so, or that prayers were a regular part of temple meetings. Nevertheless, Muhammad went on record in a 1957 prayer manual published by the University of Islam, the movement's primary and secondary school, in favor of the Sunni prayer ritual. His prayer manual outlined all of the steps common to the Islamic *salat,* the ritual prayer performed five times daily by most pious Muslims. The only difference was that Muhammad instructed his followers to say the prayers in English, rather than the traditional Arabic, which would be taught to them "some day in the near future." The manual contained descriptions of the proper prayer times, ritual cleansing or ablutions, the call to prayer, and the components of prayer. Most of the manual explained *how* to perform prayer properly, rather than telling believers *why* it was important to do so.[35]

But when the edited versions of "The Prayer Service in Islam" appeared in *Muhammad Speaks* in 1962, Muhammad interpreted the meaning of the prayers strictly within the confines of his own dispensationalist Islam. When discussing the Qur'anic injunction that *all* Muslims face Mecca while in prayer, for example, Muhammad claimed that the injunction actually "refers to the lost and found people of Islam," meaning the members of the NOI: "Before their return," Muhammad wrote, "they must turn in the direction with clean hands and hearts, bow in submission to the Will of Allah alone with the righteousness that they may be welcomed to take their place again among their own people." This passage also connected the "resurrection" of black Muslims to proper ritual performance, which was explained using the same logic that informed Muhammad's advocacy of a good diet and decent clothes. Believers, Muhammad claimed, must be clean both inside and out in order to submit properly to Allah. Then, they can turn their whole selves towards Mecca, which symbolized *and* enacted their submission to the will of God. In 1965, when edited versions of "The Prayer Service" column became a chapter in *Message to the Blackman in America,* Muhammad promised that "he who cleanses himself in and out leaves no filthiness."[36]

One should pray especially, Muhammad said, for freedom from worldly desires, which he equated to a desire for food. Quoting a story from Exod. 16, the leader argued that "the want of bread and meat . . . gave Moses and Aaron much trouble trying to lead the people into spiritual knowledge of Jehovah and self-independence." This hunger led people to regret that God had even bothered to bring them out of Egypt (Exod. 16:3). In the case of black Americans, however, it was the "want of the slave-masters' bread, meat and luxuries [that] is depriving the so-called

Negroes today of their independence." What blacks coveted, he implied, was not a full belly, but the accouterments of the slavemaster's culture, including liquor, cigarettes, pork, and other prohibited foods. To remedy this desire, he said, one should pray, beseeching God for deliverance. Drawing from Qur'an 1:6–7, Muhammad wrote that the "Muslims pray in their oft-repeated prayer to seek Allah's help in guiding them on the right path, the path of those whom God has favored and not on the path of those who have caused His anger to descend upon them (the Jews and Christians)."[37]

In the later editions of "The Prayer Service," Muhammad also argued that the *fard* or obligatory components of the prayers were references to the founder of the Nation of Islam, W. D. *Fard*. This claim was wholly beyond the pale of any traditional Islamic understanding of the concept of the word *fard*. "All praise is due," Muhammad wrote, "to our Lord and Saviour, Master Fard Muhammad. To Him do we submit; to Him we fly for refuge from the evils of Yacub's civilization." Unlike the black Christian, the Messenger taught, the Muslim "prays in the Name of Allah and not to a mystery God that he nor anyone else has seen, nor does such exist. Neither does he pray in the name of dead prophets." The leader's "prayer service" also introduced some innovations into the traditional Islamic ritual. Muhammad instructed believers that in addition to reciting of the *fatiha*, or the first *sura* of the Qur'an, they should add these words: "O Allah! I seek refuge from anxiety and grief, and I seek Thy refuge from lack of strength and laziness, and I seek Thy refuge from cowardice and niggardliness, and I seek Thy refuge from being overpowered by dept [*sic*] and the oppression of men; O Allah! suffice Thou me with what is lawful to keep me away from what is prohibited, and with Thy grace make me free from want of what is besides Thee." This prayer obviously emerged not out of any previously Islamic text, but out of Muhammad's own prophetic teachings.[38]

FROM AN ABSOLUTIST PARTICULARISM TO AN ABSOLUTIST UNIVERSALISM

The changes in Muhammad's writings on prayer showed that by the early the 1960s, Islamic legitimacy within the NOI was defined solely in relationship to the Messenger himself. As the last and only legitimate representative of W. D. Fard, God in the flesh, Muhammad had not only rejected Christianity, he had also rejected the right of anyone to interpret

Islamic traditions except himself. In a sense, this decision can be viewed as a pragmatic one. Perhaps Muhammad was aware of his own limitations. He had little formal education and his familiarity with Old World Islamic traditions was modest. In fact, he possessed no knowledge of Arabic. If Muhammad had agreed to debate rival Muslims using the terms of Old World Islamic traditions, he would have been entirely outmatched. But by rejecting their challenges and offering his own interpretations of Islam, he effectively ended any possible debate and asserted his own prophetic authority. He embraced a particularistic form of Islam that he could control.

For many of his believers, who felt extremely devoted to Muhammad, this intellectual insularity was not only justified, it was also desirable. After all, many credited the Messenger and his vision with saving their lives—for them, he was their conduit to Islam. It was his Islam of self-reliance, black chosenness, and divine retribution that many saw as their pathway to liberation from oppression, self-hatred, and hopelessness. It was his Islam rather than the Islam of his critics that made their lives new.

But other followers were more independent of Muhammad and questioned his authority on various grounds. For some of them, like Malcolm X, Muhammad's thought became the particularistic springboard for other visions of Islam that embraced universalism in equally absolutist ways. In fact, one of the ironies of movement history was that in trying to defend his teacher, Malcolm confronted Muhammad's critics on their own terms—that is, by trying to use Old World Islamic traditions to justify Muhammad's beliefs. In so doing, however, he came to care far more about Muslims outside of the movement and about the traditions of Old World Islam. This seminal intellectual moment in the history of African-American Islamic thought had vital, if unforeseen consequences, as the next chapter shows.

Chapter 5

Islamic Universalism, Black Particularism, and the Dual Identity of Malcolm X (1925–1965)

INTRODUCTION

This chapter argues that at the end of his life, Malcolm X faced what he called a "double burden"—namely, to be true to his universalistic inter-pretation of Islam while also promoting the particularistic goals of pan-Africanism. Unlike Blyden, Drew Ali, or Muhammad, Malcolm came to define Islam in strictly universalistic ways. Accepting the "Islam" of his Arab Muslim sponsors, he never questioned whether Islam might be a ve-hicle for black nationalism, messianism, or any other form of particular-ism. For Malcolm, as I show below, Islam was no more relevant to "black" people than it was to "white" people; it was a "human" tradition that ap-plied equally to all human beings. At the same time, however, Malcolm did not look to this universalistic Islam as any sort of strategy in his fight for black liberation; instead, he espoused a pan-African struggle led exclu-sively by and for blacks. Moreover, like Blyden, Drew Ali, and Muham-mad, he believed in an essentialist black identity, characterized by shared biological and intellectual traits, that linked together all persons of African descent into a common community.

Because Malcolm viewed his own black identity as different from and nearly antithetical to his Muslim identity, his thought exhibited a form of what W. E. B. DuBois famously called "double consciousness." In fact, Mal-colm's simultaneous commitments to identities that he viewed as contradic-tory shaped much of his thought, including his discussion of "religion" and "politics." On the one hand, he championed a particularistic black politics that sought to bring blacks together based on their common cultural and biological traits. On the other, he believed in an Islam that, by definition, could have nothing to do with particularistic movements or struggles. Consequently, he said, he must keep his religion and politics separate. The result of his doubleness was that his Islam, which had been a powerful force in his life, could have nothing to do with his struggle for black freedom, which had been an equally, if not more significant force in his life.

In order to understand how Malcolm developed his self-confessed dual identity, this chapter begins with a brief biographical sketch of Malcolm's life before 1960. I then focus on the intellectual issues surrounding Malcolm's separation from Elijah Muhammad and demonstrate how Malcolm's interaction with and eventual sponsorship by Muslim missionaries during the early 1960s led him to embrace a universalistic definition of the "true" Islam. In the next section, I explore Malcolm's embrace of pan-Africanism as an approach to the struggle for black freedom and show how this commitment led him to distinguish between his "religion" and his "politics." I conclude with a discussion of how, until his brutal assassination, Malcolm committed himself to starkly dichotomous views of Islamic universalism and black particularism.

MALCOLM X BEFORE 1960

Of all the figures examined in this study, no one has been a more important symbol in American and Afro-American popular culture than Malcolm X. Malcolm's mythological place in black culture emerged soon after his death, brought about in part by the release of the *Autobiography of Malcolm X.* This work quickly became a bestseller and since then a classic of American literature. In addition, figures in the black power struggle of the second half of the 1960s appropriated Malcolm as an icon of black liberation, making him even more significant in death than he was in life. In the 1990s, Spike Lee's biographical movie, based largely on the *Autobiography,* both renewed and reflected popular fascination with the famous hustler turned Muslim. Also during the past decade, authors like James Cone have seized Malcolm as a didactic contrast to Martin Luther King, Jr., and his advocacy of nonviolence.[1]

Partly because of his symbolic and mythological significance, Malcolm has received an enormous amount of scholarly attention in the American academy. In addition to the vast number of articles about Malcolm, a number of full-length treatments have been devoted to his life and its historical meaning. Peter Goldman's biography, for example, stands as a useful introduction to Malcolm. The extensive and controversial biographies of Eugene Wolfenstein and Bruce Perry employ psychohistory to illuminate nearly every event in his life. Both Robin Kelley and Clayborne Carson, on the other hand, have examined Malcolm in the context of the social and cultural history of both World War II and the postwar period. Finally, paying more attention to Malcolm's life of faith than any previous author, Louis DeCaro's biography speaks to Malcolm's double conversion, first to Elijah Muhammad's Nation of Islam, then to Sunni Islam.[2] Because Malcolm's biographical data has been extensively studied by these authors, I begin with only a brief summary of his life before the 1960s, after which I develop my own argument about the importance of his dual identity during his final years.

According to Malcolm's autobiography, he was born into an activist family. His mother, Louise, was a Caribbean émigré from Grenada and, like her husband, a committed Garveyite. While Malcolm's father, Earl, organized UNIA activities in Omaha, Louise contributed material to the *Negro World*, the UNIA's official periodical. By the late 1920s, the Littles had moved to East Lansing, Michigan. In 1931 Earl was tragically run over by a streetcar and died; later Malcolm said that, according to rumors he had heard, the accident was intentional. In 1939, broken by the Great Depression, his mother Louise was no longer able to care for her children and was declared legally insane. Malcolm spent the next few years in various foster homes, eventually moving to the East Coast.[3]

At various times from 1940 to 1944, Malcolm lived both in Boston and New York. In those cities, he joined the ranks of a wartime black youth culture that donned the zoot suit, did the lindy hop, and listened to bebop. Many of these young men avoided work, slept around, dodged the draft, and often embraced hustling, the numbers rackets, and drugs. According to Robin Kelley, their modes of dress, speech, and behavior, if criminal, were also subtle forms of resistance against middle-class norms, especially those of middle-class blacks. For Malcolm, however, this alternate world of cultural resistance came to an end in 1946, when he was indicted for larceny, firearm violations, and breaking and entering. In March, after being convicted, he entered a Massachusetts state prison. It was during this incarceration that Malcolm's first conversion took place. While he was in Concord Reformatory in 1947, Philbert and Reginald Little, two of Malcolm's siblings, encouraged their brother to learn about the teachings of the Honorable Elijah Muhammad. Malcolm's conversion, dramatically portrayed as both sudden and blinding in Spike Lee's film,

actually occurred over a period of months as Malcolm became more familiar with the Nation's teachings.[4]

After Malcolm was paroled in 1952, he quickly rose to prominence
within the Nation. The next year, Elijah Muhammad appointed him assistant minister at the Detroit temple. For the following three years, Malcolm led the temples in Boston, Philadelphia, and New York. Employing
revival-type meetings and other sophisticated evangelistic techniques to
attract young African Americans to the NOI, he quickly became the
movement's most able and well-known evangelist. In 1957, he also gained
the attention of black New Yorkers and New York City authorities, when
he successfully demanded that a fellow Muslim receive medical attention
after a beating by some police officers in Harlem's twenty-eighth precinct.
Then during 1959, Malcolm garnered national attention when Mike
Wallace's *The Hate that Hate Produced* aired on WTNA-TV. Afterwards,
Malcolm regularly appeared on a number of television and radio programs, often debating the merits of separatism with advocates of integration. During this period, according to his autobiography, Malcolm was
a loyal servant of Elijah Muhammad, never questioning the leader's approach to civil rights or matters of belief. Only after Malcolm's suspension
from the Nation, the *Autobiography* indicated, did Malcolm truly question
the leader's approach to these issues. The *Autobiography* also characterized
Malcolm's attraction to Sunni Islam and his activist politics as phenomena
that occurred after the break with Elijah Muhammad. While Malcolm
himself may have genuinely felt this way about his activities during the last
year of his life, quite a different pattern emerges from the available sources.
In fact, it is quite clear that Malcolm had begun to have his doubts about
the Messenger by the late 1950s, as the following section argues.[5]

MALCOLM'S SECOND CONVERSION AND THE
CRUCIAL ROLE OF MUSLIM MISSIONARIES

By 1959, as seen in chapter 4, several mainstream Islamic groups launched
attacks on the legitimacy of Elijah Muhammad and the NOI. As national
spokesman for Elijah Muhammad, Malcolm defended the Messenger and
his teachings. Unlike his mentor, however, he tried to shield the NOI from
criticism by appropriating elements of Islamic discourse, especially passages from the Qur'an, to legitimate Muhammad's beliefs. In a letter dated
November 24, 1962, for example, Malcolm wrote to the New York
Amsterdam News to protest one Afghani Muslim's critique of the NOI.

He cited Qur'an 20:102 as proof for the Islamic legitimacy of Muhammad's view that all white people were blue-eyed devils destined to face divine retribution at the end time. "The day when the trumpet is blown," Malcolm quoted the verse, "and we shall gather the guilty, blue-eyed, on that day." In a 1963 edition of the *New York Times Magazine*, however, Robert Payne argued that Malcolm's use of the text was faulty and that "all sinners, not only blue-eyed ones, are implicated in the judgement." Indeed, though Malcolm's translation of the verse was perfectly legitimate, he seemingly had no idea how the "guilty, blue-eyed" persons mentioned in the text had been traditionally defined in *tafsir,* or classical Qur'anic commentary. The "blue-eyed," or *zurqa,* according to some commentators, can refer to the image of blue- or blind-eyed persons with black faces—a definition that, if he had known about it, might have made Malcolm think twice before using this verse in support of an antiwhite theology. Moreover, the "guilty," according to some tafsir, can refer to criminals, polytheists, sinners, or disbelievers in the oneness of God—another fact of which Malcolm seemed to have been unaware. The important point is that, despite Malcolm's intentions, he simply lacked the intellectual resources to make a forceful defense of Muhammad using the terms of Old World Islamic traditions.[6]

Malcolm also criticized Muhammad's naysayers as whites or "Uncle Tom" Muslims who had done nothing to advance the interests of blacks. They failed to recognize, as Malcolm said in a March 24, 1961 speech at the Harvard Law School, that Elijah Muhammad had a "new dispensation." Comparing the NOI leader to Moses and Jesus, Malcolm argued that Muhammad had been "raised up among his enslaved people at a time when God was planning to restore them to a land of their own where they could give birth to a new civilization." Those whites who criticized the legitimacy of this man, he said, were simply trying to "separate us from the Muslim world." As for immigrant critics of Muhammad, they had not been successful "in converting one thousand Americans to Islam." Elijah Muhammad, on the other hand, "has hundreds of thousands of his fellow ex-slaves turning eastward toward Mecca five times daily giving praises to the great God Allah." Of course, this claim was an exaggeration, if not an outright falsehood. As observed in the previous chapter, very few members actually practiced the Islamic *salat,* despite the fact that Muhammad had encouraged them to do so in his prayer manual.[7]

But in another sense, the fact that Malcolm now cited the daily practice of prayer, one of the five pillars of Islam, as proof of the movement's legitimacy, showed just how much mainstream criticisms of the movement were beginning to affect him. Particularly disturbing to Malcolm were the Muslim students who often confronted him about the differences between the "true" Islam and the NOI. Concerned that NOI theology might be mistaken for their own beliefs about Islam, these students often accosted Malcolm on the streets of New York and along the college lecture circuit. In 1962, one immigrant Muslim student at Dartmouth, Ahmed Osman, traveled to NOI Mosque No. 7 to question Malcolm about Islam. After grilling Malcolm in the question and answer section of his talk, Osman came away "unsatisfied." Malcolm himself seemed affected by the encounter, for when Osman began to send Malcolm literature from the Islamic Centre in Geneva, Switzerland, he read it and asked for more. In another incident, Arab students from UCLA surrounded Malcolm after a March 1963 appearance on the *Ben Hunter Show* in Los Angeles. After hearing the students argue that his belief in white devils was un-Islamic, Malcolm became quite disturbed, according to journalist Louis Lomax, who was accompanying Malcolm at the time.[8]

While Malcolm continued to defend Elijah Muhammad and his Islamic dispensationalism throughout 1963, it is clear that by this time his separation from his spiritual father had already begun. During a March 3 appearance on the Chicago television show, *At Random,* Malcolm redefined "white devils" to mean any human being who "intentionally or consciously carries into practice the attributes or characteristics of the devil." While this was not yet a full denial of the belief that whites were by their very nature evil, such a statement came a few months later when Malcolm spoke on the Washington, D.C., radio program, *Focus,* aired over WUST on May 12. "When you are a Muslim," Malcolm said, "you don't look at the color of a man's skin . . . you look at the man and judge him according to his conscious behavior." This was the practice of Muslims in the Islamic lands, he argued, and it should also be the practice of black Muslims in the United States. "[M]any people in this country think we are against the white man because he is white . . . [but] we are against the white man because of what he has done to the black man."[9]

Though Malcolm remained the loyal national spokesman of Elijah Muhammad throughout 1963, he was also questioning the morality of his leader. The previous year, Malcolm had visited three of Muhammad's secretaries, all of whom had given birth to the Messenger's illegitimate children. In April, he apparently confronted the Messenger about these relationships at Muhammad's house in Phoenix. Furthermore, Malcolm was clearly becoming frustrated by Muhammad's prohibition against any political activities. While Malcolm both dutifully publicized and obeyed

Muhammad's directive that no member of the NOI support or participate in the March on Washington that year, Malcolm appeared at the march as a "critical observer." Notwithstanding his comments about the march as a "farce" on Washington, Malcolm seemed to be unable to resist the chance to be at this important event.[10]

Finally, on December 1, Malcolm officially rebelled by disobeying Elijah Muhammad's directive that no Muslim minister comment on the assassination of President Kennedy. On December 4, Muhammad suspended Malcolm from his duties as national spokesman and demanded his silence. Malcolm initially expressed acquiescence toward the order, but statements made previously that year showed that part of Malcolm had already accepted the necessity of a separation from Muhammad long before this time. On March 8, 1964, Malcolm announced that he was leaving the movement for good. Four days later, he outlined his intentions for the future at the Park Sheraton in New York. In his statement, Malcolm announced that he would embrace cooperation with other black leaders interested in pursuing an activist strategy toward black liberation. "We must control the politics and the politicians of our community," he argued. At the same time, Malcolm unveiled his plans to create the Muslim Mosque, Inc. "I am and always will be a Muslim," he said. "I am going to organize and head a new mosque in New York City." While Malcolm embraced black nationalism as his political ideology, he upheld Islam as "the spiritual force necessary to rid our people of the vices that destroy the moral fiber of our community." Speaking at Harvard College ten days later on March 18, 1964, Malcolm explicated his new position a bit further, stating that "we believe that the religion of Islam combined with Black Nationalism is all that is needed to solve the problem" of the black community. Here Malcolm defined black nationalism as a comprehensive approach to social life that included economic self-determination, moral renewal, racial pride, and political involvement—a platform that sounded very much like the program of Marcus Garvey.[11]

In the meantime, however, Malcolm was also exploring Sunni Islam and beginning to make more intimate contact with immigrant Muslims. In particular, Malcolm turned to Dr. Mahmoud Youssef Shawarbi, a University of Cairo professor in the United States on a Fulbright grant to teach at Fordham University. Malcolm knew of Shawarbi through the numerous immigrant and foreign Muslims, especially Muslim students, who had accosted him during his various lectures and appearances before the media. "Those orthodox Muslims whom I had met, one after another, had urged me to meet and talk with a Dr. Mahmoud Youssef Shawarbi," he said in his *Autobiography.* Shawarbi encouraged Malcolm to make the *hajj,* the annual pilgrimage to Mecca, and instructed him in the fundamental elements of Sunni Islam.[12]

Most scholars present the relationship between Shawarbi and Malcolm as a product of Malcolm's reaching out toward Sunni Islam. While this was certainly the case, it was not a one-way relationship. In fact, Malcolm converted to Sunni Islam at arguably the most important moment in the history of Muslim missionary activity, or *da'wa,* in North America. In the first half of the twentieth century, most Muslims focused on da'wa as an activity to be conducted among other Muslims. Groups like the Muslim Brothers in Egypt and the Society of the Call and Guidance in South Asia aspired mostly to change Islamic practices within *dar al-islam,* or Islamdom. Only the Ahmadiya movement committed serious resources to spreading Islam among all non-Muslims and North Americans, especially. After World War II, however, da'wa became entangled in world politics as the former European protectorates emerged into Arab nation-states. On one level, da'wa was emphasized as a part of these new states' foreign policy in the West. By sponsoring Muslim missionaries in non-Muslim states, they hoped to spread their influence abroad and soften derogatory images of Islam.[13]

In a more direct way, however, da'wa was one of the secondary fronts of what Malcolm Kerr called the "Arab Cold War," especially the conflict between the Kingdom of Saudi Arabia and Egypt. These two states were locked in ideological and military struggles from 1958 through the 1960s. The ideological battle began shortly after Egyptian President Gamal Abd al-Nassir successfully entered into a political union with Syria in the winter of 1958. The United Arab Republic (UAR), as the two states became known, signaled the growth of both revolutionary socialism and pan-Arabism, the movement to unite all Arab peoples into one political entity. A few months later, when revolution overturned the Iraqi monarchy and an uprising occurred against President Sham'un in Lebanon, monarchs throughout the Middle East feared that Nassirism might actually succeed. But, due to the failure of the UAR and the constantly shifting alliances that characterized Middle Eastern politics, their fears were never realized. The idea of Arab unity remained only a symbol—albeit one of paramount importance—in Arab political culture during the following decade. As such, aspiring revolutionaries aligned with Nassir might always use it to upset the neocolonialist status quo. But while this ideological struggle provided the general context of tensions between Egypt and Saudi Arabia, the two states also engaged in an actual military conflict through their involvement in the Yemeni revolution of 1962. Here, too, monarchical forces faced the challenge of a socialist revolution that Nassir supported by sending thousands of Egyptian troops.[14]

This conflict most certainly influenced the missionary efforts sponsored by Saudi Arabia, which established a new university in Medina committed to the training of Muslim missionaries in 1961. The following year, as tension over Yemen escalated, the government supported the founding of the Muslim World League, whose statement of purpose included a commitment to daʿwa. An impressive array of Muslim personages attended the organization's inaugural meeting, including the Grand Mufti of Saudi Arabia, Said Ramadan of Egypt, Allal al-Fasi of Morocco, and Mawlana Maududi of Pakistan. Not surprisingly, the conference was strongly anti-Nassirist, promoting a vision of pan-Islam that hoped to counter the powerful Arab populist. Ramadan, like many other Arab missionaries, was a member of the Muslim Brothers, a politically minded religious group that had been forcefully repressed by Nassir.[15]

A politicization of Islam also occurred among Muslim students in the West. These were the same Muslims who continually hounded Malcolm as he traveled the campus lecture circuit. In 1963, several students from a variety of countries gathered at the University of Illinois, Champaign-Urbana to establish the Muslim Students Association (MSA). Among the founding members were three Muslim Brothers from Egypt. Using their positions on college campuses, these activists helped to make the MSA one of the most successful immigrant-led organizations in the propagation of Islam throughout North America.[16]

By seeking the guidance of Mahmoud Youssef Shawarbi, another Egyptian reportedly disliked by the Nassir regime, Malcolm unknowingly thrust himself into the center of this new Saudi-financed missionary activity. After training Malcolm in the rudiments of Sunni Islamic thought and practice, Shawarbi gave Malcolm a letter of recommendation, a copy of *The Eternal Message of Muhammad* by the renowned pan-Islamicist Abd al-Rahman Azzam, and the phone number of Azzam's son, who happened to be married to the daughter of Saudi Prince Faysal. The elder Azzam was one of pan-Islam's most important figures. A father of Arab nationalism and a distinguished Egyptian diplomat, Azzam was a chief architect of the Arab League and served as its first secretary general from 1945 to 1952. But like so many others, he lost favor after Nassir came to power, finding refuge in Saudi Arabia, where he became a leading pan-Islamic polemicist and author.[17]

His *Eternal Message of Muhammad,* still available in a 1993 edition, was a primary example of a popular modern Islamic polemic that both defended Islam against Western critics and advocated a vision of the ideal

Islamic nation-state. Islam, Azzam said, was a "faith, a law, a way of life, a 'nation,' and 'state.'" Contrary to Western assumptions, Azzam implied, Islam was a highly modern religious tradition that promoted tolerance, removed superstition, and encouraged mercy, charity, industriousness, fairness, and brotherhood in the hearts and minds of its adherents. Islam, according to Azzam, also required that all political leaders enjoy the consent of their fellow citizens. Islam, he implied, intrinsically possessed many elements of Western liberalism, but incorporated them into a theocratic form of governance. The West, he argued, based its social life on materialism, which produced modern colonialism and class struggle; as a theocratic system, Islam eliminated such problems.[18]

Whether or not Malcolm ever read this book is unclear. But Malcolm did come under the influence of Azzam himself during the pilgrimage. On April 13, 1964, Malcolm departed JFK International Airport with a one-way plane ticket to Jedda, Saudi Arabia. When Malcolm arrived on the Arabian peninsula, Saudi authorities detained him for special interrogation. After fretting for some time, Malcolm thought to telephone Azzam's son, Dr. Omar Azzam. Upon hearing word of Malcolm's difficulties, the Azzams immediately interceded with the proper authorities. They vouched for Malcolm when he faced an examination by the hajj court, the legal entity that decides whether one is a legitimate Muslim able to participate in the pilgrimage. In fact, Prince Faysal himself probably communicated with the court on Malcolm's behalf. In addition, the elder Azzam insisted that Malcolm stay in his suite at the Jedda Palace Hotel. Later, the Saudi government officially extended its welcome when the Deputy Chief of Protocol, Muhammad Abdul Azziz Maged, gave Malcolm a special car in which to travel during his time in the kingdom.[19]

The Azzams, Malcolm claimed in the *Autobiography*, had nothing to gain by their hospitality. This was surprising, Malcolm said, since he had never known such light-complexioned people to be so generous to a black man without expectation of advantage or favor. According to Malcolm, this act led him to "reappraise the 'white man.'" It was the first moment, he said, in which "I first began to perceive that 'white man,' as commonly used, means complexion only secondarily; primarily, it described attitudes and actions." Though Malcolm had expressed such sentiments in 1963, well before he separated from the Nation of Islam or traveled to the Middle East, the *Autobiography* did not include such information. Instead, it depicted the pilgrimage as a truly watershed moment in Malcolm's spiritual life. Malcolm also desired his trip to be viewed as such. In a letter from Mecca that Malcolm sent to both friends and the press, he said that the hajj represented the first occasion in his life during which he had experienced real brotherhood between peoples of all races. The pilgrims, Malcolm said, "were of all colors. . . . But we were all participating in the same ritual, displaying a spirit of unity and brotherhood that my experiences in America had led me to believe never could exist between the white and the non-white." Islam, he said, had seemingly removed racism from the white mind. All of America, he concluded, needed to believe in the oneness of God if this kind of unity was to be realized across the Atlantic. For the first and perhaps last time, Malcolm imagined that Islam might have the power to change people's attitudes towards race.[20]

This is exactly what his Saudi hosts hoped to hear. According to Malcolm, the elder Azzam had expressed such sentiments during dinner with Malcolm before he left Jedda for Mecca. During that occasion, Azzam argued that Islam was a tradition free of racial prejudice from its very beginning. He illustrated the point by claiming that the Prophet Muhammad himself was a man of both black and white ancestries. He also confronted the charge by Western critics that racism was as difficult a problem in Islam as it was in the West by blaming Western influence. "[T]he problems of color which exist in the Muslim world," Azzam said, "exist only where, and to the extent that, that area of the Muslim world has been influenced by the West." Racism is foreign to the very nature of Islam, Azzam indicated, and has only been practiced where Muslims have acted in an un-Islamic fashion—that is, like Westerners. Even Prince Faysal joined in the effort to help Malcolm understand the "true" meaning of Islam. After Malcolm completed the pilgrimage, Prince Faysal invited him for an audience at which, once again, Malcolm was assured that his special treatment was offered freely, without any expectation of a quid pro quo. Of course, the Prince then proceeded to quiz Malcolm about the Nation of Islam, carefully suggesting that if what he had read in Egyptian papers were true, they did not practice the "true" Islam. Further, the prince reminded Malcolm that due to the abundance of English literature on Islam "there was no excuse for ignorance, and no reason for sincere people to allow themselves to be misled." Prince Faysal, in other words, wanted to make sure that the message of his hospitality was clear: now that Malcolm had experienced the "real" Islam, the royal implied, he should be able to represent it properly in the United States.[21]

Malcolm seemed to accept his Saudi hosts as sincere. If calculated, the interest shown in Malcolm by those connected to Saudi interests, like Azzam, was by no means nefarious. While Azzam and the Saudi authorities hoped to gain an ally in the United States, they were also assisting

Malcolm to achieve legitimacy and acceptance as a Sunni Muslim and an international black leader. The problem for Malcolm was that even in the mystical Holy Land, he could not ignore the power of race as a sociological reality. Observing the masses of pilgrims at Mecca, Malcolm concluded in a letter sent back to his followers in the United States that "there was a color pattern in the huge crowds [of pilgrims] . . . where true brotherhood existed among all colors, where no one felt segregated, where there was no 'superiority' complex, no 'inferiority complex'—then voluntarily, naturally, people of the same kind felt drawn together by that which they had in common." No matter how strong the universalistic impulses of Islam might shape its adherents, he implied, some natural impulse still led humans to seek out their own color group. Moreover, in this same letter Malcolm also wrote that he had continued to publicize the "evils and the indignities that are suffered by the black man in America." He had even done so while on Arafat, which for many is the climax of the hajj.[22]

While the hajj had been a personally meaningful event in Malcolm's life, it led him neither to question his essentialist views of race nor to develop a strategy for black liberation based on a universalistic interpretation of Islam. Islam, he concluded, may have the power to make all humans feel equal to one another, but it did not lessen their desire to divide themselves into separate groups based on color. He also mentioned that Islam seemingly removed racism from the white mind and publicized the fight for black liberation among his fellow pilgrims. But he did not reflect upon a politics that might utilize Islamic universalism nor did he articulate any specifically pan-Islamic strategy for black liberation. In fact, after Malcolm left the sanctuary of the pilgrimage in April 1964, any liberating potential of Islam for race relations in the United States seemed more distant in his mind as he came to reflect more deeply on pan-Africanism during his tour of the newly emerging African states.

PAN-AFRICANISM, MALCOLM'S PIVOTAL AFRICAN TOUR, AND BLACK LIBERATION STRATEGY

In 1945, George Padmore helped to launch postwar pan-Africanism by organizing an important conference in Manchester, England. Largely controlled by delegates from British colonies, this conference differed from past pan-African gatherings as indigenous Africans upstaged African-American and West Indian representatives, including W. E. B. DuBois, one of the fathers of the movement. During the 1950s, the intellectual center of pan-Africanism moved from London to Africa itself as the former colonies emerged as new nation-states. The Egyptian revolution of 1952, the Algerian struggle for independence, the 1955 Afro-Asian Conference in Bandung, and the establishment of Guinea as an independent state in 1958 all contributed to this phenomenon. Above all, however, the career of Kwame Nkrumah propelled the new energy behind pan-Africanism. Elected as Prime Minister of the Gold Coast in 1951, Nkrumah quickly became an international figure, appearing in front of adoring crowds throughout the world, including one in Harlem in 1956. In 1957, Nkrumah became even more important to the history of pan-Africanism after he led his country's transition from the Gold Coast to the independent state of Ghana. Nkrumah appointed George Padmore chief of the Bureau of African Affairs, the umbrella under which Padmore organized a 1958 conference of the independent African states, including Ethiopia, Liberia, Morocco, Tunisia, Libya, Egypt, Sudan, and Ghana. At the end of the same year, Padmore inspired the first All-African Peoples' Conference to which representatives from every African state and colony were invited. In 1963, the Organization for African Unity succeeded the Conference as the major transnational body of African states. Postwar pan-Africanism thus developed in the shadow of decolonization. As such, the one common characteristic that it shared was a "common rejection of white predominance and colonialism." But many of its West African proponents, in particular, also interpreted the movement as a call for racial solidarity and cultural unity. It was this brand of pan-Africanism that Malcolm discovered during his visit to Ghana following the pilgrimage.[23]

After spending more than two weeks in Saudi Arabia, Malcolm departed for Beirut on April 30, 1964. From Beirut, where he delivered a talk on the failures of the civil rights movement, Malcolm traveled to Lagos, Nigeria (via Cairo and Alexandria). There he underwent what might be fruitfully seen as yet a third conversion. On May 8, Malcolm addressed a group of Ibadan University students, first at Trenchard Hall, then at the Student Union. At the second talk, students gave Malcolm a new name, "Omowale," meaning "the son who has come home." According to Malcolm, he responded enthusiastically, telling them that he had never "received a more treasured honor." In fact, Malcolm consistently used words like "thrilling" and "speechless" to narrate his trip in West Africa.[24]

Writing from Lagos on May 10, Malcolm began to promote pan-Africanism as his preferred strategy for black liberation. But he did not abandon his role as African-American Muslim spokesperson, either. While he still expressed the "hope that my Hajj to the Holy City . . . will establish the religious affiliation of the Muslim Mosque, Inc., with the 750 million Muslims of the world once and for all," he also asserted that the black struggle had an importance that went beyond concerns of confessional affiliation. In fact, he argued that Muslims should concern themselves with oppression against blacks because it was a violation of the "*human rights*" of persons of African descent. "The Koran," Malcolm wrote, "compels the Muslim world to take a stand on the side of those whose human rights are being violated, no matter what the religious persuasion of the victims is." In this passage, he again indicated that he conceived of Islam as an essentially universalistic tradition that required concern for humans as humans. In effect, he said, Muslims should not support pan-Africanism because they are pro-black or pro-Muslim; they should support pan-Africanism because they are pro-human.[25]

Still, Malcolm was beginning to think that his main mission in life should be to develop support for pan-Africanism. In fact, his trip to Ghana only cemented this commitment further. On May 10, the same day that he dated his letter, Malcolm flew to Accra, Ghana, where he became an official guest of state. The newspaper compared his arrival to that of W. E. B. DuBois, the American expatriate whom Nkrumah had treated as black royalty. Malcolm met with Ghanaian officials, addressed the parliament, and was honored at both a state dinner and by the Algerian and Chinese ambassadors. "I can only wish," he wrote, "that every American black man could have shared my ears, my eyes, and my emotions throughout the round of engagements which had been made for me." By the end of the trip, Malcolm uncharacteristically proclaimed that "I no longer had any words." In Malcolm's meeting with President Nkrumah on May 15, both agreed, according to Malcolm, that "Pan-Africanism was the key . . . to the problems of those of African heritage." In a letter penned four days earlier from Accra, Malcolm made his advocacy of pan-Africanism even more explicit, comparing the black unity to that of worldwide Jewry. "Just as the American Jew is in harmony (politically, economically, and culturally) with world Jewry," Malcolm wrote, "it is time for all African-Americans to become an integral part of the world's Pan-Africanists." Blacks need not physically immigrate to Africa, he said, as much as "we must 'return' to Africa philosophically and culturally and develop a working unity in the framework of Pan-Africanism."[26]

But Malcolm was concerned that his views would spark criticism among his Muslim benefactors, who might assume that he had reverted to his old racist beliefs or that he had no intention of spreading the universalistic message that they attempted to convey to him. In his *Autobiography*, he assured them that "my reacting as I did presented no conflict with the convictions of brotherhood which I had gained in the Holy Land." At the same time, Malcolm maintained that a pan-African political agenda was the most realistic strategy for awakening the revolutionary consciousness of black America. Mass conversion to Islam, he seemed to say, was simply an impractical solution to the race problem. This was because of Christianity's strong hold on the soul of black America. "America's Negroes," he said, "are too indelibly soaked in Christianity's double standard of oppression" for Islam to have an adequate impact on them. What he meant by this was a bit opaque. Did he believe that something other than "religion" was needed to awaken black America? Or did he mean that one could never expect enough black Americans to convert to Islam to make a real difference? In this passage, at least, no clear answer emerged.[27]

Malcolm soon became a leading voice for pan-Africanism, filling a gap in the ideological spectrum that had existed throughout the previous decade, when no major group emerged in black America to trumpet the values of Nkrumah's and Padmore's pan-Africanism. After visiting Senegal, Morocco, and Algeria, Malcolm returned from this pivotal trip to New York on May 21, 1964. Back in the United States, he also celebrated his new status as a bona fide Sunni Muslim leader. Moreover, Malcolm stepped up his criticism of Elijah Muhammad, making it seem as if he were now ready to challenge the authority of his former mentor. Malcolm's rhetorical jousting, however, was a dangerous game. After Malcolm let it be known on June 8 that as many as six women were involved in the Messenger's sex scandal, he began to receive death threats. While Malcolm managed to announce the formation of an Organization of Afro-American Unity (OAAU) on June 28, 1964, problems with the NOI only escalated. Malcolm took others' advice to disappear again and left New York for Cairo on July 6, 1964. On this trip to the Middle East and Africa, Malcolm attempted to juggle his commitment to pan-Africanism as a liberation strategy with his newfound identity as a Sunni Muslim missionary. It became clear, however, that Malcolm would not relinquish the fight for pan-African liberation, no matter what his Arab hosts said.[28]

THE BIFURCATION OF POLITICS AND RELIGION: PAN-AFRICANISM *VS.* ISLAM

On July 17, 1964, Malcolm attended the African Summit Conference in Cairo as a representative of the OAAU. Practically every African head of state was present at the meeting, which was the second such gathering sponsored by the Organization of African Unity. President Nassir's welcoming address, a kind of retrospective of the past year, lauded the passage of the 1964 civil rights bill in the United States. Others at the conference also gave the impression that they had better let American blacks take care of their own problems. Malcolm sought to challenge both of these positions. As an official observer at the conference, Malcolm submitted an eight-page memorandum that tried to convince African leaders that "our problem is your problem." America, Malcolm said, was good at "trickery" when it came to civil rights, but the United States was actually "the century's leading neo-colonialist power." Further, Malcolm asked African support for measures to guarantee the human rights of Afro-Americans by bringing the problem before the United Nations. In closing, Malcolm beseeched the conferees not to replace European colonialism with American dollarism.[29]

Malcolm suspected, however, that his Muslim hosts and pro-Saudi allies would once again take him only for a black nationalist. In a speech on July 27 before Cairo's Shubaan al-Muslimeen, a youth organization much like the YMCA, Malcolm reassured his audience that his fight for black liberation did not contradict his desire to be a good Muslim. "[M]y fight is two-fold, my burden is double, my responsibilities multiple . . . material as well as spiritual, political as well as religious, racial as well as non-racial," he declared. "I will never hesitate to let the entire world know the hell my people suffer from America's deceit and her hypocrisy, as well as her oppression." Throughout the summer, Malcolm continued to press his case in Egypt, speaking in Alexandria on August 4 and attending a second African Summit Conference on August 21. It was during this second tour that the Egyptian-sponsored Supreme Council of Islamic Affairs (SCIA) granted Malcolm twenty scholarships for study at the University of al-Azhar, arguably the most prestigious Islamic university in the world.[30]

While Malcolm was clearly adopting pan-Africanism as the animating force behind his politics, he did not relinquish his own personal interest in Islam either. In September 1964, Malcolm left for another pilgrimage to Mecca. During this 'umra, or lesser pilgrimage, Malcolm underwent training as an evangelist by the World Muslim League. Shaykh Muhammad Sarur al-Sabban, secretary general of the organization and a descendant of black slaves, oversaw his training. The University of Medina, like the SCIA, granted Malcolm several scholarships for study there. According to Richard W. Murphy, then second secretary at the American embassy in Jedda, Malcolm granted an interview to a Jeddan newspaper, al-Bilad, in which he "took pains . . . to deprecate his reputation as a political activist and dwelt mainly on his interest in bringing sounder appreciation of Islam to American Negroes." It is difficult to tell whether Malcolm was simply telling his Saudi hosts what they wanted to hear or whether the account of the Saudi newspaper on which Murphy based his memorandum distorted Malcolm's words. Perhaps this is what he actually believed at the time. Whichever interpretation is correct, however, Malcolm clearly relished another opportunity to focus on his "personal spiritual development . . . far away from politics."[31]

In October and November, however, it was back to politics. Throughout these two months, Malcolm met with eleven African heads of state and other VIPs, including Kenyan President Jomo Kenyatta and Ugandan Milton Obote. Concerned that factionalism might tear Africa apart, Malcolm returned to New York on November 24, 1964, with a renewed determination to fight for the ideals of pan-African unity. From this point until his death in February, Malcolm's speeches became harshly critical not only of United States policy towards American blacks, but towards African blacks, as well. Malcolm focused, in particular, on United States support for Moise Tshombe's junta in the Congo. In late 1960, CIA Director Allen Dulles spearheaded the effort to depose Patrice Lumumba, the leader of the movement that had helped to win Congolese independence from Belgium. In his place, the United States supported Moise Tshombe, whose forces murdered Lumumba in January 1961. From November 1964 until February 1965, Malcolm cited the Congolese intervention as one of the worst forms of United States deceit and wondered aloud whether he should recruit a force of black American freedom fighters to tip the balance in favor of the anti-Tshombe forces.[32]

In describing other reasons for his support of a pan-African struggle, Malcolm also reaffirmed his essentialist view of black identity as a container for cultural and biological traits shared by all persons of African descent. He voiced these views, for example, during a speech on Afro-American history given at Harlem's Audubon Ballroom on January 24, 1965. Following the lead of both Padmore and Nkrumah, Malcolm saw black history as replete with evidence of the cultural unity of black humankind. Furthermore, he viewed knowledge of this past as essential to knowledge of one's true identity, knowledge of which would inspire new "energy" and "incentive" in the struggle for black liberation. But to see the real historical achievements of blacks, Malcolm said, one would have to ignore the "Negro History Week" version of "cotton pickers, orange growers, mammies, and uncles."[33]

Curiously, the version of black history that Malcolm offered in its place sounded much like that of Noble Drew Ali and Elijah Muhammad.

Before the age of colonialism, Malcolm said, the ancestors of modern blacks who peopled Africa, the Middle East, and India built great civilizations. While whites sat naked in Europe consumed by the hunger for "raw meat," blacks developed astronomy, the earth sciences, and architecture. Slavery, he argued, stole this cultural inheritance from the Africans. "They came here," Malcolm stated, "from a civilization where they had high morals; there was no stealing, no drunkenness, no adultery, fornication; there was nothing but high morals." When the slaves arrived, however, "they found a country that had the lowest morals" since it was filled "by prostitutes, by cutthroats." Slaveholders, Malcolm asserted, turned civilized Africans into their slaves by breaking up black families and contenting slaves with Jesus. The result was a people who "had no language, no history, no name."[34]

But, Malcolm argued in the style of Elijah Muhammad, the powerlessness and immorality of modern black Americans ran counter to their true nature as Africans. Echoing the essentialist racialism of Blyden and Elijah Muhammad, Malcolm stated:

> The Black man by nature is a builder, he is scientific by nature, he's mathematical by nature. Rhythm is mathematics, harmony is mathematics . . . you've gotten away from yourself. But when you are in tune with yourself, your very nature has harmony, has rhythm, has mathematics. You can build. You don't ever need anybody to teach you how to build. You play music by ear. You dance by how you're feeling.[35]

This was quite similar to a statement that Malcolm had made just weeks earlier on December 16, 1964, at a gathering sponsored by the Harvard Law School: "When you hear a black man playing music, whether it is jazz or Bach, you still hear African music. The soul of Africa is still reflected in the music played by black men. In everything else we do we still are Africans in color, feeling, everything. And we will always be that whether we like it or not."[36] That Malcolm continued to view black identity in biologically and culturally essentialist terms was also indicated by his comments on intermarriage during this period. When asked by an interviewer for the British magazine *Flamingo* whether "mixed marriages promote better human relations," Malcolm answered thus: "Mixed marriages don't solve anything. What are the Black men trying to prove? Such 'Toms' really need psychoanalysis." In another interview with Pierre Berton taped on January 19, 1965, at CFTO-TV in Toronto, Malcolm conceded that intermarriage was "one human being marrying another human being," but also asserted that it was an unnatural phenomenon—a "reaction that develops among the people who are victims of . . . [a] negative society."[37]

While Malcolm continued to define black identity in essentialist terms, he also argued for an Islam that transcended the bonds of any group identity. In fact, he almost presented Islam as a necessary corrective to his own racialism. "It is only being a Muslim which keeps me from seeing people by the color of their skin," Malcolm said during a speech given at the London School of Economics on February 11. "And the real religion of Islam doesn't teach anyone to judge another human being by the color of his skin . . . but the man's deeds, the man's conscious behavior, the man's intentions." Malcolm echoed this exact sentiment at nearly every speaking engagement during his last month, including a February 15 meeting at the Audubon Ballroom and a speech at the Cory Hill Methodist Church in Rochester, New York, on February 16.[38]

But Malcolm was always just as quick, as he was in Mecca, to remind his audiences that his commitment to this nonracialist tenet of Islam did not preclude his participation in a specifically black liberation struggle. In an address given on December 16, 1964, at the Harvard Law School, Malcolm stressed that "despite being a Muslim, I can't overlook the fact that I'm an Afro-American in a country which practices racism against black people. . . . [W]hether I'm Muslim, Christian, Buddhist, Hindu, atheist or agnostic, I would still be in the front lines." While religion preaches brotherhood, Malcolm consistently said, most whites in America did not practice it. In an address at the Ford Auditorium in Detroit on February 14, 1965, Malcolm argued that "I'm for the brotherhood of everybody, but I don't believe in forcing brotherhood upon people who don't want it." Religion, Malcolm told *New York Post* reporter Timothy Lee on February 18, "is not enough. Today the problems of the Negro go beyond religion."[39]

This comment did not mean that Malcolm disbelieved in Islam or devalued his Islamic identity. But it did indicate that he defined Islam as a "religion" or a creed that could have limited impact in the achievement of his political goals. As a result, he chose pan-Africanism for his "politics" while grasping Islam as his "religion"; Malcolm viewed both identities as part of his own authenticity. But in holding to both, Malcolm made it impossible to integrate his "religious" values with his "political" beliefs, since his assumptions about the meaning of both pan-Africanism and Islam pitted them against each other in his own mind. On the one hand, his pan-Africanism was informed by a classic form of racial essentialism—hence the comment that the black man's African behavioral traits would always be a part of him whether he liked it or not. On the other hand, Malcolm viewed Islam as a religion that could have nothing to do with a specifically racialist political struggle, given its emphasis on non-racial unity. While it might be argued that Malcolm had found a perfectly reasonable method of balancing his "political" commitment to the black struggle with his "religious" beliefs in Islam, his bifurcation of religion and politics had important consequences for his ability to determine the direction of his own Islamic commitments.

THE MEANING OF MALCOLM'S DOUBLENESS

Malcolm had ceded the authority to define the meaning of Islam (and hence, the authority to decide what was legitimately Islamic) to his missionary sponsors like Shawarbi and Azzam. For Malcolm, these men were synonymous with the "real" Islam. They spoke the language of the Qur'an, while he did not. They were also Arabs, a people whose "image is almost inseparable from the image of Islam," as Malcolm put it.[40] And they held the keys to Mecca, where Malcolm had experienced his second conversion and gained confidence in his own legitimacy as a "real" Muslim. It should come as little surprise, then, that Malcolm allowed them to define what was or was not the true Islam. Ramadan, Shawarbi, Azzam, and even Prince Faysal had made it clear to Malcolm that Islam paid no heed to race. If Malcolm were to practice the "true" Islam, they said, he could not appropriate Islam in an explicitly black struggle. Where Malcolm surrendered the ideological ground was in accepting this argument. Once he adopted their ideological requirements as a fundamental part of his own Islamic identity, he could use Islam only in a universalistic way to support a more general "human" liberation. He could not make an argument that appropriated Islam in any particularistic way. Put another way, if Islam could have nothing to do with issues of race, and Malcolm were a true Muslim, then he could not mix his Islam with his pan-Africanism.

A written exchange between Said Ramadan and Malcolm illustrated the fact that Malcolm seemed unable to break free of the ideas of his sponsors. Ramadan, the director of the Saudi-sponsored Islamic Centre in Geneva, had asked Malcolm in September 1964 whether it was true that "you still hold Black color as a main base and dogma for your drive under the banner of liberation?" If so, Ramadan wanted to know, "[h]ow could a man of your spirit, intellect, and worldwide outlook fail to see in Islam . . .

a message that confirms . . . the ethnological oneness and equality of all races, thus striking at the very root of . . . racial discrimination?" Sometime between February 13 and 20, 1965, Malcolm composed a rather spirited reply, stating that "as a Black American I do feel that my first responsibility is to my twenty-two million fellow Black Americans." Malcolm then turned the tables on Ramadan, accusing the Muslim world of ignoring racism in the United States. He also repeated a charge that he had made while still in the NOI that Muslim missionaries focused on whites rather than blacks.[41] But Malcolm had no answer to Ramadan's main assertion, which was that Islam strikes at the "very root" of "racial discrimination" and thus represents the best solution for America's race problem. Malcolm believed such an assertion to be unrealistic. But because he had tied his legitimacy to Ramadan's own Islamic universalism, he could not offer any sort of *Islamic* approach to a more particularistic struggle.

At the same time, because of his essentialist views of black identity, he could not imagine a black struggle that operated across racial lines or that did not accentuate the particular needs of blacks. Since blacks around the world shared a common experience and common traits, he argued, they should join in a common struggle led by and for blacks. Such views blinded Malcolm to other possible strategies for black liberation that might pay more attention to the historical rather than essentialist meanings of blackness. If the need to defend an essentialist black identity had not been so great in his mind, perhaps he might have considered other strategies for liberation that were pan-Islamic, multiracial, or socialist.

In contemplating the meaning of Malcolm's assassination for American and Afro-American politics, some have speculated about how Malcolm would have reacted to the radicalization of the anti-war effort and the black struggle. It was, after all, less than a year since he had announced his official independence from Elijah Muhammad. I wonder, on the other hand, whether Malcolm might not have also broken away from his Muslim sponsors to develop his own Islamic response to black oppression that paid more attention to race without reifying any "essential" black traits. But assassins' bullets silenced Malcolm at the Audubon Ballroom on February 21, 1965. After this loss, it would take exactly a decade before another prominent African-American Muslim thinker would confront Malcolm's dilemma.

Chapter 6

Wallace D. Muhammad (b. 1933), Sunni Islamic Reform, and the Continuing Problem of Particularism

INTRODUCTION

While Malcolm X has received the most scholarly attention of all the figures covered in this study, W. D. Muhammad has received the least.[1] Born the seventh son of Elijah and Clara Muhammad in 1933, Wallace grew up in the Nation of Islam as a member of Muhammad's "royal family." Like Malcolm, however, the future leader questioned the legitimacy of his faher's teachings as early as the 1950s. By the 1960s, he had broken with his father in order to embrace Sunni Islam. Then, after the death of Malcolm X, he reconciled with the Messenger. Throughout that decade, he repeated the entire process, separating from the NOI at least twice, only to seek readmission into his father's flock. It was almost miraculous that by 1974 Wallace positioned himself as his father's successor.[2]

In this chapter, I will show how Wallace Muhammad inherited the mantle of leadership from his father in 1975 and then led the movement through a remarkable transformation toward the universalistic interpretation of Islam that Malcolm had promoted in his final year. Specifically, this chapter will explore how, in less than a decade, Wallace Muhammad debunked the myth of Yacub, became an advocate of American patriotism, and aligned the NOI with Sunni Islamic teachings and the Arab Islamic world. In so doing, Wallace Muhammad faced questions not unlike those confronted by Malcolm X. How, for example, would he advocate a universalistic reading of Islam and simultaneously fight for black liberation? Would he abandon black particularism altogether or, like Malcolm, try to keep his "religion" separate from his "politics"?

I will argue that unlike Malcolm, Wallace Muhammad first attempted to blend elements of black particularism with his belief in a universalistic Islam. Appropriating themes from the black consciousness movement, the leader linked the Muslim identity of his followers to that of an African Muslim ancestor named Bilal. But in associating Islam with this particularistic identity, he faced powerful opposition from his immigrant Muslim allies, who accused him of continuing the race-based Islam of his father. In the face of that criticism, the leader abandoned these black consciousness teachings by the 1980s, reaffirming what his immigrant allies argued was the only "true" Islam—a universalistic Islam impossible to associate with any particular group of human beings.

But in the 1980s, the leader again tried to put his own stamp on the practice of Islam among black Americans. Rather than explicitly combining black particularism with his universalistic vision of Islam, however, he claimed the right to interpret the seminal texts of Sunni Islam, including both the Qur'an and Sunna, in view of the particular historical circumstances in which African-American Muslims lived and practiced. This was a key moment in African-American Islamic thought and suggested a number of new directions. For Wallace Muhammad, it meant that African-American Muslims should avoid relying solely on immigrant and foreign interpretations of Islamic texts and instead form a comprehensive vision of Islam that focused on specifically black issues.

I will also argue, however, that as Imam Muhammad, as he would come to be called, set out to create his own original body of Islamic thought, he offered two competing visions of social change that seemed to pit a universalistic Islam against a particularistic black struggle. On the one hand, his official "Islamic" view stressed individual responsibility as the primary engine of lasting social change. On the other hand, when the Imam discussed various solutions to problems plaguing black people, he promoted collectivist solutions almost identical to those of his father. Whether these two differing visions were complementary in the Imam's mind was never made clear. Even more importantly, the Imam did not explain or justify his collectivist thought in terms of any interpretation of Islam. Though he had sounded the call for an African-American Islam that incorporated aspects of particularism into an overarching vision of universalism, he did not offer any details on how collective black struggle might be informed by or understood in terms of an Islamic perspective.

WALLACE MUHAMMAD
AS NOI APOSTATE AND LEADER

Born in Detroit, Michigan, in 1933, this son of Elijah Muhammad entered life at a tumultuous time for the Nation of Islam. Disputes among the leadership forced Elijah out of Detroit the following year, prompting the leader to seek refuge at Temple No. 2 in Chicago. As outlined in chapter 4, Chicago also proved to be a difficult place for Elijah Muhammad, who became an itinerant preacher from 1934 until the early 1940s. Then, in 1942, Elijah Muhammad was sent to prison, where he remained until 1946. As a result, Wallace Muhammad barely knew his father as he was growing up. His mother became his sole parent. During this time, Clara Muhammad also played a key role in sustaining the movement in her husband's stead and inculcated NOI values and beliefs in her children, as well.[3]

Once Elijah Muhammad rejoined the family in 1946, the movement began to expand significantly due in large part to the leader's successful efforts to build an organizational infrastructure. These efforts included the establishment of the University of Islam, where Wallace Muhammad attended school. An elementary and secondary school, the "University" offered standard subjects, religious education, and Arabic language. In addition to working sporadically at the Oxford Electric Co. from 1952 to 1954, Wallace Muhammad received his only formal education at this parochial institution. There, he studied Arabic with a number of native speakers, including a Palestinian named "Ibrahim," an Egyptian named "Kamil," and another Palestinian named Jamil Diab. Though Diab later led a movement in Chicago to discredit Elijah Muhammad, during this period Diab was actually in the employ of the Nation of Islam. According to Wallace Muhammad, Diab mostly taught Arabic language, although he occasionally introduced traditional Islamic concepts through his teaching.[4]

As a result, Wallace looked more and more to the Qur'an as a source of divine guidance. As a newly appointed minister of the NOI temple in Philadelphia, he began in 1958 to introduce his own Qur'an-based teachings to local followers. According to Wallace Muhammad, many NOI members expressed interest in this new focus on Qur'an, especially since he made certain that none of his statements directly contradicted his father's doctrines. According to E. U. Essien-Udom, his use of the Qur'an also increased his prestige as a movement leader among some members in Chicago. In fact, despite Malcolm's growing popularity with the mainstream media, the "word" within the movement was that Wallace would succeed his father as leader of the NOI. Essien-Udom, whose account of the NOI remains the best ethnographic source on the movement during the 1950s and early 1960s, claimed that "[s]everal followers have told the writer that Muhammad assured them that 'Allah has chosen Minister Wallace to succeed him.'" Malcolm X himself may have believed this, as he seemed to indicate on December 12, 1958, when he introduced Wallace Muhammad as the son who was "following in the footsteps of his father." When Essien-Udom asked Wallace himself about the rumor, Wallace replied that the "followers have come to look upon me as the second man."[5]

In 1961, however, Wallace Muhammad's important moves toward leadership of the NOI temporarily came to an end when he had no choice but to serve out a prison sentence for draft evasion. His incarceration followed a long saga in the courts, which began in 1953, when Wallace had become eligible for the draft. At that time, he appealed to his local Chicago draft board for conscientious objector status and was successful. In 1957, he was then ordered to serve two years civilian duty at the Illinois State Hospital in Elgin. After he failed to report, however, the federal government brought charges against him during the following year in United States District Court, where he was indicted and convicted of draft evasion. In April 1960, Muhammad was sentenced to three years, and after a failed appeal, reported to the Sandstone Correctional Institution in Minnesota on October 31, 1961, to serve out his sentence.[6]

The NOI responded by depicting Wallace's sentence as the unjust persecution of the righteous. The December 1961 edition of *Muhammad Speaks* carried a story whose headline announced that "Courts Jail Muslim Ministers; Taught Negroes In Faith of Islam Religion!" Framing Muhammad's conviction as a religious issue, the paper went on to say that these religious "teachings . . . have been held to be criminal, although . . . demonstrations of racial violence such as lynchings . . . are regarded as 'loyal Americanism.'" Whether Wallace accepted such statements as true cannot be known, although he later described his time in prison as important to his own spiritual development. Sandstone, Wallace said, had afforded him the opportunity to study the Bible and the Qur'an more extensively than he had ever done before. It was also the first time, he stated, that he had begun seriously questioning his father.[7]

Nevertheless, after he was paroled on January 10, 1963, Wallace Muhammad continued to support the elder Muhammad's movement. At the annual Savior's Day convention held on February 26, Wallace attempted to address the gathered followers, only to be thwarted by Malcolm X, who had been left in charge due to Elijah Muhammad's ill health. This incident, among others, created tension between Malcolm and the rest of the "royal family," who felt that Malcolm was becoming far too powerful within the movement. Malcolm himself knew this and later that spring sought to defuse the situation by writing an apologetic letter to Elijah Muhammad. Curiously, however, the *Autobiography of Malcolm X* depicted the relationship between Wallace and Malcolm during this period as being a harmonious one. After Malcolm became convinced that Elijah Muhammad was guilty of adultery in late 1962, he turned to Wallace, of whom he "always had a high opinion. . . . I felt that Wallace was Mr. Muhammad's most strongly spiritual son," he wrote. "Always, Wallace and I shared an exceptional closeness and trust." According to Malcolm, Wallace simply confirmed during this meeting that his father was indeed the immoral man whom Malcolm had described and doubted whether anything could be done to defend him.[8]

After Malcolm's suspension in December 1963, Wallace became even more embroiled in the controversy surrounding his father's sexual behavior. According to Malcolm, it was Wallace who had told him about the Messenger's improprieties. On January 2, 1964, Elijah Muhammad sent a message to his son that Malcolm had implicated him in the whole mess. Wallace Muhammad then requested a trial before his father, but he was denied. After nearly half a year of isolation from the NOI, Wallace broke with his father in May 1964, a couple months after Malcolm had announced his own independence in March. While working odd jobs to pay his own bills, he also established the Afro-Descendant Upliftment Society, which he hoped to use to support himself. The organization was never a success, probably because Wallace was too busy worrying about his own safety. Like Malcolm, Wallace feared that he might be murdered, and on August 4, 1964, he went to the FBI and the local police hoping to obtain some protection from what he described as the "punch-your-teeth-out" squads in the NOI.[9]

After the assassination of Malcolm on February 21, 1965, Wallace kept quiet—at least for a little while. Five days later, on February 26, Wallace Muhammad approached the podium at the annual Savior's Day gathering in Chicago to reaffirm the legitimacy of his father's teachings. A short speech of five minutes, Wallace's mea culpa included a plea to be accepted once again by the NOI membership as a "brother." Such statements seemed quite disingenuous, given both the duress under which Wallace must have been operating and his actions in the following years.

From 1965 until 1971, Wallace was expelled from the movement at least twice and perhaps as many as three to four times. Whatever personal animosity existed between him and his father seemed to take the form of a running debate about the Islamic legitimacy of the elder Muhammad's teachings and the need to introduce more Sunni Islamic concepts into the movement.[10]

Given this, it is all the more remarkable and even curious that Wallace eventually inherited the mantle of leadership from his father. While Elijah Muhammad never publicly appointed a successor, he seemed to defer quietly to his son's efforts to secure his right to the throne throughout 1974 and early 1975. In New York, Wallace flatly told National Secretary Abass Rassoull and National Spokesman Louis Farrakhan that he would succeed his father and specifically warned Farrakhan not to interfere. By 1975, it seems that he had garnered the support of key members, including Muhammad Ali, Herbert Muhammad, Raymond Sharrieff, Farrakhan, and Elijah Muhammad, Jr.[11]

Mattias Gardell speculates that the FBI might have helped Wallace gain this position through its COINTELPRO operations. COINTELPRO was a child of the Cold War era, when the FBI regularly conducted counterintelligence operations against suspected Communists, white hate groups, and the New Left. These operations often worked in the following way: Bureau agents would penetrate the upper echelons of various social or political movements, spread dissension, and plant false information, hoping to destroy the movement from within. Beginning in 1967, however, the FBI expanded its COINTELPRO operations to include "Black Nationalist-Hate Groups." Encompassing nearly 360 separate operations, this effort represented the second largest COINTELPRO of all. And, according to Frank Donner, the Nation of Islam was at the top of the Bureau's list.[12]

In 1968, the FBI's field office in Chicago identified Wallace Muhammad as "the only son of Elijah Muhammad who would have the necessary qualities to guide the NOI in such a manner as would eliminate racist teachings." How much the FBI actually assisted Wallace in his bid for the position cannot be known due to key deletions in their files. But the Bureau seemed to do what it could. In a January 7, 1969 letter from the Director's officer to Chicago Agent Marlin Johnson, a Bureau official stated that after the death of Elijah Muhammad "a power struggle can be expected. . . . We should plan now to change the philosophy of the NOI to one of strictly religious and self-improvement orientation, deleting the race hatred and separate nationhood aspects." The Bureau also reiterated that it viewed Wallace Muhammad as uniquely qualified to fulfill this task. Chicago Agent Johnson responded by initiating an investigation into Herbert Muhammad's tax returns, hoping to remove him "as a possible successor to his father as head of the militant black nationalist NOI."[13]

WALLACE MUHAMMAD'S SUNNI REFORMATION OF THE NOI

Whether or not the efforts of the FBI helped Wallace Muhammad inherit the leadership of the NOI, he did carry out a program of Sunni Islamic reform that, in a few short months, almost completely changed the character of the NOI. The new leader made his first appearance as his father's successor during the annual Savior's Day convention on February 26, 1975, one day after the death of the seventy-seven-year-old Muhammad. In an address to an audience of more than twenty-five thousand people at the Chicago Amphitheater, he slowly laid the foundation of his "second resurrection" by beginning to debunk the beliefs regarding the divinity of NOI founder W. D. Fard. Fard, he explained, was not God himself but "the manifestation of God to the Honorable Elijah Muhammad." Over the following few years, he similarly reinterpreted almost all of his father's doctrines, claiming all the while that he was merely preserving the elder Muhammad's true legacy. The front page of the March 14, 1975 edition of *Muhammad Speaks* emphasized this idea, featuring a large photograph of Elijah Muhammad smiling down on his son, who was pictured in both meek and authoritative poses. The headline proclaimed, "He Lives On!"[14]

And yet, Elijah Muhammad's intellectual legacy, especially his idea of black chosenness, was clearly doomed. According to Wallace Muhammad, being black did not mean that one was a god or even a member of the chosen race; being black meant having the "black mind," which was a symbol for closeness to God. Moreover, he said, the Messenger never preached against another human being because of his or her skin color. No person, he paraphrased his father, should be hated on the basis of skin color alone: "The Honorable Elijah Muhammad has said Himself, and this is on record: 'We do not teach hate.'" Furthermore, Wallace continued, white people were not actually devils. "I'm not calling those people 'devil.' I'm calling the mind that has ruled those people and you 'devil.'" Killing the white devil, said Wallace, did not mean physically snuffing out his or her life. It meant making a white person relinquish his or her devilish ways. "You can destroy a devil," he asserted, "by destroying the mind that the person has grown within them. If you can destroy the mind, you will destroy the devil." This allegorical destruction of racism was also similar, he argued, to what his father *really* meant in predicting the end of the world. Reinterpreting the passage of Ezekiel on which Muhammad based his belief that a Mothership would obliterate white humankind, Wallace argued that "Ezekiel saw this body as a wheel (Nation of Islam) in a wheel (world community), the Revelator saw it as . . . a divinely revealed community." It was this community's sheer moral force, the leader implied, that would destroy all the evil that whites had brought about in the world.[15]

Then, in a June 15, 1975 address to twenty thousand people at Chicago's McCormick Place, he announced that whites would be allowed to join the NOI. "There will be no such category as a white Muslim or black Muslim. All will be Muslims. All Children of God," said Wallace Muhammad. In explaining the change in a CBS News interview with Randy Daniels, Muhammad said that the NOI had banned whites previously because of their obsession with race or "color." While the NOI would continue to fight such thinking among whites, the leader said, "those . . . who identify with our thinking can come in and join us . . . in giving moral direction to the world." Of course, Wallace Muhammad realized that the number of white members wanting to join would never be very high. The decision was a symbolic one, allowing him to uphold the idea of nonracialism while knowing full well that his movement would remain predominantly black.[16]

Muhammad also concentrated on promoting the practice of the Old World Islamic tradition of Ramadan. As announced in an August 29, 1975 edition of *Muhammad Speaks,* he directed his followers to celebrate the dawn-to-dusk fast during the lunar month of Ramadan rather than during the Christian Advent season. While he acknowledged the usefulness of his father's policy of giving black Muslims something to celebrate in place of Christmas, Muhammad said that it had now come time to observe "the victorious completion of this fast with our Muslim Brothers and Sisters the world over." Later that year, on October 17, 1975, Muhammad used the front page of his movement's popular newspaper to invite "all Muslims in Chicago" to gather at McCormick Place for the traditional prayers preceding '*id al-fitr*, the festival marking the end of Ramadan. Also in October, the leader demanded that *salat*, the ritual prayer performed by pious Muslim five times daily, be learned and practiced by movement members. Then, in 1977, as many as three hundred of Muhammad's followers performed the hajj as guests of the Saudi government. The experience, as St. Louis resident Ahmed Ghani put it, was "a chance to see al-Islam in its universal perspective."[17]

In addition, Muhammad sought to align himself with the Arab Islamic world, including Egypt, Saudi Arabia, and the Gulf States, who identified in Wallace yet another potential black Muslim ally. On June 29, 1975, Muhammad addressed a crowd of thousands at Madison Square Garden in New York. Many foreign dignitaries attended the gathering, although the movement newspaper singled out Amin Hilmy, ambassador of the Arab League, as particularly important. When President Anwar Sadat of Egypt visited the United States in October 1975, the movement newspaper covered the trip in three separate issues, highlighting pictures of movement members and President Sadat taken at receptions and in greeting lines. The November 14, 1975 edition dramatically depicted the movement's new focus on its partnership with the Arab Islamic world by including an illustration of Arab and African-American males stretching their hands out to each over the Atlantic Ocean. Above this picture was written, "The Universal Nation of Islam." Interestingly, under Elijah Muhammad, the movement paper had previously featured a similar image of two black men stretching their hands out to each other. These identical men were situated in Asia and Africa respectively and their hands met over America, signifying the important role of American blacks in Elijah Muhammad's millennial vision. Under Wallace Muhammad's leadership, however, the image was used to stress interracial Muslim unity and the nonracial character of Islam. President Sadat officially recognized the relationship between Egypt and the organization by awarding the group twelve scholarships to Egyptian universities.[18]

Another change implemented by the leader involved his relationships with black Christians. Instead of attacking black Christian leaders, he sought closer ties with them, a transformation that produced more than a few ironies. For instance, at a tribute to the late Elijah Muhammad held on March 14, 1975, *Muhammad Speaks* columnist Ali Baghdadi sat on the dais next to the Reverend Jesse Jackson, whom he had harshly criticized only two months earlier in one of his columns. That same year, Jackson's Operation Push recognized the organization for its efforts to save the black family. In 1977, Ibrahim Pasha, one of Muhammad's closest advisers, joined the Reverend Benjamin Hooks, then executive director of the NAACP, in an interfaith tribute to the late Dr. Martin Luther King, Jr. King, who had been dubbed a "foolish Uncle Tom" by the old Nation of Islam, was now recognized as one of the great African-American leaders. In 1978, Wallace Muhammad also called for interfaith cooperation in accomplishing similar social goals. Paraphrasing Qur'an 5:48, he called on believers to join "together as in a race toward all that is good. Not only Muslim with Muslim, but Muslim with Jew, Muslim with Christian. Let us all go together."[19]

By the 1976 celebration of Savior's Day, the leader even called for Muslims to involve themselves in American politics and flew the American flag over the meeting. Two years later, Wallace announced that the organization would celebrate "New World Patriotism Day" on July 4. It was, according to the movement newspaper, "another great and significant move in the reformation of the membership into outstanding examples of model American citizens." The American flag also appeared on the front page of the newspaper. And children attending the movement's school system recited the pledge of allegiance every morning. Then, in January 1979, a company run by Muslims closely associated with Wallace Muhammad called Salaam International inked a twenty-two million dollar contract with the United States Department of Defense to produce food packs for the military.[20]

To symbolize these changes, Muhammad also altered the nomenclature of the movement. He was no prophet, he announced in a March 21, 1975 interview in *Muhammad Speaks,* but a *mujaddid,* literally a renewer of the faith. Moreover, he eschewed the title of "Minister" to become an "imam," a word in the African-American context that has come to mean a spiritual and administrative Muslim leader. By July 1975, he no longer called his father the "Messenger," but the "Master." And in February 1976, he renamed Temple No. 7 in Harlem after Malcolm X, who had done so much to build that institution but who had left it to become a Sunni Muslim. Then, in late October, the leader changed the name of the organization itself to the World Community of al-Islam in the West (WCIW). "We are not Black Muslims and never have been," he said in an interview with the *New York Times.* "We're not black separatists. We're a world community—a community that encompasses everybody . . . we are all just Muslims." In 1977, the Imam announced that movement temples would henceforth be called *masjids,* the Arabic word for mosque.[21]

Despite this new era of interfaith cooperation and universalism, however, Muhammad did not abandon every perceivably particularistic aspect of the movement. Like his father, Imam Muhammad continued to criticize the harmful psychological effects of Christianity's depiction of Jesus as a white man. To counter this, Muhammad founded CRAID, the Committee to Remove All Images of the Divine in places of worship. CRAID was quite active during the latter half of the 1970s, staging protests nationwide. Muslims would travel to high-traffic urban areas and display signs that linked feelings of white superiority and black inferiority to pictures of the white Jesus. CRAID thus offered a suggestive synthesis of Islamic theology and the struggle for black liberation. CRAID allowed believers to capitalize on older critiques of white Christianity as psychologically harmful to blacks. But rather than simply replace the white Jesus with a black version, as some African-American Christians and other African Americans had done since the nineteenth century, CRAID sought to banish images of God altogether. The goals of CRAID, then, were both particularistic and universalistic: on the one hand, protesters hoped to rid black America of the negative psychological consequences of a white God; on the other, they were also advancing their belief in the One God and their theological opposition to *shirk*, or the association of God with anything other than the Divine itself. In so doing, CRAID created a version of Islamic universalism that paid attention to specifically black concerns.[22]

A UNIVERSALISTIC MUSLIM IDENTITY WITH PARTICULARISTIC ASPECTS

The same was true for the Imam's effort to redefine black Muslim identity. Though Imam Muhammad divorced himself from his father's biological views of blackness, he did adopt a definition of group identity that stressed black ties to the African continent and to an African Muslim ancestor in particular. In so doing, the Imam's leadership showed the influence of larger historical trends in the reconstruction of black identity during the 1960s and 1970s. The death of Malcolm X in 1965 marked the beginning of a period in which blackness came to be defined as a "cultural" identity that included "authentically black" expressions of art, literature, music, cuisine, coiffure, and language, among other traditions. Many African Americans, while still hoping to integrate into the economic and political fabric of America, embraced what they argued was a distinct African-American culture within the United States. For many, "soul," which might be manifested in "giving skin" or cooking traditional Southern dishes, became an essential element of African-American authenticity as did the specifically "African" aspects of blackness. Many young African Americans donned new "Afro" hairstyles and sported "bubas, caftans, agbadas, djellabas, and geles" designed with "colors and fabrics that would have seemed exotic even to their most resplendently attired [African] forebears." New rituals that emphasized this "cultural" definition of black identity were also created during this period. In December 1966, US leader Ron Karenga celebrated the first Kwanzaa, an alternative holiday to Christmas that included the exchange of heritage symbols, the ritualistic lighting of candles, and communal drinking from the unity cup. In addition, Karenga advocated the teaching of Swahili to African-American youth.[23]

While the late 1960s are often associated in American historical memory with black political radicalism, it was these "cultural" aspects of the black revolution that attracted the most support from African Americans themselves, at least according to public opinion polls. For example, 21 percent of a pool of black interviewees polled by *Newsweek* in 1969 thought that a separate black nation-state should be formed. Thirteen percent of the same pool stated that they favored "community control" over integration as a way to succeed in America. In contrast, a 1970 *Time* poll conducted by Louis Harris showed that 85 percent of his interviewees endorsed black studies programs as important signs of "black identity and pride," while nearly half of the pool approved of the new Afro hairstyles. Around 40 percent of blacks polled in Detroit in 1968 indicated their approval of dashikis while 80 percent said they enjoyed soul food and music. Even if one discounts the accuracy of such instruments, the support for a culturally distinct black identity seemed remarkable.[24]

Black writers also sought to identify and contribute to this "self-consciously distinct and meaningful black culture in the United States" by contributing to a number of black publications, including *The Black World, The Journal of Black Studies, The Black Scholar,* and *Black Books Bulletin.* In addition, black intellectuals seized black history as one of the main forums of debate about black identity. These intellectuals focused both on the oppressive nature of slavery and how the African spirit survived and even triumphed through this oppression; characters like Gabriel Prosser, Nat Turner, and Harriet Tubman became key figures in this new black consciousness. Journalist Alex Haley made perhaps the most significant popular contribution to this genre of historical literature in writing his massive *Roots.* First published in *Reader's Digest* during 1974, the 688-page book told the story of how Haley's search for his own ethnic heritage led him back to a particular West African ancestor named Kunta Kinte. Releasing the book in 1976 after twelve years of research, Haley dedicated *Roots* "as a birthday offering to my country within which most of *Roots* happened."[25]

The irony of Haley's dedication should not be lost. *Roots* was not primarily a story about slavery, but an immigrant narrative that showed the journey of the African-American people from West Africa to North America. Of course, the book gave a vivid account of the horrors of slavery, but it concluded as a triumphant narrative about the promise of America. "The story ends," wrote Nathan Huggins, "with that onward, upward, progressive vision fundamental to the American faith. Through *Roots*, black people could find a collective memory and be mythically integrated into the American dream." Haley did not celebrate his ancestor's story to illuminate differences between himself and white Americans but to show the similarities of their long journeys. "It is, ironically, because Americans take so much for granted among themselves that they can dramatize their differences comfortably," Werner Sollors has suggested. "Ethnic revivalism . . . only works in a context where values, assumptions, and rhetoric are shared."[26]

Also seeking to highlight the authentic "immigrant" identity of blacks, Imam Muhammad incorporated this brand of ethnocentrism into his own movement. On November 1, 1975, he announced that he would call himself "Bilalian," a term referring to Bilal ibn Rabah, an African companion of the Prophet Muhammad and the first *muadhdhin*, or prayer-caller, in Islam. Like Haley, Muhammad identified this ancestor as an exemplary model for African-American identity. According to Muhammad, Bilal was "a Black Ethiopian slave who was an outstanding man in the history of Islam. He was the first *muezzin* (Minister) [*sic*] of Prophet Muhammad (may peace be upon Him). He was so sincere and his heart was so pure that the Prophet Muhammad and the other leaders of Islam under him addressed him as 'Master Bilal.'" African-American Muslims, the Imam argued, had a "double connection with Bilal because he was a Muslim and he was also a so-called African."[27]

The appropriation of Bilal, then, was not meant to separate black Muslims from their nonblack Muslim brothers and sisters, but merely to stake out a special place for them within the history of Islam. That Bilal was East African, and not from West Africa, where most African Americans claim their roots, was of no consequence. He was a viable symbol of black Muslim success. Bilal had thrown off the shackles of slavery by refusing to serve his master after taking the *shahada*, the declaration of faith that makes a person Muslim. His example was lauded in a number of sources, including biographies that are still read in various African-American Muslim communities.[28] Bilalian styles of dress, including the "Bilalian" fez, were marketed in the newspaper, which was also renamed in Bilal's honor. The *Bilalian News* children's page even featured a word puzzle about the historic figure. Printed next to an illustration of a man performing the call to prayer, the puzzle read: "I was once a slave / Who was very brave / I was a man without fear / who gave the first prayer / in a land where Arabia lay / and though there were great odds / I was not afraid / to proclaim the religion of God. Who am I?"[29] Following the example of their leader, nearly every active member of the movement came to call themselves "Bilalian." Some outsiders, including the Reverend Al Sharpton, may have used the title as well.[30]

Around 1978 or shortly thereafter, however, opposition to Muhammad's appropriation of the African Muslim ancestor developed within the immigrant and foreign Muslim communities. This criticism emerged at the very time during which Muhammad had begun to cultivate closer ties with Sunni Islamic groups, including the Muslim World League. Muhammad Ali al-Harkan, secretary general of the League from 1976 to 1983, had praised Imam Muhammad for the changes that he had implemented within the NOI. As a result, the Imam became an official consultant and trustee of *da'wa* activities sponsored by the Gulf States in America. Moreover, Wallace Muhammad developed a working relationship with the U.S.-based Muslim Students Association (MSA). Since its founding in 1963 at the University of Illinois, the MSA had become one of the best-organized Muslim associations in the United States. In the middle 1970s, it purchased a huge farm in Plainfield, Indiana (located between Indianapolis and Terra Haute), which would serve both as the headquarters of the MSA and its successor organization, the Islamic Society of North America, founded in 1982. Functioning as an umbrella organization through the 1970s, the MSA established a network of Islamic publishing concerns, properties, and member organizations including the North American Islamic Trust, the Islamic Teaching Center, the American Muslim Scientists and Engineers, and the American Muslim Social Scientists. In order to increase the number of formally educated Islamic clerics and missionaries in the United States, the MSA also helped to place these figures in various locations around the country.[31]

Wallace Muhammad hosted one such missionary. Through a relationship with El Tigani A. Abugideiri, a leading figure within the MSA, Imam Muhammad arranged for a Medina-trained Sudanese shaikh named Muhammad Nur Abdallah to serve as imam of his mosque in Chicago. In 1978, Abdallah first spent two weeks in Indiana with Abugideiri and then left for his assignment at the main mosque of the new WCIW. Once installed as imam, Abdallah preached the Friday *khutba,* or sermon, wrote articles for *Bilalian News,* and taught believers the rudiments of Sunni

Islamic practice, including the prayers.[32] By installing Abdallah as the imam of his main mosque in Chicago, Imam Muhammad showed how serious his ties to the immigrant Muslim community had become. And when quiet opposition to "Bilalism" was voiced in the immigrant community, he decided to yield.[33] "We were experimenting . . . trying to find a solution to our identity problem," Wallace Muhammad said in a 1993 interview. "But Bilalian didn't work for us. We were charged with a division in Islam, of making Bilal our leader rather than the Prophet."[34] By redefining black identity in a way that claimed a particular historical space within the universalistic Islamic heritage, the Imam jeopardized his relations with some of his immigrant Muslim allies.

But rather than abandon the title immediately, the Imam defended the title on the grounds that it had little to do with Islam. "Bilalian," the leader tried to explain in an interview that appeared in the *Bilalian News* on November 16, 1979,

> is not a religious name. We have adopted the name Bilalian as an ethnic name to replace other terms that we think are not as rich, ethnically speaking. They are not as rich because to identify with skin color is not as rich ethnically speaking as to identify with an ancestor who identified with a great ideology. . . . We don't identify with Bilal only because he was Muslim, it's mainly because he was an African ancestor.

Of course, this statement ignored his original intent in 1975 to offer a label that would incorporate his followers' "double connection" with Bilal, who was seen as equally black and Muslim. By 1979, the Imam claimed that he had actually chosen the term "mainly because he [Bilal] was an African ancestor" who also happened to serve as an exemplary ideologue. The explanation, however, did not satisfy Muhammad's critics. While many of his followers continued to call themselves "Bilalian" for some time afterward, Wallace Muhammad abandoned his ancestor, changing the name of the *Bilalian News* to *World Muslim News* in 1980.[35]

By giving up on this project during the early 1980s, Wallace Muhammad showed the extent to which he would go to maintain his integrity as a Sunni Islamic reformer in the eyes of his Muslim Arab allies. The costs in terms of African-American autonomy, however, could be quite high. Like Malcolm X, Wallace Muhammad relinquished an opportunity to insist on an interpretation of the Islamic heritage that paid attention to the particular interests and needs of many African Americans.

ISLAMIC MODERNISM, CONTEXTUALIZED ISLAM, AND BLACK LIBERATION

But while he no longer tried to link any type of black particularism to his universalistic vision of Islam, he did lay a theoretical foundation for another kind of difference within Islam. This possibility emerged in the 1980s, as the Imam touted what might be seen as a form of "Islamic modernism." Originally crafted during the latter nineteenth and early twentieth centuries by Islamic reformers like Jamal al-Din al-Afghani and Muhammad Abduh of Egypt, Sayyid Ahmad Khan of India, and Allal al-Fasi of Morocco, Islamic modernism aspired to synthesize what its ideologues identified as the fundamental ideals of modernity with Islam. As John Esposito summarizes, "Islamic modernism did not seek to restore a pristine past but instead wished to reformulate its Islamic heritage in response to the political, scientific, and cultural challenge of the West. It provided an Islamic rationale for accepting modern ideas and institutions, whether scientific, technological, or political (constitutionalism and representative government)." Moreover, for al-Afghani especially, "Islam was the religion of progress and change, of reason and science, a religion with a strong work ethic." Perhaps most importantly for the history of Islamic thought, Islamic modernists often proposed to reinterpret centuries of Islamic tradition, including the *shari'a,* or the body of Islamic laws and ethics, by using *ijtihad,* or individual interpretation. While Islamic modernism was in part an apologetic, justifying the usefulness of Islam in a world where Muslims seemed increasingly irrelevant or powerless, it also represented an important attempt to preserve and reinterpret aspects of the Islamic heritage in light of radically changing historical conditions.[36]

In a move reminiscent of many Islamic modernists, Imam Muhammad presented Islam throughout the 1980s as a tradition compatible with notions of personal freedom, individualism, and democracy. "America," the Imam argued in a Pittsburgh television program taped in 1983, "is perhaps a place where the idea of freedom is developed to its highest degree." In one sense, he argued, this was advantageous, since "a person can come and can live their life and do whatever they want as long as they respect the laws of the land." But in another sense, he stated, one also has the freedom to be "uncivilized . . . to be tossed about in the winds." The proper antidote to the more destructive side of freedom, he said, was *jihad,* "not for the purpose of conquering lands or overthrowing nations . . . [but] for the purpose of liberating the higher instincts, the higher aspirations of man." A proper *jihad* might include the struggle to become better educated, to lead by moral example, or to succeed in business. While this meant that change was left to the individual, he admitted, such voluntary effort was far better for a society than any imposed moral or religious codes.[37]

The individual's struggle for a life richer in things both sacred and profane is at the very heart of Islam, the Imam claimed in a 1987 interview on the same television program. Equating Islam to American democracy, the Imam argued that "our religion focuses on the individual as the best safeguard [for society]." The Qur'an, the Imam said, "is not a Book to call nations to a mission; it's a Book that calls individuals to life." By providing individuals with clear rules and daily rituals, the Imam stated, the holy book shows individuals how to "give their whole life to God. And in so doing, God lets you have your whole life." The perpetuation of Islamic religion itself also rests on the strength of an individual's practice, according to the Imam: "[An individual] should be able to come into a town where there's no Muslims and practice his religious life. . . . He should be able to conduct himself properly as a Muslim in business, properly as a citizen in the country, as a neighbor to his neighbor who is non-Muslim . . . he should be able to do all of that by himself." In defending his attitudes toward individualism, freedom, and democracy, the Imam turned both to the Qur'an and the *sunna*, the traditions of the Prophet Muhammad. Imam Muhammad argued that "if we find ourselves faced with great difficulty, we should turn not only to the Word of God in Qur'an, but we should also turn to the Seerah," or the biography of the Prophet. Prophet Muhammad, the Imam said, was a "universal model" whose reaction to any given circumstance could be used to understand and solve contemporary problems and dilemmas.[38]

For example, he applied the *sunna* to the question of Muslim participation in American democracy. Imam Muhammad argued that Islam "promotes democratic processes. It sanctions and encourages the democratic processes. In fact, our religion is a democracy." While he did not make clear exactly what it meant that Islam was a democracy, he said it was incumbent on Muslims to become active in politics and he suggested holding political awareness seminars to accomplish this end. "Our religion teaches us that we should be active and supportive of all the good things that a society has established," Muhammad stated in 1984 on the same program in Pittsburgh. This also meant that the Muslim should support the state by paying taxes and joining the military. In explaining the Islamic legitimacy of these views, the Imam utilized an important historical parallel to the early history of Islam. Muslims in America, he said, were religious minorities, much like the Jews and Christians of Islamic Arabia. The Prophet Muhammad, according to the Imam, guaranteed these minorities the right to practice their religion as long as they contributed "to the common needs of that new society that was formed" including, for example, the payment of a mandatory tax. The arrangement made between the early Islamic state and its religious minorities offered an instructive lesson for Muslims in the United States, according to the Imam. "[I]f a Muslim state requires of non-Muslim citizens participation in the support for the general welfare of the state, then if a Muslim is in a non-Muslim state, he should accept to do the same." Such cooperation with the state assumed, the Imam noted, that the government "permits him to practice his religion" and to live a Muslim life. If, for some reason, the state no longer observed its duty to the Muslim citizen in this regard, the Imam said, then he or she was no longer obligated to support the state. In fact, the Muslim should be willing to take up arms in the fight for religious freedom. But for American Muslims, he argued, such a possibility was unrealistic. "[W]e trust," Muhammad stated, "that this country will remain civilized and protect the rights of Muslims, as it protects the rights of other minorities."[39]

The articulation of these arguments represented an important moment in the history of African-American Islamic thought. By looking to the *sunna* as a primary source for his own thought, the Imam hoped to apply the Prophet Muhammad's reasoning to the historical circumstances of African-American life. The Imam also argued that African Americans should confront these sources themselves, rather than relying on others to interpret them. Criticizing what he characterized as an unhealthy reliance by African Americans on charismatic leaders, including Father Divine and his own father, Imam Muhammad emphasized that believers needed only the Qur'an in their search for God. "They say, 'Well, what do you have here, Brother Imam, that makes you so special?" the Imam asked rhetorically. "The Qur'an, the Word of God," he said. "You mean to tell me that just you, and the Word of God . . ." "That's right," the Imam interrupted himself. "Just me and the Word of God." For Imam Muhammad, the act of independent interpretation also required that blacks rely less on their non-black brothers and sisters. "It is not enough for God to tell us through another race, we still feel insecure," the Imam said. "We feel unapproved that we still have not been validated as a man. They are the master, and we are the boys." Obviously referring to immigrant Muslims, the Imam criticized an act of which he himself was clearly guilty—that is, relying on immigrant sponsors to determine what behavior was or was not legitimately

Islamic. In fact, he also called for the development of an African-American school of *fiqh,* or Islamic jurisprudence.[40]

But having defended his right to interpret the texts of Islam in his particular historical circumstances, he did not articulate any new "Islamic" approaches to the question of a particularistic black liberation. In fact, he downplayed issues of race and racism, arguing that blacks had suffered too long under an inferiority complex. Paraphrasing the Prophet Muhammad's last sermon, the Imam argued that "there is no superiority of a white over black or black over white. There is no superiority of . . . an Arab over a non-Arab. The only criteria in this religion is . . . Taqwa—faith in God and in good deeds." Denying that his own color had been a burden to him, the Imam implied that racism was like a mental ailment that the oppressed could treat with positive thinking. While he conceded that African Americans were "treated differently" than persons of other racial backgrounds, the Imam countered that "if you don't accept that anyone has the right to treat you differently, and as long as the law protects you, I think you shouldn't feel any burden." The courts had been doing their part, the Imam said; it was time for blacks to do theirs.[41]

At the same time, however, he argued that blacks should develop and celebrate a stronger sense of group identity. The Imam asserted, for example, that the "Prophet Muhammad (PBUH) was very careful not to undermine or take away the native characteristics of people." According to the Imam, the Prophet indicated that people need not distance themselves from "any healthy development and growth that they had, whether it was ethnic or nationalistic." Rather, he continued, they should preserve their identity, as the Qur'an itself states: "[I]t is Allah who has made you a distinct people, tribes, etc., that you should know one another." God, according to the Imam, also showed divine approval for diversity by permitting the Quraysh, the tribe of the Prophet, to remain a distinct people after the advent of Islam. According to the Imam, someone might have said, "This is going to be a Universal message. I am going to get rid of this importance on Quraish." The Prophet did not do so, said the Imam. In fact, he argued, God even named a chapter in the Qur'an after the tribe.[42] Of course, the Imam did not remark—or choose to remark—just how much controversy the special status of the Quraysh generated in the era of classical Islam, a phenomenon mentioned in chapter 1. He also did not comment on the fact that he had argued elsewhere for the view of Islam as a "Universal message."

Moreover, when forced to articulate how this sense of group identity might benefit blacks, his own program of social change contained no allusions whatsoever to Islam. In fact, his platform sounded exactly like that of Elijah Muhammad. In a Harlem address, Imam Muhammad decried the lack of "social unity" among blacks, which he identified as "what is wrong with us." In fact, the Imam stated, "if you were really Black as a race, if you were Black as an ethnic people, you would be able to progress in this country." In addition, the Imam said, many African Americans were immoral people, whose "dope traffic, prostitution, gambling, Black on Black crime . . . [and] unnatural sex" had rendered them impotent to effect social change. Moreover, the Imam advocated collective self-reliance and "bootstrapping" to correct the economic disparities between African Americans and other racial groups in the United States.[43]

Denying the existence of any fundamental disadvantage for blacks within the economic "system" of the United States, Muhammad called in 1983 for less dependence on the federal government and more cooperative ventures between African Americans. In fact, the year earlier he had begun a kind of cooperative buying club called the AMMCOP, the American Muslim Mission Committee to Purchase 100,000 Commodities Plus. While the cooperative was not officially dissolved until 1986, it never managed to achieve much success. Nevertheless, the Imam said, it was the responsibility of African Americans and not the government to reestablish a "tax base" in the inner city. "Muslims," he explained, "can't accept to live in the world and see other people develop in business and . . . just be employed waiting for other people to create an opening for them. Allah says: 'Seek the Hereafter with all means I've given you, but don't neglect your share of responsibility in the physical world.'"[44]

In effect, the Imam seemed to be advocating two methods of social change animated by different assumptions and values. On the one hand, his Islamic modernism placed the responsibility of moral and economic progress on the individual, who had been identified by the Qur'an, according to Wallace Muhammad, as the "best safeguard" for society. For the Imam, this focus on the individual reflected his notions of Islamic social justice and equality; that is, the Imam understood Islam as a tradition that values a person for his or her individual character and actions rather than any group affiliation. On the other hand, the Imam also understood Islam to sanction "ethnic" cohesiveness, which he said was lacking among African Americans. Here he seemed to indicate that the onus of social change was on the black community and not simply black individuals. But rather than offering his own solutions to the problems of black Americans *as a group,* the Imam advocated the implementation of his father's program for black uplift—and he did not explain, as he had done so well in defending individualism, how this made sense in terms of Islam.

Put another way, the Imam understood values of individualism, acquisitiveness, and democracy as universalistic Islamic themes. Morality, economic success, and freedom were not the values of a particular people; they were the very organizing principles of humanity. And yet, African-American deficiency in these values, according to the Imam, was related to their blackness. African Americans, he said, possessed social problems that seemed to be particularly *black*. But since (for him) Islam could not signify values of social change tailored for one group or another, the Imam seemed unable to compose a program of social change in which Islamic values served as the basis for communal action. Rather, he relied on the race-oriented programs of his father, while still upholding the race-less values of Islamic universalism.

IMAM MUHAMMAD'S LEGACY

In the span of less than a decade, Wallace Muhammad attempted to dismantle the black particularistic tradition of Islam that had been the most prominent strain of Islamic thought among African Americans since World War II. In its place, he asserted the primal importance of Sunni Islamic traditions and norms. Even more than Malcolm X, he distanced himself from the black messianist foundations of African-American Islam, including any essentialist notions of what it meant to be black. Instead, he attempted to redefine black identity in a way that incorporated blacks into both an American immigrant narrative and Islamic history. When forced to abandon this effort, he then sought to achieve a different goal: to create an interpretation of Islam specifically suited to the needs of contemporary African Americans. While he did not work out the details of this idea with regard to a collective black struggle for liberation, he had claimed an important right. Blacks, he said, should find an Islam whose meaning would be determined within the black community and whose focus would be on the betterment of black life. The defense of this idea represented a significant moment in the history of African-American Islamic thought, a moment whose implications I explore further in the following conclusion.

Chapter 7

Toward an Islam for
One People and Many

LOUIS FARRAKHAN AND THE
RECAPITULATION OF PARADOX

It would be wrong to conclude from the previous chapter that particularism has vanished in African-American Islamic thought. In fact, its ongoing presence can be seen quite clearly in the career of Minister Louis Farrakhan, leader of a reconstituted Nation of Islam (NOI). Born Louis Eugene Walcott in Bronx, New York, on May 11, 1933, the future NOI leader first learned about the teachings of Elijah Muhammad through Malcolm X, who was helping to start a temple in Boston at the time. Converting to the NOI in the middle 1950s, Louis X, as he came to be called, quickly achieved a great deal of success as a movement leader. Originally serving as Malcolm's assistant minister in Boston, the former calypso singer composed a number of movement songs, including "A White Man's Heaven is a Black Man's Hell," in addition to authoring two important movement plays called *Orgena, a Negro Spelled Backwards* and *The Trial.* In 1964, after Malcolm left the movement, Elijah Muhammad appointed Louis X as the Minister of Harlem's Temple No. 7. He was even mentioned as a successor to Elijah Muhammad, as Malcolm X had been.[1]

When Elijah Muhammad died in 1975, the man who had since become Louis Farrakhan initially expressed his support of Wallace Muhammad. But tensions between the two men grew, especially after Muhammad had Farrakhan replaced as minister of Temple No. 7 and brought him to Chicago, where he could be watched more closely. After being sent on a good will tour of the Caribbean, Farrakhan had had enough. Rallying several NOI confidants around him, he planned a resurrection of the old NOI in 1977. Attacking Wallace Muhammad's Sunni Islamic reforms as a misguided departure from Elijah Muhammad's teachings, Minister Farrakhan charged that the new policies ignored the issue of racism. Any form of integration was, he said, a "lullaby." Racism was a global problem, he argued in another interview. "I have visited Christian, Muslim, Socialist, and Communist countries," Farrakhan said. "Wherever I found a plurality of races, I consistently found the Black man on the bottom."[2]

Elijah Muhammad's black dispensationalist Islam, he stated in effect, was the only realistic answer to this problem. In fact, from the late 1970s until today, Farrakhan has retained many aspects of the elder Muhammad's thought, especially by emphasizing the importance of Elijah Muhammad's prophetic status. In the early 1990s, Minster Farrakhan sought to legitimate his own leadership of the NOI by describing his unique links to the Messenger. He cited, for example, his kinship to Muhammad through the marriage of two daughters to members of Elijah Muhammad's family. He also compared his relationship to Elijah Muhammad to that between Jesus the Messiah and Paul, the great evangelist. Finally, he reported having experienced spiritual visions—including one in which he visited a UFO during a trip to Mexico in 1985—that confirmed the validity of Muhammad's teachings.[3]

Like Elijah Muhammad before the early 1960s, Farrakhan justified these views through interpretations of Islamic texts. He also incorporated several elements of Sunni Islam into his movement, telling his followers, for example, to observe the Ramadan fast not at Yuletide, as Elijah Muhammad said, but according to the lunar calendar followed by other Muslims. In addition, the Minister began to hold the main prayer meeting on Friday rather than Sunday and encouraged followers to make the hajj. Finally, Farrakhan used historical parallels to the life example of the Prophet Muhammad to illuminate the meaning of his own mission. When Farrakhan purchased the Stoney Island mosque in 1988 for some two million dollars, he compared this act to the Prophet Muhammad's triumphant return to Mecca after a ten-year absence. When, in another example, he tried to explain his belief that Elijah Muhammad is not actually dead but in hiding, he likened Elijah Muhammad's disappearance to that of the Prophet's escape from Mecca before establishing his political community in Medina.[4]

More recently, however, Minister Farrakhan has received a great deal of attention from the national press not for the continuing presence of such particularism, but for his participation in interracial and interfaith dialogue and activism. In a way, Farrakhan's ecumenism might be dated to April 18, 1993, when he performed the Mendelssohn violin concerto in Winston-Salem, North Carolina, as a way "to try to do with music what cannot be done with words and try to undo with music what words have done." Farrakhan was referring to the anti-Semitic remarks and attitudes that had been expressed by him and other leaders of the Nation of Islam during the 1980s and early 1990s. Felix Mendelssohn, of course, was born a Jew, and by playing his violin concerto, Farrakhan was attempting to offer a symbolic gesture of reconciliation.[5]

But in the last few years, Minister Farrakhan and his representatives have gone beyond such symbols, actively organizing demonstrations and conferences with persons of different faiths and racial backgrounds. Moreover, the leader has explained such activity as an embodiment of universalistic Islamic principles. In fact, many of these efforts have been directed toward other Muslims, including Imam Wallace Muhammad, the man with whom Farrakhan separated in the late 1970s. On February 26, 1999, while Minister Farrakhan was suffering from prostate cancer, Wallace Muhammad was invited to attend the NOI's annual Savior's Day convention in Chicago. "Embraced with cheers, hugs and kisses," according to the official NOI press release, Imam Muhammad participated in Friday prayers "in an effort to continue the process of resolving differences between the communities of the followers of the Honorable Elijah Muhammad since 1975." For his part, the Imam was quoted as saying that he "couldn't resist coming here knowing that the (Nation of Islam) was observing this day [of prayers]" and added that the time when he and Farrakhan would be one was coming "inshallah." Interpreting the event through the lens of Islamic universalism, Minister Farrakhan's son, Mustapha, explained that it represented "an invitation of unity and brotherhood to the whole Muslim ummah that wants to see freedom, justice, and equality."[6]

Similarly, Farrakhan has sought to strengthen ties to foreign Muslim leaders and dignitaries by using the language of universalistic Islam. On February 25, 2000, during the Second International Islamic Conference in Chicago, an event held concurrently with the annual Savior's Day convention, Farrakhan proclaimed, "I love Allah, Prophet Muhammad, may the peace and blessing of Allah be upon him. I love every Muslim on this earth, no matter where they are, [or] what their color is." A multiracial crowd that included a representative of "Sheik Tantawi, the Grand Sheikh of Egypt's Al-Azhar University," warmly received his remarks, according to the official NOI press release. Speaking through a translator, "Sheik Farhat . . . urged the Muslims to put aside their differences, unify themselves and prepare for what's being planned against those (striving to submit to Allah's will)."[7] The final communiqué issued on behalf of the Conference stressed the need for Muslim unity, solidarity, and networking in responding to the oppression of Muslim persons around the world. It also resolved to "regard, treat, and respect all Muslims as part and parcel of the one and same Ummah (Community of Muslims)" and to "affirm that the Brotherhood and Sisterhood and unity of Islam transcend all barriers and difference of colors, language, place of residence or citizenship, and schools of law." Finally, the document called on Muslims to "promote mutual understanding and peaceful coexistence with other faith communities through interfaith dialogue and joint action for the common good of all."[8]

These messages of racial harmony, interfaith dialogue, and "joint action for the common good" informed much of Minister Farrakhan's participation in the Million Family March, an event held later that year in Washington, D.C., on October 16. Supported in part by the Reverend Sun Myung Moon and the Unification Church, the march brought a multiracial and multifaith crowd of thousands to the west front of the U.S. Capitol to hear Farrakhan, among others, speak on a variety of political, social, and moral issues. In his address, Farrakhan argued that the achievement of world peace and social justice depends on interfaith unity and he chastised the children of Abraham who "recognize . . . God as a father, and then turn around and slaughter each other." The leader also criticized the extent to which ethnic, racial, and national division had led to violence and oppression around the globe. Paraphrasing Qur'an 49:13, Farrakhan proclaimed that God "created you into tribes and families that you may know one another and, parenthetically, not despise one another." One people is not better than another because of their race or their creed, Farrakhan declared, but because of their "righteous conduct. . . . God is just, and he's no respecter of persons. It doesn't matter what your color is, what your race is, with God it is righteousness that He is after." That righteousness, he said, must become manifest in the fight for social justice and a more equal distribution of world resources. But if humans truly want a more just world, he continued, they must "rise above symbols [of difference] into the substance of the oneness of God."[9] Using similarly universalistic arguments in his introduction to the Million Family March National Agenda, Farrakhan drew on interpretations of both the Bible and the Qur'an to argue that the family is the primary institution of all human society. All families, he said, must be strengthened through increased access to basic financial and educational resources and opportunities.[10]

Despite this progressive political agenda and the use of universalistic Islamic language to support it, however, Minister Farrakhan has not abandoned various components of Elijah Muhammad's particularistic Islam. Rather, Minister Farrakhan's particularistic interpretations of Islam often appear alongside his new universalism without any further comment. For example, as of this writing, the official Nation of Islam website features a version of the Muslim Program that contains statements that might be viewed by most Muslims as entirely contradictory. In the second section of that document, entitled "What the Muslims Believe," the last numbered item reiterates the traditional NOI belief in W. D. Fard's divinity: "We Believe that Allah (God) appeared in the Person of Master W. Fard Muhammad, July, 1930; the long-awaited 'Messiah' of the Christians and the 'Mahdi' of the Muslims." Then, immediately after this sentence, the following appears: "We believe further and lastly that Allah is God and besides HIM there is no god and He will bring about a universal government of peace wherein we all can live together."[11] For the vast majority of Muslims around the world, the first statement of belief in Fard's divinity constitutes a form of *shirk*, or the association of something with God— an act often seen by Islamic scholars throughout history as the worst form of unbelief. The second statement, however, contains a proclamation of God's Oneness in universalistic language with which most other Muslims would agree. In the historical terms of scholarly Sunni Islamic discourse, these statements seem wholly inconsistent: it is not possible to believe simultaneously that a human being appeared as God and that God is One. But no further explanation is given in the NOI document, perhaps implying that for Minister Farrakhan, there is no contradiction in the two statements. At the least, the inclusion of the statement of belief in God's Oneness allows NOI members to claim that their basic theological orientation is not fundamentally different from that of most Muslims.

In making this claim, Minister Farrakhan has left behind the attempt to define the Islamic legitimacy of the movement solely in terms of Elijah Muhammad's prophetic authority. In fact, Farrakhan's use of Qur'an and of basic Sunni theological principles are reminiscent of Malcolm X's attempts to bolster the Islamic authenticity of the NOI in the midst of Sunni criticism during the late 1950s and early 1960s. Such attempts, it will be recalled, did not result in the abandonment of particularism, but in fact in its perpetuation. Similarly, Farrakhan now combines particularistic and universalistic elements in a system of Islamic thought that links universal human redemption with black chosenness. In his address to the participants of the Million Family March, for instance, Farrakhan still stressed an Ethiopianist interpretation of the Bible that posits a special role for black people in God's plan. Describing American slavery as "the worst form of slavery ever in the history of the world," Farrakhan repeated themes familiar within particularistic African-American Islamic discourse: "[T]here have never been a people," he said, "that have lost their names, their language, their culture, their religion, cut off from their history and the knowledge of God and their religion, then sold as chattel slaves for 300 years." Asking how a just God could allow such horror—even after legal emancipation—the Minister argued that the suffering of African Americans was a sign of their chosenness. "But I respectfully say to you that it is written in the Bible," he preached, "that God would choose a . . . people who were despised and rejected . . . none fits that description of the lost sheep or lost people or lost brother more than the black man and woman of America and the Western Hemisphere."[12]

While Farrakhan did not linger on this theme during his Million Family March speech, he has expanded on this vision in other speeches currently available through the official website of the NOI. In "Giving New Meaning to Race," for example, Minister Farrakhan reinterprets Elijah Muhammad's myth of Yacub to argue that the triumph of the chosen does not mean the destruction of whites, but the end of racial division and "race" itself. Repeating Elijah Muhammad's claim that the black man was the original man, Farrakhan asserts that race per se did not exist until "the white man came to our planet and gave meaning to race." That meaning, he argues, "created hatred and mischief among the family of man." But "now we (Black people) are being called upon by Allah through the Honorable Elijah Muhammad to give new and true meaning to race." Though Elijah Muhammad's first task was to uplift the black man and convince him of his own worth, argued Minister Farrakhan, "we must [now] understand that race has a beginning and race will have an ending." In fact, Minister Farrakhan argues that the end of racism and of race itself was exactly what Elijah Muhammad had prophesied: "[N]ationalism will have an end: racism will have an end: sexism will have an end: and humanity will then have a new beginning." But black people, he concludes, must play a special role in this divine plan. "We must give new meaning to race and end it forever. Black people must take it upon ourselves to end racism once and for all."[13]

In espousing this black messianist vision of universal human redemption, Farrakhan evokes the earliest voices of African-American Islamic thought. Like Blyden and Ali, he adopts both universalistic and particularistic interpretations of Islam without exploring any of the contradictions or tensions that these positions create. It is as if the opening themes of African-American Islamic thought are recapitulated in a symphony whose final movement sounds very much like its first. The questions raised by Farrakhan's more recent pronouncements are the same questions raised in examining the thought of the first African-American Islamic thinkers: Is there any important difference between being a black Muslim and being a human Muslim? What is the nature of that difference, if there is any? Is there any way of reconciling these two forms of Muslim identity, or is the paradox evoked by these different representations of Islamic identity actually desirable?

In analyzing why such questions have not been more explicitly addressed by most of the thinkers covered in this study, I would like to suggest that the use of certain essentialist interpretations of Islam and black identity has been key to the unfolding of modern black Islamic thought. Employed by black thinkers themselves, these constructs have acted as intellectual constraints within which African-American Islamic thought has operated and developed throughout its history. My concluding remarks retrace the genealogy of black Islamic thought by highlighting the prevalence of such essentialism and by showing how more recent historically minded interpretations of Islam implicitly challenge this style of Islamic thought.

ESSENTIALISM AND THE RECONSTRUCTION OF AFRICAN-AMERICAN ISLAMIC THOUGHT

The essentialist style of Islamic thought, which can be seen most clearly in Drew Ali, Elijah Muhammad, and Minister Farrakhan, contains starkly ahistorical constructions of both black identity and Islam. For example, as shown in chapter 3, Noble Drew Ali described Islam as a natural phenomenon that inextricably bound Islam to the very being of all nonwhite persons. For Drew Ali, to be white was to be Christian; to be Asiatic was to be Muslim. Hence, "Moors," a national subgroup of the larger Asiatic race, were also by nature Muslim. Moreover, despite the fact that Drew Ali attempted to escape the prison of race by redefining black identity in terms of a nationalistic Moorish mythology, the effects of his system of thought were to reinforce essentialist conceptions of black identity, including an emphasis on racial purity. Though Elijah Muhammad did not adopt Drew Ali's Moorish mythology, I showed in chapter 4 how he espoused similarly essentialist and racialist views of both Islam and blackness. Reaffirming the inseparability of Islam from the identity of black people themselves, Muhammad helped to establish a long-lasting intellectual legacy of African-American Islamic particularism. In fact, after immigrant Muslims challenged Elijah Muhammad, he retreated further into an ontologically particularistic interpretation of Islam. He seemed to have no answer to his critics other than to entrench himself more deeply into his own black Islamic metaphysic.

This essentialist style of thought can also be seen in Malcolm X, who rejected the substance of Elijah Muhammad's particularistic teachings, but perpetuated many of his racialist assumptions about black identity, including the belief in inherent black traits and characteristics. Based in part on these views of black identity, Malcolm supported a particularistic approach to black liberation through his advocacy of pan-Africanism. At the same time, Malcolm advanced an absolutist view of Islamic universalism that, by definition, could not be used to support any sort of particularistic struggle. At best, as outlined in chapter 5, Malcolm could claim a "double burden"—both to his "race" and to his faith. In other words, as a result of his essentialist views of both black identity and Islam, Malcolm seemed unable to synthesize his "religion" with his "politics." His essentialist worldview became an intellectual barrier to appropriating Islam within the context of a particularistic struggle for black liberation.

At the same time, this essentialist style did not limit the thought of Blyden in such profound and direct ways. Like Minister Farrakhan in the early 2000s, Blyden seemed far more comfortable with the ambiguity created by his incongruous mix of both particularistic and universalistic themes. Or perhaps he simply did not notice the logical contradictions and the open-ended questions that his thought suggested. For example, he never made clear whether Islam was a tradition well-suited for blacks because of particularistic reasons, like its tendency to encourage an explicitly black self-determination, or because of universalistic reasons, like (what was for Blyden) its essential message of human justice, dignity, and equality. Blyden also made an *historical* argument for the "salutary" effects of Islam on the African character, coming closer than his American counterparts to rejecting overwhelmingly essentialist constructions of Islam. For most of his life, however, Blyden remained an essentialist with regard to matters of race, reaffirming nineteenth-century notions of both romantic and scientific racialism. As shown in chapter 2, this orientation led Blyden to adopt the idea that blacks were by nature "softer" and more "spiritual," and thus were necessary players in the salvation of the world that would emerge as a result of the redemption of Africa.

Nevertheless, the fact that Blyden shifted rhetorical strategies so often shows that, unlike Malcolm and Elijah Muhammad, his creativity seemed somewhat less squelched by his own essentialist assumptions. In a sense, this was also true for Noble Drew Ali, who maintained that while Islam was an exclusively nonwhite tradition, it also contained what Ali claimed were the true teachings of "Love, Truth, Peace, Freedom and Justice being taught universally to all nations, in all lands."[14] Of course, it was unclear whether non-Muslims, who were by definition white, could experience any true liberation, since only "Moorish Science" offered the gnosis necessary to achieve such a state of being. But, like Blyden, Drew Ali seemed quite comfortable with advocating contradictory or at least paradoxical positions about the "nature" of Islam. For him, Islam contained both egalitarian and racialist elements. Whether Blyden and Drew Ali meant to construct these paradoxical formulations is difficult to know. Clearly, if either had desired a more logically consistent style of argument, then some other explanations would have been needed.

My point here, however, is not to criticize the contradictions and ambiguities expressed in their views. Nor am I trying to suggest that their paradoxical formulations are necessarily subtler than the static definitions of Islam offered by Elijah Muhammad and Malcolm X. But I do want to analyze the critical differences between their essentialist style of thought and the intellectual orientation suggested by the thought of Wallace Muhammad. More than any of these other thinkers, Wallace Muhammad took seriously the role of historical context in articulating his visions of both black identity and of Islam. The key moment in his shift away from essentialism came, as I observed in chapter 6, when Wallace Muhammad began to reconstruct black identity within the Nation of Islam during the middle 1970s. Appropriating themes from the black consciousness movement, Muhammad linked the Muslim identity of his African-American followers to that of an African Muslim ancestor named Bilal. In effect, he said that the true meaning of being black could be found in the proud history of black culture. For him, part of that history was also Islamic.

While Imam Muhammad abandoned "Bilalism" by the early 1980s, he did not divorce himself from the idea that African-American Islam must be seen in the light of its own particular historical context. For Imam Muhammad, this commitment to history also involved a reinterpretation of Qur'an and hadith in light of his own historical circumstances. For example, he compared Muslims in America to the Jews and Christians of early Islamic Arabia. Relations between the early Islamic state and its minorities offered an instructive lesson for Muslims in the United States, the Imam said: "[I]f a Muslim state requires of non-Muslim citizens participation in the support for the general welfare of the state, then if a Muslim is in a non-Muslim state, he should accept to do the same." Applying one of the traditions of the Prophet Muhammad, Imam Muhammad argued that the United States should guarantee minorities the right to practice their traditions as long as they contributed "to the common needs of that new society that was formed" including, for example, the payment of a mandatory tax.[15]

On the one hand, one might view this style of interpretation as yet another form of essentialism. After all, one could see the Imam as identifying within the Sunna a certain essential principle—which in this case involves the obligations of all citizens regardless of confessional affiliation or minority status—and then applying this principle within a specific historical context. On the other hand, one might also interpret the Imam's hermeneutic as radically historicist. In other words, his use of the text might also imply that the meanings of sacred text actually change, depending upon the human context in which one interprets the text. When followed to its logical conclusion, such thinking implies that there is no essential meaning within Islamic texts—or that these core meanings remain beyond human grasp—and to take this one step further, no essential definition of Islam. Farid Esack, a South African Muslim scholar-activist, argues that such historicist interpretation is inevitable, whether conscious or not: "Because every reader approaches the Qur'an within a particular context it is impossible to speak of an interpretation of the qur'anic text applicable to the whole world. Meaning is always tentative and biased."[16] For Esack, then, the expression of "essential" Islamic principles will necessarily reflect the biases of the person in support of them. Of course, this itself is an ontological position, reflecting a belief in the contingency of all human life. Moreover, some Muslims, including Abdal-Hakim Murad, have criticized Esack's approach as an incoherent rejection of Sunni Islamic tradition that recasts the Qur'an as a "miraculous prefigurement of late twentieth-century Western ideals."[17]

But without deciding finally whether the Imam's thought is essentialist or historicist, the key point for this study is that his style of thought suggests new directions in confronting the tension between universalism and particularism. For his attention to the role of historical context in determining the meaning of black identity and Islam suggests that difference, in all its forms, might be accepted and embraced more heartily by Muslims challenged to respond both to the contingency of human life and to what many Muslims view as the timeless core of the Islamic message. Because circumstances change, the Imam's thought implies, what might be the most Islamic thing to do in one situation may not be the most Islamic thing to do in another. Of course, such thinking could lead to a crude relativism if Muslims do not agree on something common to all of them. Put another way, if Islam is radically deconstructed, one might end up only with competing forms of particularism. This situation could be avoided, however, if participants in the discourse decide that something is universal to them all—like a commitment to social justice or the centrality of the Qur'an and the hadith.

Still, while a more historical view of Islam may help to carve out a larger space for difference within Islamic thought, it does not mean that the tension between universalism and particularism would suddenly disappear. After all, it seems quite inevitable that as historical circumstances shift, new particularistic challenges would be issued to norms that had become temporarily authoritative among certain groups and individuals. The difference is that the debate over these norms might be more deliberately reflective of its own contingency. Practically speaking, one of the issues that participants might debate is the role of difference itself in Islam. Just how much particularism should be allowed? For example, would a particularism that expressed chauvinism be tolerated? How would one oppose such exclusionary arguments? Are there certain acceptable ways of conducting an argument? In one sense, this very discussion has taken place among some African-American Muslim leaders. For example, according to Wallace Muhammad, he and Minister Farrakhan disagree about the most fundamental tenets of Islam, but also expressly forbid their followers from attacking each other based on these differences—a phenomenon that was a real threat during the 1980s.[18] Perhaps more frequent and more equitable dialogue can also take place among African-American Muslims and their immigrant and foreign brothers and sisters. This dialogue might consider more seriously the historical importance of race and slavery not only in the United States but in the Old World Islamic lands, as well. In addition, more attention might be paid to the particular challenges within African-American Muslim communities and the meaning of those problems for the practice of Islam in black America.

At the same time, making room for more historical contextualization in Islamic thought need not lead to the demise of strong principles—things worth dying for. Nor would the recognition of the contingency of one's thought need render one's principles less meaningful or sincere. The difference in recognizing the contingency of a principle is that one *chooses* to adhere to a certain idea, rather than feeling compelled by tautological necessity. That is, one is able to articulate several interrelated reasons for believing the way one does, rather than simply saying that this is what the tradition says to do. Of course, all the while one is defining what is "essential" about Islam, but without reifying it outside of time and space.

For example, one might look at the tension between universalism and particularism and conclude that paradox is needed to confront this question. But unlike Blyden and Drew Ali, one would make explicit one's contradictions and explain them in terms of a larger vision that accounts for one's context. It could be argued, for instance, that humans should always be dealt with as both one and many. To treat all humans as one, for instance, may be explained as an expression of the egalitarian impulse so central to Islamic history. To treat humans as many, however, may mean to practice this ideal by focusing on the liberation of a particularly oppressed minority, much in the same way that affirmative action is meant to advance equality of opportunity among all. Perhaps an embrace of difference may mean not to differ over issues of public policy but to allow for variation in ritual practice. Whatever the example, this simultaneous defining of Islam as both one and many may represent no real contradiction; in fact, it may be the only practical way to achieve the ideals of Islam as defined by the Muslim community.

Imam Muhammad's dynamic style of interpretation could very well yield such approaches to problems still facing the contemporary African-American Muslim community. Or perhaps other African-American Muslim thinkers can rise to the level of national leadership in giving voice to an African-American Islam that confronts the continuing challenges of inequality and diversity—not only in terms of race, but also in terms of class, gender, sexual orientation, disability, and more. Realistically, any strong challenge to the oppression of African Americans must emerge not only from the small number of black Muslims in America, but from fellow black Christians and persons without confessional affiliation, as well. So, some sort of hermeneutical confrontation with interfaith activity and secularism will also be necessary in this struggle. The vitality of Islam in black America itself may depend upon the abilities of its adherents to face such questions in a bold and creative manner. "For the numerous Muslims who experience existence as marginalized and oppressed communities or individuals," writes Farid Esack, the venture of Islam "has to take place amidst their own Meccan crucibles of the engagement between oppressor and oppressed, the Abyssinian sojourn amidst the gracious and warm hospitality of 'the other' and the liberating praxis in Medina."[19] In African-American Islamic thought, such a journey has only begun—not because it has taken a long time to develop, but because the journey ought always to be new.

Notes

NOTES TO CHAPTER 1

1. See C. Eric Lincoln, *The Black Muslims in America,* 3rd ed. (Grand Rapids: William B. Eerdmans, 1994). The other classic scholarly work on the movement is E. U. Essien-Udom, *Black Nationalism: A Search for an Identity in America* (Chicago: University of Chicago Press, 1962). More recent overviews of African-American Islam include Aminah Beverly McCloud, *African American Islam* (New York: Routledge, 1995) and Richard Brent Turner, *Islam in the African-American Experience* (Bloomington: Indiana University Press, 1997). Recent monographs on more limited topics include Louis A. DeCaro, *On the Side of My People: A Religious Life of Malcolm X* (New York: New York University Press, 1996); Mattias Gardell, *In the Name of Elijah Muhammad: Louis Farrakhan and the Nation of Islam* (Durham: Duke University Press, 1996); and Claude Andrew Clegg III, *An Original Man: The Life and Times of Elijah Muhammad* (New York: St. Martin's Press, 1997).

2. Lawrence H. Mamiya, for example, calls the book "the best social history of the Nation of Islam available" in an annotated bibliography of the movement. See "Nation of Islam," in *The Oxford Encyclopedia of the Modern Islamic World,* ed. John L. Esposito (New York: Oxford, 1995), 3:235–8.

3. See Lincoln, *Black Muslims,* 26, 43, 63, 210.

4. Talal Asad, *Genealogies of Religion: Discipline and Reasons of Power in Christianity and Islam* (Baltimore: Johns Hopkins University Press, 1993), 39, 42, 47.

5. Abdulkader Tayob, *Islam in South Africa: Mosques, Imams, and Sermons* (Gainesville: University Press of Florida, 1999), 10.

6. See L. Gardet, "Din," in the *Encyclopedia of Islam* (Leiden: E. J. Brill, 1962), 2:293–6, and L. Gardet, "Islam," in the *Encyclopedia of Islam* (Leiden: E. J. Brill, 1978), 4:171–4.

7. Alisdair C. MacIntyre, *After Virtue: A Study in Moral Theory* (Notre Dame: University of Notre Dame Press, 1984), 222.

8. Gustave E. von Grunewald, ed., *Unity and Variety in Muslim Civilization* (Chicago: University of Chicago Press, 1955), 17.

9. See Edmund Burke III's conclusion to Marshall G. S. Hodgson, *Rethinking World History* (New York: Cambridge University Press, 1993), 302, 315.

10. Marshall G. S. Hodgson, *The Venture of Islam: Conscience and History in a World Civilization* (Chicago: University of Chicago Press, 1974), 2:80–1, 83, 87.

11. Talal Asad as quoted in the introduction to Barbara D. Metcalf, ed., *Making Muslim Space in North America and Europe* (Berkeley: University of California Press, 1996). But see also Asad, *Genealogies of Religion*, 18, 210–11. Asad suggests the necessity of an "historical" essentialism: "It is like saying that the constitutive rules of a game define its essence—which is by no means to assert that the game can never be subverted or changed; it is merely to point to what determines its essential historical identity, to imply that certain changes (though not others) will mean that the game is no longer the same game." This analogy helps to illuminate my distinction between Islam, which can signify anything that Muslims say it signifies, and certain traditions of Islam, like Sunni and Shi'i Islam, which have been characterized by specific constitutive elements throughout their history.

12. Ernesto Laclau, "Universalism, Particularism, and the Question of Identity," in *The Politics of Difference*, eds. E. N. Wilmsen and P. McAllister (Chicago: University of Chicago Press, 1996), 52, 57. And here my approach differs from that of Hodgson, who argued that a "tradition does not lend itself indifferently to every possible opinion or practice." See Hodgson, *The Venture of Islam*, 1:86.

13. Wilfred Cantwell Smith, *Toward a World Theology: Faith and the Comparative History of Religion* (Maryknoll, NY: Orbis, 1981), 4–5, 27–28.

14. Hodgson, *Venture of Islam*, 1:26.

15. The third edition of Lincoln's *Black Muslims* still insists on labeling the Nation of Islam a Moslem sect. See Lincoln, *Black Muslims*, 217.

16. The most comprehensive work on the presence of African Muslims in the United States during the 1800s is Allan D. Austin, *African Muslims in Antebellum America: Transatlantic Stories and Spiritual Struggles* (New York: Routledge, 1997).

17. See Louise Marlow, *Hierarchy and Egalitarianism in Islamic Thought* (Cambridge: Cambridge University Press, 1997), 2–3, 97.

18. See H. T. Norris, "Shu'ubiyyah in Arabic Literature," in *'Abbasid Belles-Lettres*, ed. J. Ashtiany et al. (Cambridge: Cambridge University Press, 1990), 32; Hodgson, *The Venture of Islam*, 223; Roy P. Mottahedeh, "The Shu'ubiyya Controversy and the Social History of Early Islamic Iran," *IJMES* 7 (1976): 180–1; and Norris, "Shu'ubiyyah," 36.

19. Marlow, *Hierarchy and Egalitarianism*, 35–6.

20. See Hamid Dabashi, *Authority in Islam: From the Rise of Muhammad to the Establishment of the Umayyads* (New Brunswick: Transition, 1989), 6–7; Mottahedeh, "Shu'ubiyya Controversy," 164; and Dabashi, *Authority in Islam*, 131.

21. See Dabashi, *Authority in Islam*, 129; Hodgson, *Venture of Islam*, 1:487–8; and E. A. Salem, "Political Theory and the Institutions of the Khawarij," *Johns Hopkins University Studies in Historical and Political Science* 74 (1956): 63.

22. See Julius Wellhausen, *The Religio-Political Factions in Early Islam*, trans. R. Ostle and S. Walzer (Amsterdam: North Holland, 1975), 20–1; Salem, "Political Theory," 32; Hodgson, *Venture of Islam* 257–8; and G. Levi Della Vida, "Kharidjites," *Encyclopedia of Islam* (Leiden: E. J. Brill, 1978), 4:1075.

23. H. A. R. Gibb, *Studies on the Civilization of Islam* (Boston: Beacon, 1962), 10–13.

24. Mottahedeh, "The Shuʿubiyya Controversy," 175–8.

25. See especially Edward W. Said, *Orientalism* (New York: Vintage, 1979), and *Culture and Imperialism* (New York: Alfred A. Knopf, 1993).

26. See Yvonne Y. Haddad and Jane I. Smith, ed., *Muslim Communities in North America* (Albany: State University of New York Press, 1994), xxv.

27. See C. Eric Lincoln and Lawrence H. Mamiya, *The Black Church in the African American Experience* (Durham: Duke University Press, 1990), 12–13.

28. See Orlando Patterson, *Ethnic Chauvinism: The Reactionary Impulse* (New York: Stein and Day, 1977), 67; Wilson J. Moses, *The Golden Age of Black Nationalism, 1850–1925* (New York: Oxford, 1978), 20; and Eddie S. Gaude, Jr., *Exodus: Religion, Race, and Nation in Early Nineteenth-Century Black America* (Chicago: University of Chicago Press, 2000).

29. See Barbara J. Fields, "Ideology and Race in American History," in *Region, Race, and Reconstruction: Essays in Honor of C. Vann Woodward,* eds. J. Morgan Kousser and James M. McPherson (New York: Oxford, 1982), 143–58; Michael O. Emerson and Christian Smith, *Divided by Faith: Evangelical Religion and the Problem of Race in America* (New York: Oxford, 2000), 7; and David R. Roediger, *The Wages of Whiteness: Race and the Making of the American Working Class* (London: Verso, 1992), 9–15.

30. See Sterling Stuckey, "Identity and Ideology: The Names Controversy," in *Slave Culture: Nationalist Theory and the Foundations of Black America* (New York: Oxford, 1987), 193–244.

31. See further George M. Fredrickson, *Black Liberation: A Comparative History of Black Ideologies in the United States and South Africa* (New York: Oxford, 1995).

32. See Wilson J. Moses, *Black Messiahs and Uncle Toms: Social and Literary Manipulations of a Religious Myth* (University Park, PA: Penn State University Press, 1993), 1.

33. See Evelyn Brooks Higginbotham, *Righteous Discontent: The Women's Movement in the Black Baptist Church, 1880–1920* (Cambridge: Harvard University Press, 1993), 4–13.

NOTES TO CHAPTER 2

1. Hollis Lynch, *Edward Wilmot Blyden: Pan-Negro Patriot, 1832–1912* (London: Oxford University Press, 1967), 4–5.

2. Ibid., 16–17.

3. Ibid., 6.

4. Wilson J. Moses, *The Golden Age of Black Nationalism, 1850–1925* (New York: Oxford, 1988), 11.

5. Lynch, *Edward Wilmot Blyden,* 13.

6. Edward W. Blyden, "The Call of Providence to the Descendants of Africa in America," in *Negro Social and Political Thought, 1850–1920,* ed. Howard Brotz (New York:

Basic Books, 1966), 117–118. This piece was originally published in Edward W. Blyden, *Liberia's Offering* (New York: J. A. Gray, 1862).

7. Reproduced in the *New York Colonization Journal* 12 (July 1862) as quoted in Lynch, *Edward Wilmot Blyden*, 28–29.

8. Blyden, "Call of Providence," 117–8.

9. See Ira M. Lapidus, *A History of Islamic Societies* (Cambridge: Cambridge University Press, 1988), 489–522.

10. Lynch, *Edward Wilmot Blyden*, 32–33.

11. Blyden to Rev. John L. Wilson, Board of Foreign Mission of the Presbyterian Church, 4 August 1860, *Selected Letters of Edward Wilmot Blyden*, ed. Hollis Lynch (Millwood, NY: KTO Press, 1978), 42.

12. Lynch, *Edward Wilmot Blyden*, 15, 42. See also how Blyden downplays the wrenching conflicts between the "natives" and colonials in "Call of Providence," 123.

13. Blyden to Walter Lowrie, London, 21 June 1858, in *Selected Letters*, 75.

14. Edward W. Said, *Orientalism* (New York: Vintage, 1979), 3.

15. Edward W. Blyden, *From West Africa to Palestine* (Manchester: John Heywood, 1873), 37–42, 159–62, 180.

16. Ibid., 194–6, 145–9, 127.

17. Ibid., 104–5.

18. Blyden to Major Alexander Bravo, Acting Governor of Sierra Leone, Report of the Expedition to Timbo, 10 March 1873, *Selected Letters*, 133–4.

19. Ibid., 138.

20. Edward W. Blyden, *Christianity, Islam, and the Negro Race* (1887; reprint, Edinburgh: Edinburgh University Press, 1967), 173–88.

21. Lynch, *Edward Wilmot Blyden*, 142–3.

22. See George W. Stocking, Jr., *Victorian Anthropology* (New York: Free Press, 1987), 233–7.

23. Blyden, *Christianity, Islam, and the Negro Race*, 10–13.

24. Ibid., 37, 64.

25. Ibid., 242–4.

26. See Bernard Lewis, *Race and Slavery in the Middle East: An Historical Enquiry* (New York: Oxford, 1990), 99–102.

27. Edward W. Blyden, *The African Problem and Other Discourses Delivered in America in 1890* (London: W. B. Whittingham and Co., 1890), 83.

28. Edward W. Blyden, "Islam in Western Soudan," *Journal of the African Society* 2 (Sept. 1902): 21, 24, 33.

29. George M. Fredrickson, *Black Liberation: A Comparative History of Black Ideologies in the United States and South Africa* (New York: Oxford, 1995), 69–70; Blyden, *The African Problem*, 34; and Moses, *The Golden Age of Black Nationalism*, 49. See also

George M. Fredrickson, *The Black Image in the White Mind: The Debate on Afro-American Character and Destiny, 1817–1914* (Hanover, NH: Wesleyan University Press, 1987).

30. Lynch, *Edward Wilmot Blyden*, xv, 53, 106, 111–12.

31. Blyden, *Christianity, Islam, and the Negro Race*, 113.

32. Ibid., 110–11.

33. Ibid., 224–26.

34. In his Qur'anic commentary, al-Tabari related that Luqman was "a thick-lipped, flat-footed slave." See B. Heller and N. A. Stillman, "Lukman," in *Encyclopedia of Islam*, new ed. (Leiden: E. J. Brill, 1983), 5:811–13.

35. Blyden, *Christianity, Islam, and the Negro Race*, 228–31, and Edward W. Blyden, "The Koran in Africa," *Journal of the African Society* 14 (Jan. 1905): 162–3.

36. Blyden, *Christianity, Islam, and the Negro Race*, 233.

37. Ibid., v.

38. Lynch, *Edward Wilmot Blyden*, 70–77.

39. Edwin S. Redkey, *Black Exodus: Black Nationalist and Back-to-Africa Movements, 1890–1910* (New Haven and London: Yale, 1969), 48, and Blyden, *The African Problem*, 14–15, 32.

40. Blyden, *The African Problem*, 80–81.

41. Redkey, *Black Exodus*, 54, 66–69, and *Congressional Record*, 21, 1890, pt. 1: 622–30.

42. See Edward W. Blyden, "Dedication," in *The Jewish Question* (Liverpool: Lionel Hart, 1898) and p. 5 in the same.

43. Ibid., 8.

44. Ibid., 18–20.

45. Lynch, *Edward Wilmot Blyden*, xvi; Blyden, "Islam in the Western Soudan," 20; and Blyden, *The Jewish Question*, 11–13.

46. Blyden, *The Jewish Question*, 16, 21–24. Blyden seemed to ignore the prophecy in Zephaniah 2:12: "You also, O Ethiopians, / shall be slain by my sword."

47. See Edward Wilmot Blyden, *African Life and Customs* (1908; reprint, Baltimore: Black Classic Press, 1994).

NOTES TO CHAPTER 3

1. Peter Lamborn Wilson, *Sacred Drift: Essays on the Margins of Islam* (San Francisco: City Lights Books, 1993), 6–7.

2. Ibid., 15–19.

3. See, for example, C. Eric Lincoln, *The Black Muslims in America*, 3rd ed. (Grand Rapids: William B. Eerdmans, 1994), 48; E. U. Essien-Udom, *Black Nationalism: A Search for an Identity in America* (Chicago: University of Chicago Press, 1962), 33;

and Aminah Beverly McCloud, *African American Islam* (New York: Routledge, 1995), 10. All of these books rely heavily on Arthur H. Fauset, *Black Gods of the Metropolis* (Philadelphia: University of Pennsylvania Press, 1944).

4. Col. J. T. Bissell to J. Edgar Hoover, 3/2/1943, HQ 62–25889, section 3 in *FBI File on the Moorish Science Temple of America* (Wilmington, DE: Scholarly Resources, 1995), 413–415.

5. My copy of the *Holy Koran of the Moorish Science Temple* was reproduced from the Moorish Science Temple's FBI file, which also contains other movement documents and the movement newspaper, *Moorish Voice*, published after Noble Drew's death. For Noble Drew's scripture, see File 100–3095, 1/28/42, in HQ 62–25889, sect. 1 of the version published by Scholarly Resources.

6. Much of Arthur Fauset's oft-cited account of the Moors in *Black Gods of the Metropolis* is derived from his involvement with the movement during this time. But in order to reconstruct the origins and meanings of Moorish Science in the 1920s, we must be careful not to assume that Fauset's findings from 1944 apply to the 1920s. See File 100–3095, 1/28/42, and Bissell to Hoover, 3/2/43, in the FBI file. For an account of the MST after 1925, see also Wilson, *Sacred Drift*, 29–50.

7. See Richard Brent Turner, *Islam in the African-American Experience* (Bloomington: Indiana University Press, 1997), 90.

8. See Robert Hill's introduction to *The Marcus Garvey and United Negro Improvement Associations Papers*, ed. Robert A. Hill (Berkeley: University of California Press, 1983), xxxv–xl; Beryl Satter, "Marcus Garvey, Father Divine, and the Gender Politics of Race Difference and Race Neutrality," *American Quarterly* 48, no. 1 (March 1996): 44; and George M. Fredrickson, *Black Liberation: A Comparative History of Black Ideologies in the United States and South Africa* (New York: Oxford, 1995), 153–60. While Garvey's was the largest black nationalist group, his was not the largest black organization, as Fredrickson claims. According to Higginbotham, that distinction belonged to the National Baptist Convention, which had over 2.9 million members in 1916. See Evelyn Brooks Higginbotham, *Righteous Discontent: The Women's Movement in the Black Baptist Church, 1880–1920* (Cambridge: Harvard University Press, 1993), 6.

9. Randall K. Burkett, *Garveyism as a Religious Movement* (Metuchen, NJ: Scarecrow Press, 1978), 48–49.

10. See *Marcus Garvey and UNIA Papers*, ed. Hill, 2:128, 311 and 3:23–4, 440, 502, 646.

11. Ibid., 3:307.

12. See Burkett, *Garveyism*, 178–81.

13. See Garvey to Sir Frederic Kenyon, Dir., British Museum, 8 October 1913 in *Marcus Garvey and UNIA Papers*, 1:27; "A Talk with Afro-West Indians. The Negro race and its Problems," Kingston, Jamaica, ca. July-August 1914, in 1:55–64; and "Catechism," in 3:310–11.

14. See Hill, "General Introduction," in *Marcus Garvey and UNIA Papers*, 1:xliv–xlv; Randall Burkett, ed., *Black Redemption* (Philadelphia: Temple University Press, 1970), 15; and Turner, *Islam in the African-American Experience*, 90.

15. Noble Drew Ali, *Holy Koran of the MST,* 59.

16. See William E. Leuchtenburg, *The Perils of Prosperity, 1914–32,* 2d ed. (Chicago: University of Chicago Press, 1993), 206–9.

17. See Roger Daniels, *Not Like Us: Immigrants and Minorities in America, 1890–1924* (Chicago: Ivan R. Dee, 1997), 132–3, 139, 143; Reed Ueda, *Postwar Immigrant America: A Social History* (Boston: St. Martin's Press, 1994), 20, 22; and Walter Benn Michaels, *Our America: Nativism, Modernism, and Pluralism* (Durham: Duke University Press, 1995), 14–15, 30–32, 78, 84.

18. *Holy Koran of the MST,* 3.

19. Ibid., 3, 56–59.

20. Ibid., 57–60.

21. Ibid.

22. Ibid., 59.

23. See Wouter J. Hanegraaff, *New Age Religion and Western Culture: Esotericism in the Mirror of Secular Thought* (Leiden: E. J. Brill, 1996), 386–489, and "Introduction I" in *Modern Esoteric Spirituality,* eds. Antoine Faivre and Jacob Needleman (New York: Crossroad, 1992), xv–xix. For the role of esotericism in the making of Mormonism, see John Brooke, *The Refiner's Fire* (Cambridge: Harvard University Press, 1994). Brooke shows how Mormonism appropriated freemasonry, divination, alchemy, polygamous marriage, and counterfeiting into a syncretistic belief system that hoped to bring about human perfection.

24. See *Chicago Defender,* 19 January and 9 February 1929.

25. Wilson reproduces a copy of the flyer in *Sacred Drift,* 30.

26. See Hans A. Baer, *The Black Spiritual Movement: A Religious Response to Racism* (Knoxville: University of Tennessee Press, 1984), 9, 82–98; and Delores S. Williams, *Sisters in the Wilderness: The Challenge of Womanist God-Talk* (Maryknoll, NY: Orbis, 1994), 222–226.

27. See Baer, *The Black Spiritual Movement,* 92; Levi H. Dowling, *The Aquarian Gospel of Jesus the Christ: The Philosophic and Practical Basis of the Religion of the Aquarian Age of the World and of the Church Universal,* 6th ed. (London: L. N. Fowler, 1920), 13; Edgar J. Goodspeed, *Modern Apocrypha* (Boston: Beacon Press, 1931), 15–17; Wilson, *Sacred Drift,* 19; and cf. Hanegraaff, *New Age Religion,* 449, 473. Wilson first pointed out that chapters 2 through 19 were from the *Aquarian Gospel,* though he could not locate a source for the first chapter. It, too, is from Dowling's text, though its source is the introduction.

28. See Dowling, *Aquarian Gospel of Jesus Christ,* 5–12, 31–32.

29. Cf. *Holy Koran of the MST,* chapters 5, 6, 7, and 11, with Dowling, *Aquarian Gospel of Jesus Christ,* chapters 18, 21, 22, and 32 on pages 44, 47–49, and 60–62.

30. Cf. *Holy Koran of the MST,* chapters 2, 4, and 13–19 with Dowling, *Aquarian Gospel of Jesus Christ,* chapters 1, 15, 47, 61, 65, 168, 178, 172, and 176 on pages 25, 40–41, 78–79, 93–94, 97–98, 239–240, 253–255, 244–246, and 250–251.

31. See "Introduction" in *The Infinite Wisdom* (Chicago: De Laurence Co., 1923). For a scholarly work on Tibetan Orientalism in the West, see Donald S. Lopez, Jr., *Prisoners*

of Shangri-La: Tibetan Buddhism and the West (Chicago: University of Chicago Press, 1998).

32. See Sri Ramatherio, ed., *Unto Thee I Grant*, rev. ed (San Jose, CA: Supreme Grand Lodge of the AMORC, 1953), 93–97; Stephen R. Prothero, "Rosicrucians," in *The Encyclopedia of American Religious History*, eds. Edward L. Queen et al. (New York: Facts on File, 1996), 575–6; Frances A. Yates, *The Rosicrucian Enlightenment* (London: Routledge and Kegan Paul, 1972), 220–223; and Harry Wells Fogarty, "Rosicrucians," in *The Encyclopedia of Religion*, ed. Mircea Eliade, (New York: Macmillan, 1987), 12: 476–77.

33. Cf. the *Holy Koran of the MST*, 32–56 with *Infinite Wisdom*, 27–102, or their exact equivalent in the AMORC edition.

NOTES TO CHAPTER 4

1. See "Genealogy of Elijah (Poole) Muhammad," and biographical information in Claude Andrew Clegg III, *An Original Man: The Life and Times of Elijah Muhammad* (New York: St. Martin's Press, 1997), 3–13. For an introduction to the New South, see the classic work by C. Vann Woodward, *Origins of the New South, 1877–1913* (Baton Rouge: Louisiana State Press, 1951); and Edward L. Ayers, *The Promise of the New South* (New York: Oxford, 1992).

2. See Paul Boyer, *When Time Shall Be No More: Prophecy Belief in Modern American Culture* (Cambridge: Harvard University Press, 1992), 1–92.

3. See Timothy E. Fulop, "The Future Golden Day of the Race: Millennialism and Black Americans in the Nadir, 1877–1901," in *African-American Religion*, eds. Timothy E. Fulop and Albert J. Raboteau (New York: Routledge, 1997), 227–254; J. Carleton Hayden, "James Theodore Holly (1829–1911): First Afro-American Episcopal Bishop: Its Legacy to Us Today," in *Black Apostles: Afro-American Clergy in the Twentieth Century*, eds. Randall Burkett and Richard Newman (Boston: G. K. Hall, 1978), 129–140; and J. T. Holly, "The Divine Plan of Human Redemption in Its Ethnological Development," *AME Church Review* 1 (Oct. 1884) as quoted in Fulop, "The Future Golden Day," 240.

4. William Seraile, *Voice of Dissent: Theophilus Gould Steward (1843–1924) and Black America* (Brooklyn, NY: Carlson, 1991), 90, and Fulop, "The Future Golden Day," 240–241.

5. Stephen Ward Angell, *Bishop Henry McNeal Turner and African-American Religion in the South* (Knoxville: University of Tennessee Press, 1992), 260–261; and Henry M. Turner, "God is a Negro," in *Black Nationalism in America*, eds. John H. Bracey Jr. et al. (Indianapolis: Bobbs Merrill, 1970), 154–55.

6. Richard W. Thomas, *Life for Us Is What We Make It: Building Black Community in Detroit, 1915–1945* (Bloomington: Indiana University Press, 1992), 26–27; and Clegg, *An Original Man*, 13–14. For Muhammad's biographical information, see FBI file 105–24822, section 12, SAC Chicago to FBI Director, 26 May 1969, in Scholarly Resources, Reel 3, 112.

7. See Thomas, *Life for Us,* 89–201.

8. Ibid., 66, and St. Clair Drake and Horace R. Cayton, *Black Metropolis: A Study of Negro Life in a Northern City,* vol. 2 (New York: Harbinger, 1970), 419, 436. While Gayraud Wilmore believed that the dissatisfaction with the Black Church was a result of its deradicalization in this period, Randall K. Burkett has made a compelling case against this argument. See "The Baptist Church in Years of Crisis: J. C. Austin and Pilgrim Baptist Church, 1926–1950," in *African-American Religion,* eds. Timothy E. Fulop and Albert J. Raboteau (New York: Routledge, 1997), 311–340.

9. See Erdmann D. Beynon, "The Voodoo Cult among Negro Migrants in Detroit," *American Journal of Sociology* 43 (1938): 895–905.

10. Mattias Gardell, *In the Name of Elijah Muhammad: Louis Farrakhan and the Nation of Islam* (Durham: Duke University Press, 1996), 51–53; Clegg, *An Original Man,* 21; and Richard B. Turner, *Islam in the African-American Experience* (Bloomington: Indiana University Press, 1997), 161–165.

11. Kemal H. Karpat, "The Ottoman Emigration to America, 1860–1914," in *IJMES* 17, no. 2 (May 1985): 175–209; Barbara Bilgé, "Voluntary Associations in the Old Turkish Community of Metropolitan Detroit," in *Muslim Communities in North America,* eds. Yvonne Y. Haddad and Jane I. Smith (Albany: State University of New York Press, 1994), 381–405; and Barbara C. Aswad, "The Lebanese Muslim Community in Dearborn, Michigan" in *The Lebanese in the World: A Century of Emigration,* eds. Albert Hourani and Nadim Shehadi (London: I. B. Tauris, 1992), 170.

12. Alixa Naff, *Becoming American: The Early Arab Immigrant Experience* (Carbondale: Southern Illinois University Press, 1985), 15; Bilgé, "Voluntary Associations," 387, 399; and Frances Twix, "Bektashi Tekke and the Sunni Mosque of Albanian Muslims in America," in *Muslim Communities in North America,* 359–380.

13. Yohanan Friedmann, "Ahmadiya," in *The Oxford Encyclopedia of the Modern Islamic World,* ed. John L. Esposito (New York: Oxford, 1995), 1:54–7.

14. See Turner, *Islam in the African-American Experience,* 110–129; Edward Curtis, "Islam in Black St. Louis," *Gateway Heritage* 17, no. 4 (Spring 1997): 33–34; and "Two Slave-Leaders of Islam—Bilal and Zaid," *Moslem Sunrise,* October 1932/January 1933, 31–33.

15. Clegg, *An Original Man,* 41.

16. SAC Chicago to FBI Director, 26 May 1969, 7–8; Clegg, *An Original Man,* 78–97; and cf. Malcolm X, *The Autobiography of Malcolm X* (New York: Ballantine, 1965), 209–210.

17. Ernest Allen, Jr., "When Japan was Champion of the Darker Races: Satokata Takahashi and the Development of Our Own, 1933–1942," *The Black Scholar* 24 (Winter 1994); Turner, *Islam in the African-American Experience,* 168–89; SAC Chicago to FBI Director, 5/26/69, 7–8; and Joseph Hanlon, "'Fifth Column' Propaganda Among Negroes in St. Louis Area Traced to Japanese," *St. Louis Post-Dispatch,* 5 March 1942.

18. See Curtis, "Islam in Black St. Louis," 33–43; E. U. Essien-Udom, *Black Nationalism: A Search for an Identity in America* (Chicago: University of Chicago Press, 1962),

70–71; and Elijah Muhammad, *Message to the Blackman in America* (Chicago: Muhammad Mosque of Islam No. 2, 1965; reprint, Newport News: U.B. and U.S. Communications Systems, 1992), 236, 241 (page citations are to the reprint edition).

19. Muhammad, *Message to the Blackman,* 170–1, 174, 200, 230.

20. For information on the production and editing of Muhammad's most famous work, see "Acknowledgements," in *Message to the Blackman.*

21. *Message to the Blackman,* 19, and Elijah Muhammad, *The Supreme Wisdom: Solution to the so-called Negroes' Problem* (1957; reprint, Newport News, VA: *National Newport News and Commentator,* n.d.), 33.

22. *Message to the Blackman,* 31, 110–122. Notice, too, how the timeline utilizes the number six, often interpreted by readers of the Book of Revelation as a sign of the Beast or Antichrist.

23. Ibid., 116–9, *The Supreme Wisdom,* 30; and cf. H. H. Garnet, "The Past and the Present Condition, And the Destiny of the Colored Race," in *Black Nationalism in America,* ed. Bracey, 115–120. In 1848, Garnet said that while Africans were basking in the light of civilization, Anglo-Saxons "abode in caves under ground, either naked or covered with the skins of wild beasts. Night was made hideous by their wild shouts, and day was darkened by the smoke which arose from bloody altars, upon which they offered human sacrifice."

24. *The Supreme Wisdom,* 16, 18, 42–43, and *Message to the Blackman,* 3, 298.

25. While it is not at all clear what Muhammad meant exactly by calling Fard the Mahdi, most Muslims believe that the Mahdi is a figure who will appear on earth to usher in an era of justice and true belief prior to the end of the world. As many traditions have it, he will hail from the Prophet's family; he will appear in a time of desperate need; and his appearance will be accompanied by fantastic signs. For Twelver Shi'ism, the most popular branch of Shi'i Islam, the Mahdi is said to be the twelfth Imam, perhaps hiding somewhere around Mecca. Some Muslims, however, have also believed in a Second Coming of Jesus Christ and have disagreed about whether this would be the same figure as the Mahdi. In addition, Muslims have posited that an Antichrist-like *Dajjal,* or deceiver, would wreak havoc on the whole earth for perhaps forty days or forty years near the end time. See Robert S. Kramer, "Mahdi," 18–19, and Abdulaziz Sachedina, "Messianism," 95–99, in vol. 3 of *The Oxford Encyclopedia of the Modern Islamic World,* in addition to William J. Hamblin and Daniel C. Peterson, "Eschatology," 440–442, in vol. 1 of the same.

26. *Message to the Blackman,* 1–11.

27. Ibid., 88, 265–291.

28. George Slusser and Eric S. Rabkin, eds., *Fights of Fancy: Armed Conflict in Science Fiction and Fantasy* (Athens: University of Georgia Press, 1993), 2; Hadley Cantril, *The Invasion from Mars: A Study in the Psychology of Panic* (Princeton: Princeton University Press, 1940), 55, 58–60, 71, 133, 180; Howard Koch, *The Panic Broadcast* (Boston: Little, Brown, and Co., 1970), 3; "Radio Listeners in Panic, Taking War Drama as Fact," *New York Times,* 31 October 1938, 1.

29. Benson Saler, Charles A. Ziegler, and Charles B. Moore, *UFO Crash at Roswell: The Genesis of a Modern Myth* (Washington, DC: Smithsonian Institution Press, 1997), 6,

10–14, 146–47; see also Leon Festinger et al., *When Prophecy Fails: A Social and Psychological Study of a Modern Group that Predicted the Destruction of the World* (New York: Harper and Row, 1956).

30. *The Supreme Wisdom,* 26, 28–30, and *Message to the Blackman,* 304.

31. Louis A. DeCaro, Jr., *On the Side of My People: A Religious Life of Malcolm X* (New York: New York University Press, 1996), 136–7, and Essien-Udom, *Black Nationalism,* 80.

32. Essien-Udom, *Black Nationalism,* 73–74, 313–19, and DeCaro, *On the Side of My People,* 146–52.

33. Essien-Udom, *Black Nationalism,* 317–19, and DeCaro, *On the Side of My People,* 161–2.

34. Clegg, *An Original Man,* 136–42, and W. D. Muhammad, public address at Washington University in St. Louis, 9 October 1996.

35. Elijah Muhammad, *Muslim Daily Prayers* (Chicago: University of Islam, 1957).

36. "The Prayer Service in Islam," in *Muhammad Speaks,* 15 October 1962, 8, and *Message to the Blackman,* 136.

37. *Message to the Blackman,* 155.

38. "The Prayer Service in Islam," in *Muhammad Speaks,* 15 November 1962, 8; 30 November 1962, 8; and 31 January 1963, 8.

NOTES TO CHAPTER 5

1. See William L. Van Deburg, *New Day in Babylon: The Black Power Movement and American Culture, 1965–1975* (Chicago: University of Chicago Press, 1992), 245–6; *Malcolm X,* Warner Home Video, Burbank, 1992; and James H. Cone, *Martin & Malcolm & America: A Dream or a Nightmare* (Maryknoll, NY: Orbis, 1993).

2. See Peter Goldman, *The Death and Life of Malcolm X* (Chicago: University of Illinois Press, 1979); Eugene Victor Wolfenstein, *The Victims of Democracy: Malcolm X and the Black Revolution* (Berkeley: University of California Press, 1981); Bruce Perry, *Malcolm: The Life of a Man Who Changed Black America* (Barrytown, NY: Station Hill, 1991); Robin D. G. Kelley, *Race Rebels: Culture, Politics, and the Black Working Class* (New York: The Free Press, 1994), 161–182; Clayborne Carson, *Malcolm X: The FBI File* (New York: Carroll and Graf, 1991), 17–53; and Louis A. DeCaro, Jr., *On the Side of My People: A Religious Life of Malcolm X* (New York: New York University Press, 1996).

3. Malcolm X and Alex Haley, *The Autobiography of Malcolm X* (New York: Ballantine Books, 1987), 1–22. See also Carson, *Malcolm X,* 57–58; DeCaro, *On the Side of My People,* 38–43; and Wolfenstein, *The Victims of Democracy,* 42–152.

4. See Malcolm X, *Autobiography,* 39–190; Kelley, *Race Rebels,* 161–182; Carson, *Malcolm X,* 58–60; and DeCaro, *On the Side of My People,* 73–85.

5. See Malcolm X, *Autobiography,* 191–235, 236–287; Carson, *Malcolm X,* 60–64; and DeCaro, *On the Side of My People,* 95–113.

6. See DeCaro, 156–158, 166–167, 322 nn. 18–19; letter of Malcolm X, *New York Amsterdam News*, 24 November 1962, 39; and letter from Malcolm X and Payne's reply, *New York Times Magazine*, 25 August 1963, 2.

7. Malcolm X, *Malcolm X: Speeches at Harvard*, ed. Archie Epps (New York: Paragon, 1991), 118–125.

8. See DeCaro, *On the Side of My People*, 159–60, 201–2.

9. Ibid., 162, and FBI file 100–399321, sec. 9, 5/23/63, in Carson, *Malcolm X: The FBI File*, 237.

10. Carson, *Malcolm X*, 67, 69–70.

11. Malcolm X, *Malcolm X Speaks*, ed. George Breitman (New York: Grove Weidenfeld, 1990), 18–21, and Malcolm X, *Malcolm X: Speeches at Harvard*, 140–142.

12. See Marc Ferris, "To 'Achieve the Pleasure of Allah': Immigrant Muslims in New York City, 1893–1991," in *Muslim Communities in North America*, eds. Yvonne Haddad and Jane I. Smith (Albany: State University of New York Press, 1994), 215; Malcolm X, *The Autobiography*, 318; Perry, *Malcolm*, 261–264; and DeCaro, *On the Side of My People*, 202–203.

13. See Reinhard Schulze, "Institutionalization [of *da'wa*]" in *The Oxford Encyclopedia of the Modern Islamic World*, ed. John L. Esposito (New York: Oxford, 1995), 1:343–346.

14. Malcolm Kerr, *The Arab Cold War, 1958–1964* (London: Oxford, 1965), 21–2, 53.

15. Reinhold Schulze, "Muslim World League," in *The Oxford Encyclopedia of the Modern Islamic World*, 3:208–210, and Perry, *Malcolm*, 352.

16. See Gutbi Mahdi Ahmed, "Muslim Organizations in the United States," in *The Muslims of America*, ed. Yvonne Y. Haddad (New York: Oxford, 1991), 14; and Larry Poston, *Islamic Da'wah in the West* (New York: Oxford, 1992), 79.

17. Malcolm X, *The Autobiography*, 320; Perry, *Malcolm*, 261–264; and Yaacov Shimoni, *Political Dictionary of the Arab World* (New York: Macmillan, 1987), 105–6.

18. See Abd al-Rahman 'Azzam, *The Eternal Message of Muhammad*, trans. Caesar E. Farah (Cambridge: Islamic Texts Society, 1993).

19. Malcolm X, *The Autobiography*, 331–333, and DeCaro, *On the Side of My People*, 206.

20. Malcolm X, *The Autobiography*, 335, 340–1.

21. Ibid., 335, 348.

22. Ibid., 344–5.

23. See Immanuel Geiss, *The Pan-African Movement: A History of Pan-Africanism in America, Europe, and Africa* (New York: Africana Publishing, 1974), 3–4, 385–430; and George M. Fredrickson, *Black Liberation: A Comparative History of Black Ideologies in the United States and South Africa* (New York: Oxford University Press, 1995), 278–284.

24. See Malcolm X, *The Autobiography*, 349–51, and Carson, *Malcolm X*, 75.

25. *Malcolm X Speaks*, 61.

26. See *The Autobiography*, 353–360; Carson, *Malcolm X*, 75; and *Malcolm X Speaks*, 62–3.

27. *The Autobiography*, 352, 364.

28. See Carson, *Malcolm X*, 76–78, and Fredrickson, *Black Liberation*, 290.

29. *Malcolm X Speaks*, 72–77.

30. See DeCaro, *On the Side of My People*, 233, 238–9.

31. Perry, *Malcolm*, 322, and DeCaro, *On the Side of My People*, 239–41, 336 n. 17.

32. See Carson, *Malcolm X*, 79–80, and Malcolm X, *February 1965: The Final Speeches*, ed. Steve Clark (New York: Pathfinder, 1992), 20–1.

33. See Malcolm X, *Malcolm X on Afro-American History* (New York: Pathfinder, 1990), 11–23.

34. Ibid., 27–46.

35. See Ibid., 30–31.

36. *Malcolm X: The Speeches at Harvard*, 182.

37. *February 1965: The Final Speeches*, 44; and *Malcolm X Speaks*, 197.

38. *February 1965: The Final Speeches*, 46, 84, 140, 148–149.

39. *Malcolm X: The Speeches at Harvard*, 164; *February 1965: The Final Speeches*, 104, 182.

40. *February 1965: The Final Speeches*, 255.

41. Ibid., 252–253.

NOTES TO CHAPTER 6

1. Since 1975, Wallace Muhammad has changed the spelling of his name a number of times in addition to using an Arabic name, "Warithuddin." For the sake of simplicity, I have used his given name throughout this chapter.

2. See Zafar Ishaq Ansari, "W. D. Muhammad: The Making of a 'Black Muslim' Leader (1933–1961)," *American Journal of Islamic Social Sciences* 2, no. 2 (1985): 248–262; and Claude Andrew Clegg III, *An Original Man: The Life and Times of Elijah Muhammad* (New York: St. Martin's Press, 1997), 245.

3. E. U. Essien-Udom, *Black Nationalism: A Search for an Identity in America* (Chicago: University of Chicago Press, 1962), 81–82; Ansari, "W. D. Muhammad," 245–253; and Clegg, *An Original Man*, 98.

4. Ansari, "W. D. Muhammad," 253–258; Wallace D. Muhammad, interview by author, 8 October 1996, St. Louis, MO; and Imam Darnell Karim, telephone conversation with author, 22 January 1997, Harvey, IL.

5. Wallace D. Muhammad, interview, 1996, and Essien-Udom, *Black Nationalism*, 81.

6. Essien-Udom, *Black Nationalism*, 267–8.

7. See *Muhammad Speaks*, December 1961, 32, and Clegg, *An Original Man*, 181–2.

8. FBI File 100–399321, sec. 8 in Clayborne Carson, *Malcolm X: The FBI File* (New York: Carroll and Graf, 1991), 68, 322, and Malcolm X and Alex Haley, *The Autobiography of Malcolm X* (New York: Ballantine, 1987), 296–7.

9. Clegg, *An Original Man*, 206; Mohr to DeLoach, 2/25/65, FBI File 100–399321, sec. 16 in Carson, *Malcolm X*, 393–4; and SAC New York to FBI Director, 8/17/64, quoted in Clegg, *An Original Man*, 222–224.

10. Clegg, *An Original Man*, 245, 333 n. 15.

11. Ibid., 273–6.

12. Mattias Gardell, *In the Name of Elijah Muhammad: Louis Farrakhan and the Nation of Islam* (Durham: Duke University Press, 1996), 101, and Frank T. Donner, *The Age of Surveillance: The Aims and Methods of America's Political Intelligence System* (New York: Knopf, 1980), 178, 212–3.

13. See SAC Chicago to FBI Director, 100–35635-B, 4/22/68, as quoted in Gardell, *In the Name of Elijah Muhammad*, 101; Donner, *The Age of Surveillance*, 213; and FBI file 100–448006–626, 1/22/69, as quoted in Gardell, *In the Name of Elijah Muhammad*, 101.

14. See "Elijah Muhammad Dead: Black Muslim Leader, 77," *New York Times*, 26 February 1975, 1, and "Saviour's Day Address," *Muhammad Speaks*, 14 March 1975, 1.

15. Gardell, *In the Name of Elijah Muhammad*, 103–5; "First Official Interview with the Supreme Minister," *Muhammad Speaks*, 21 March 1975, 12; *Muhammad Speaks*, 16 May 1975, 13, quoted in Martha F. Lee, *The Nation of Islam: An American Millenarian Movement* (Lewiston: Edwin Mellen, 1988), 85; and *Muhammad Speaks*, 11 July 1975, 13, also quoted in Lee, *The Nation of Islam*, 86.

16. Paul Delaney, "Black Muslims Will End Longtime Ban on Whites," *New York Times*, 17 June 1975, 9, and "Nation of Islam: The Alternative Culture for America," *Muhammad Speaks*, 25 July 1975, 1.

17. Muhammad Nur Abdallah, interview with the author, 12 January 1995, St. Louis, MO, and Edward Curtis, "Islam in Black St. Louis: Strategies for Liberation in Two Local Religious Communities," *Gateway Heritage* 17, no.4 (spring 1997): 39. Both Abdallah and Ahmed Ghani were interviewed as part of a larger oral history project conducted by the author in some of St. Louis' Muslim communities.

18. *Muhammad Speaks*, 18 July 1975, 4, quoted in Lee, *The Nation of Islam*, 87; *Muhammad Speaks*, 31 January 1975, 1; and Clifton E. Marsh, *From Black Muslims to Muslims: The Transition from Separatism to Islam, 1930–1980* (Metuchen: Pathfinder, 1984), 96–7.

19. *Muhammad Speaks*, 17 October 1975, 3; "Interfaith celebration to highlight M. L. King Jr. Tribute," *Bilalian News*, 14 January 1977, 20; *Bilalian News*, 28 January 1977, 2; and "Historic Atlanta Address," *Bilalian News*, 29 September 1978, 17.

20. Lee, *The Nation of Islam*, 91; D. A. Williams and E. Sciolino, "Rebirth of the Nation," *Newsweek*, 10 March 1976, 33; *Bilalian News*, 3 March 1978, 3, quoted in Lee, *The Nation of Islam*, 96; Steven T. Smith, "An Historical Account of the American Muslim

Mission with Specific Reference to North Carolina," (master's thesis, Southeastern Baptist Theological Seminary, 1984), 102; and Lee, *The Nation of Islam*, 97.

21. See "First Official Interview with the Supreme Minister of the Nation of Islam," *Muhammad Speaks*, 21 March 1975, 3; Charlayne Hunter, "Black Muslim Temple Renamed for Malcolm X; Move Reflects Acceptance of Ex-Leader," *New York Times*, 2 February 1976, 1; "Nation of Islam Changes name to Fight Black Separatist Image," *New York Times*, 19 October 1976, 10; and Lee, *The Nation of Islam*, 93.

22. Curtis, "Islam in Black St. Louis," 41.

23. See William L. Van Deburg, *New Day in Babylon: The Black Power Movement and American Culture, 1965–1975* (Chicago: University of Chicago Press, 1992), 171–2, 192–8, 245–6, 292–3.

24. Ibid., 17–8.

25. See J. David Hoeveler, Jr., *The Postmodern Turn: American Thought and Culture in the 1970s* (New York: Twayne, 1996), 120; Van Deburg, *New Day in Babylon*, 272–5, 292–3; and Alex Haley, *Roots* (Garden City: Doubleday, 1976).

26. Nathan Irvin Huggins, *Black Odyssey: The African-American Ordeal in Slavery* (New York: Vintage Books, 1990), xlviii, and Werner Sollors, *Beyond Ethnicity: Consent and Descent in American Culture* (New York: Oxford, 1986), 13–14.

27. This announcement appeared in several issues of the *Bilalian News*, including 7 November 1975.

28. See Muhammad Abdul-Rauf, *Bilal ibn Rabah: A Leading Companion of the Prophet Muhammad* (N.p.: American Trust Publications, 1977); *Bilal: The First Moezzin of Islam*, trans. Z. I. Ansari (Chicago: Kazi Publications, 1976); and H. A. L. Craig, *Bilal* (London: Quarter Books, 1977).

29. *Bilalian News*, 9 January 1976, 32; *Bilalian News*, 28 November 1975, 25.

30. Imam Samuel Ansari, interview by the author, 29 March 1994, St. Louis, MO.

31. Gardell, *In the Name of Elijah Muhammad*, 108, and Gutbi Mahdi Ahmed, "Muslim Organizations in the United States," in *The Muslims of America*, ed. Yvonne Y. Haddad (New York: Oxford, 1991), 14–16.

32. Muhammad Nur Abdallah, interview by the author, 12 January 1995, Islamic Center of Greater St. Louis (on the campus of St. Louis University), St. Louis, MO. Abdallah is now leader of a mainly immigrant mosque located on Weidman Road in the St. Louis suburbs.

33. I dub it "quiet" opposition because no extensive public record of the incident exists. Further, neither Muhammad nor Abdallah has named the immigrant critics. Apparently, the critics preferred to take care of this matter without a public row.

34. W. D. Muhammad, interview by the author, 19 December 1993, Airport Hilton Hotel, St. Louis, MO. I was invited by St. Louis leader Samuel Ansari to interview the leader with a small group of reporters before he gave a public address.

35. See Wallace Deen Muhammad, "On the name Bilalian," *Bilalian News*, 16 November 1979, 17, and Lee, *The Nation of Islam*, 98.

36. See John L. Esposito, *The Islamic Threat: Myth or Reality?* (New York: Oxford, 1992), 55–7; Albert Hourani, *Arabic Thought in the Liberal Age* (Oxford: Oxford University Press, 1970); and Marshall G. S. Hodgson, "The Islamic Heritage in the Modern World," in *The Venture of Islam* (Chicago: University of Chicago Press, 1974), 3:163–441.

37. W. Deen Mohammed, *Focus on Al-Islam: A Series of Interviews with Imam W. Deen Mohammed in Pittsburgh, Pennsylvania* (Chicago: Zakat Publications, 1988), 35–7.

38. Ibid., 95–6, 100.

39. Ibid., 4, 45, 48–9, 37.

40. W. D. Muhammad, *Imam W. Deen Muhammad Speaks from Harlem, N. Y.: Challenges that Face Man Today* (Chicago: W. D. Muhammad Publications, 1985), 29–36.

41. Mohammed, *Focus on al-Islam*, 38, 49–51.

42. Muhammad, *Imam W. Deen Muhammad Speaks from Harlem, N. Y.,* 68–70.

43. Ibid., 116–7, 123–5.

44. Lee, *The Nation of Islam*, 100, and Mohammed, *Focus on Al-Islam*, 21.

NOTES TO CHAPTER 7

1. Mattias Gardell, *In the Name of Elijah Muhammad: Louis Farrakhan and the Nation of Islam* (Durham: Duke University Press, 1996), 119–123.

2. Ibid., 125; Judith Cummings, "Black Muslim Seeks to Change Movement," *New York Times,* 19 March 1978, 12; and "Black Books Bulletin Interviews Minister Abdul Farrakhan," *Black Books Bulletin* 6, no. 1 (1978): 44.

3. Gardell, *In the Name of Elijah Muhammad,* 125, 129–33.

4. Ibid., 192, 138, 128–9.

5. "Sending a Message, Louis Farrakhan Plays Mendelssohn," *New York Times,* 19 April 1993, C11, C16.

6. "Imam W. D. Muhammad joins Farrakhan followers at Saviours' Day," *The Final Call: On-Line Edition,* 27 February 1999, ⟨www.noi.org/press-events/press02–27–99.html⟩ 19 February 2001.

7. "Farrakhan Welcomes Islamic Scholars From Around World," *The Final Call Online,* 25 February 2000, ⟨www.noi.org/press-events/press-sd2k–25–2000.htm⟩ 1 March 2001.

8. "Final Communiqué from the Second Islamic Peoples Leadership Conference Held in America," *Nation of Islam Online,* 24–27 February 2000, ⟨www.noi.org/press-events/islam_conf_communique2–28–2000.htm⟩ 19 February 2000.

9. "Remarks by the Honorable Minister Louis Farrakhan of the National [*sic*] of Islam, at the Million Family March," *Unification Home Page,* 16 October 2000, ⟨www.unification.net/news/news20001016.html⟩ 1 March 2001.

10. "Forward," in *Million Family March: The National Agenda,* ⟨www.millionfamilymarch .com/agenda/default.html⟩ 1 March 2001.

11. "The Muslim Program," *Nation of Islam Online,* ⟨www.noi.org/program.html⟩ 1 March 2001.

12. "Remarks by the Honorable Minister Louis Farrakhan," 16 October 2000.

13. "Giving New Meaning to Race," *The Honorable Minister Louis Farrakhan Speaks,* ⟨www.finalcall.com/MLFspeaks/race.html⟩ 19 February 2001.

14. Noble Drew Ali, *The Holy Koran of the Moorish Science Temple* (Chicago, 1927), 37.

15. W. Deen Mohammed, *Focus on Al-Islam: A Series of Interviews with Imam W. Deen Mohammed in Pittsburgh, Pennsylvania* (Chicago: Zakat Publications, 1988), 48.

16. Farid Esack, *Qur'an, Liberation, and Pluralism: An Islamic Perspective of Interreligious Solidarity against Oppression* (Oxford: Oneworld, 1997), 12–3.

17. "Review of *Qur'an, Liberation, and Pluralism,*" *Islamic Gateway,* 4 March 1998, ⟨www.ummah.net/bicnews/BICNews/Books/books15.htm⟩ 2 May 2001.

18. W. D. Muhammad, interview by author, 19 December 1993, St. Louis, MO.

19. Esack, *Qur'an, Liberation, and Pluralism,* 60.

Selected Bibliography

PRIMARY SOURCES

NEWSPAPERS AND PERIODICALS (VARIOUS DATES)

Bilalian News (Chicago).

Chicago Defender (Chicago).

Moorish Voice (Chicago.)

Moslem Sunrise (Chicago).

Muhammad Speaks (Chicago).

Muslim Journal (Chicago).

New York Amsterdam News (New York).

New York Times (New York).

Pittsburgh Courier (Pittsburgh).

St. Louis Globe-Democrat (St. Louis).

St. Louis Post-Dispatch (St. Louis).

GOVERNMENT DOCUMENTS

Congressional Record. Washington, D.C., 1890.

Various Federal Bureau of Investigation Files, 1942–1969.

BOOKS, ARTICLES, AND UNPUBLISHED MATERIALS

Abdul-Rauf, Muhammad. *Bilal ibn Rabah: A Leading Companion of the Prophet Muham-mad.* N. p.: American Trust Publications, 1977.

Ali, Noble Drew. *The Holy Koran of the Moorish Science Temple.* Chicago: N. p., 1927.

Ansari, Z. I., trans. *Bilal: The First Moezzin of Islam.* Chicago: Kazi Publications, 1976.

'Azzam, Abd al-Rahman. *The Eternal Message of Muhammad.* Translated by Caesar E. Farah. Cambridge: Islamic Texts Society, 1993.

"Black Books Bulletin Interviews Minister Abdul Farrakhan," *Black Books Bulletin* 6, no. 1 (1978): 42–5, 71.

Blyden, Edward Wilmot. *African Life and Customs.* 1908. Reprint, Baltimore, MD: Black Classic Press, 1994.

———. *The African Problem and Other Discourses Delivered in America in 1890.* London: W. B. Whittingham, 1890.

———. *Christianity, Islam, and the Negro Race.* 1887. Reprint, Edinburgh: Edinburgh University Press, 1967.

———. *From West Africa to Palestine.* Manchester: John Heywood, 1873.

———. "Islam in Western Soudan." *Journal of the African Society* 2 (Sept. 1902): 11–37.

———. *The Jewish Question.* Liverpool: Lionel Hart, 1898.

———. "The Koran in Africa." *Journal of the African Society* 14 (Jan. 1905): 157–171.

———. *Liberia's Offering.* New York: J. A. Gray, 1862.

———. "Mohammedanism in Western Africa," *Methodist Quarterly Review* 53 (Jan. 1871): 62–78.

———. *Sierra Leone and Liberia; Their Origin, Work and Destiny, A lecture Delivered in Freetown, April 22, 1884.* London: John Heywood, 1884.

Carson, Clayborne. *Malcolm X: The FBI File.* New York: Carroll and Graf, 1991.

Craig, H. A. L. *Bilal.* London: Quarter Books, 1977.

Dowling, Levi H. *The Aquarian Gospel of Jesus the Christ: The Philosophic and Practical Basis of the Religion of the Aquarian Age of the World and of the Church Universal.* 6th ed. London: L. N. Fowler, 1920.

Farrakhan, Louis. *A Torchlight for America.* Chicago: FCN Publishing, 1993.

Garvey, Marcus. *Marcus Garvey: Life and Lessons.* Edited by Robert A. Hill et al. Berkeley: University of California Press, 1987.

———. *More Philosophy and Opinions of Marcus Garvey.* Edited by E. U. Essien-Udom and Amy Jacques-Garvey. Totowa, NJ: Frank Cass, 1977.

———. *Philosophy and Opinions of Marcus Garvey.* Edited by Amy Jacques-Garvey. 1923. Reprint, New York: Atheneum, 1986.

———. "A Talk with Afro-West Indians. The Negro race and its Problems." Kingston, Jamaica, ca. July–August 1914.

Haley, Alex. *Roots.* Garden City, NJ: Doubleday, 1976.

Hill, Robert A., ed. *The Marcus Garvey and United Negro Improvement Associations Papers.* Berkeley: University of California Press, 1983.

The Infinite Wisdom. Chicago: De Laurence Co., 1923.

Lynch, Hollis, ed. *Selected Letters of Edward Wilmot Blyden.* Millwood, NY: KTO Press, 1978.

Malcolm X. *By Any Means Necessary: Speeches, Interviews and a Letter by Malcolm X.* Edited by George Breitman. New York: Pathfinder, 1970.

———. *Black Man, Listen.* Detroit: Broadside Press, 1969.

———. *The End of White World Supremacy: Four Speeches by Malcolm X.* Edited by Benjamin Goodman. New York: Merlin House, 1971.

———. *February 1965: The Final Speeches.* Edited by Steve Clark. New York: Pathfinder, 1992.

———. *The Last Year of Malcolm X.* Edited by George Breitman. New York: Schocken, 1968.

———. *Malcolm X on Afro-American History.* 1967. Reprint, New York: Pathfinder, 1990.

———. *Malcolm X: The Last Speeches.* Edited by Bruce Perry. New York: Pathfinder, 1970.

———. *Malcolm X: The Man and His Ideas.* Edited by George Breitman. New York: Merit Publishers, 1965.

———. *Malcolm X Speaks.* Edited by George Breitman. New York: Grove Press, 1966; New York: Grove Weidenfeld, 1990.

———. *Malcolm X: Speeches at Harvard.* Edited by Archie Epps. New York: Paragon, 1991.

———. *Malcolm X Talks to Young People.* 2d ed. New York: Pathfinder, 1969.

Malcolm X and Alex Haley. *The Autobiography of Malcolm X.* New York: Ballantine, 1965.

Muhammad, Elijah. *Accomplishments of the Muslims.* Chicago: Muhammad's Mosque No. 2, 1974.

———. *The Fall of America.* 1973. Reprint, Newport News, VA: National Newport News and Commentator, 1990.

———. *How to Eat to Live.* Book 1. 1967. Reprint, Newport News, VA: National Newport News and Commentator, n.d.

———. *How to Eat to Live.* Book 2. 1972. Reprint, Newport News, VA: National Newport News and Commentator, n.d.

———. *Message to the Blackman in America.* Chicago: Muhammad's Mosque No. 2, 1963.

———. *Muslim Daily Prayers.* Chicago: University of Islam, 1957.

———. *The Muslim Flag.* Chicago: Muhammad's Mosque of Islam No. 2, 1974.

———. *Our Saviour Has Arrived.* 1974. Reprint, Newport News, VA: National Newport News and Commentator, 1993.

———. *The Supreme Wisdom: Solution to the So-Called Negroes' Problem.* 1957. Reprint, Newport News, VA: National Newport News and Commentator, 1992.

Muhammad, Wallace D. *An African American Genesis.* Chicago: Progressions Publishing Co., 1986.

———. *As the Light Shineth from the East.* Chicago: WDM Publications, 1980.

———. *Book of Muslim Names.* Chicago: Honourable Elijah Muhammad Mosque No. 2, 1976.

———. *Focus on al-Islam.* Chicago: Zakat Publications, 1988.

———. *Imam W. Deen Muhammad Speaks from Harlem, N.Y.: Challenges that Face Man Today.* Chicago: W. D. Muhammad Publications, 1985.

———. *Al-Islam Unity and Leadership.* Chicago: Sense Maker, 1991.

———. *Lectures of Emam Muhammad.* Chicago: Zakat Propogation [sic] Fund Publications, 1978.

———. *The Man and Woman in Islam.* Chicago: The Honourable Elijah Muhammad Mosque No. 2, 1976.

———. *Prayer and al-Islam.* Chicago: Muhammad Islamic Foundation, 1982.

———. *Religion on the Line: Al-Islam, Judaism, Catholicism, Protestantism.* Chicago: W. D. Muhammad Publications, 1983.

———. *The Teachings of W. D. Muhammad (Elementary Level).* Chicago: The Honourable Elijah Muhammad Mosque No. 2, 1976.

———. *The Teachings of W. D. Muhammad (Secondary Level).* Chicago: The Honourable Elijah Muhammad Mosque No. 2, 1976.

Ramatherio, Sri, ed. *Unto Thee I Grant.* San Jose, CA: Supreme Grand Lodge of the AMORC, 1953.

SECONDARY SOURCES

BOOKS, ARTICLES, AND UNPUBLISHED MATERIALS

Ahlstrom, Sydney E. *A Religious History of the American People.* New Haven: Yale, 1972.

Angell, Stephen Ward. *Bishop Henry McNeal Turner and African-American Religion in the South.* Knoxville, TN: University of Tennessee Press, 1992.

Ansari, Zafar I. "Aspects of Black Muslims Theology." *Studia Islamica* 53 (1981): 137–76.

———. "W. D. Muhammad: The Making of a 'Black Muslim' Leader (1933–1961)." *American Journal of Islamic Social Sciences* 2, no. 2 (1985): 245–253.

Asad, Talal. *Genealogies of Religion: Discipline and Reasons of Power in Christianity and Islam.* Baltimore: Johns Hopkins University Press, 1993.

Austin, Allan D. *African Muslims in Antebellum America: Transatlantic Stories and Spiritual Struggles.* New York: Routledge, 1997.

Baer, Hans A. *The Black Spiritual Movement: A Religious Response to Racism.* Knoxville, TN: University of Tennessee Press, 1984.

Baldwin, James. *The Fire Next Time.* New York: Dell, 1962.

Beynon, Erdmann D. "The Voodoo Cult among Negro Migrants in Detroit." *American Journal of Sociology* 43, no. 6 (1938): 894–907.

Boyer, Paul. *When Time Shall Be No More: Prophecy Belief in Modern American Culture.* Cambridge, MA: Harvard University Press, 1992.

Bracey, John H., Jr. et al., eds. *Black Nationalism in America.* Indianapolis, IN: Bobbs-Merrill, 1970.

Brooke, John L. *The Refiner's Fire.* Cambridge, MA: Harvard University Press, 1994.

Brotz, Howard, ed. *Negro Social and Political Thought, 1850–1920.* New York: Basic Books, 1966.

Burkett, Randall, ed. *Black Redemption.* Philadelphia: Temple University Press, 1970.

———. *Garveyism as a Religious Movement.* Metuchen, NJ: Scarecrow Press, 1978.

Burkett, Randall, and Richard Newman, eds. *Black Apostles: Afro-American Clergy in the Twentieth Century.* Boston: G. K. Hall, 1978.

Cantril, Hadley. *The Invasion from Mars: A Study in the Psychology of Panic.* Princeton, NJ: Princeton University Press, 1940.

Clegg III, Claude Andrew. *An Original Man: The Life and Times of Elijah Muhammad.* New York: St. Martin's Press, 1997.

Cone, James H. *Martin & Malcolm & America: A Dream or a Nightmare.* Maryknoll, NY: Orbis, 1993.

Curtis, Edward. "Islam in Black St. Louis: Strategies for Liberation in Two Local Religious Communities." *Gateway Heritage* 17, no. 4 (spring 1997): 30–43.

Dabashi, Hamid. *Authority in Islam: From the Rise of Muhammad to the Establishment of the Umayyads.* New Brunswick and London: Transaction, 1989.

Daniels, Roger. *Not Like Us: Immigrants and Minorities in America, 1890–1924.* Chicago: Ivan R. Dee, 1997.

DeCaro Jr., Louis A. *On the Side of My People: A Religious Life of Malcolm X.* New York: New York University Press, 1996.

Denny, Frederick M. *An Introduction to Islam.* 2d ed. New York: Macmillan Publishing Co., 1994.

Donner, Frank T. *The Age of Surveillance: The Aims and Methods of America's Political Intelligence System.* New York: Knopf, 1980.

Drake, St. Clair, and Horace R. Cayton. *Black Metropolis: A Study of Negro Life in a Northern City.* Vol. 2. New York: Harbinger, 1970.

Esack, Farid. *Qur'an, Liberation, and Pluralism: An Islamic Perspective of Interreligious Solidarity against Oppression.* Oxford: Oneworld, 1997.

Esposito, John L. *The Islamic Threat: Myth or Reality?* New York: Oxford, 1992.

Esposito, John L., ed. *The Oxford Encyclopedia of the Modern Islamic World.* New York and Oxford: Oxford University Press, 1995.

Essien-Udom, E. U. *Black Nationalism: A Search for an Identity in America.* Chicago: University of Chicago Press, 1962.

Faivre, Antoine, and Jacob Needleman, eds. *Modern Esoteric Spirituality.* New York: Crossroad, 1992.

Fauset, Arthur H. *Black Gods of the Metropolis.* Philadelphia: University of Pennsylvania Press, 1944.

Festinger, Leon, et al. *When Prophecy Fails: A Social and Psychological Study of a Modern Group that Predicted the Destruction of the World.* New York: Harper and Row, 1956.

Fredrickson, George M. *The Black Image in the White Mind: The Debate on Afro-American Character and Destiny, 1817–1914.* Hanover, NH: Wesleyan University Press, 1987.

———. *Black Liberation: A Comparative History of Black Ideologies in the United States and South Africa.* New York: Oxford University Press, 1995.

Fulop, Timothy E., and Albert J. Raboteau. *African-American Religion.* New York: Routledge, 1997.

Gardell, Mattias. *In the Name of Elijah Muhammad: Louis Farrakhan and the Nation of Islam.* Durham, NC: Duke University Press, 1996.

Gates, Henry L., Jr. "A Reporter at Large: The Charmer." *New Yorker* (29 April and 6 May 1996): 116–131.

Geiss, Immanuel. *The Pan-African Movement: A History of Pan-Africanism in America, Europe, and Africa.* New York: Africana Publishing, 1974.

Goldman, Peter. *The Death and Life of Malcolm X.* Chicago: University of Illinois Press, 1979.

Goodspeed, Edgar J. *Modern Apocrypha.* Boston: Beacon Press, 1931.

Gould, Stephen Jay. *The Mismeasure of Man.* New York: W. W. Norton, 1981.

Haddad, Yvonne Y., ed. *The Muslims of America.* New York: Oxford, 1991.

Haddad, Yvonne Y., and Jane I. Smith, eds. *Muslim Communities in North America.* Albany, NY: State University of New York Press, 1994.

Hanegraaff, Wouter J. *New Age Religion and Western Culture: Esotericism in the Mirror of Secular Thought.* Leiden: E. J. Brill, 1996.

Hanna, Samir A. and George H. Gardner. "Al-Shu'ubiyyah Up-Dated: A Study of the 20th Century Revival of an Eighth Century Concept." *Middle East Journal* 20 (1966): 335–52.

Higginbotham, Evelyn Brooks. *Righteous Discontent: The Women's Movement in the Black Baptist Church 1880–1920.* Cambridge: Harvard University Press, 1993.

Hodgson, Marshall G. S. *Rethinking World History: Essays on Europe, Islam, and World History.* Edited by Edmund Burke III. New York: Cambridge University Press, 1993.

————. *The Venture of Islam: Conscience and History in a World Civilization.* 3 vols. Chicago: University of Chicago Press, 1974.

Hoeveler, J. David, Jr., *The Postmodern Turn: American Thought and Culture in the 1970s.* New York: Twayne, 1996.

Hourani, Albert. *Arabic Thought in the Liberal Age.* Oxford: Oxford University Press, 1970.

Hourani, Albert, and Nadim Shehadi, eds. *The Lebanese in the World: A Century of Emigration.* London: I. B. Tauris, 1992.

Huggins, Nathan Irvin. *Black Odyssey: The African-American Ordeal in Slavery.* New York: Vintage Books, 1990.

Karpat, Kemal H. "The Ottoman Emigration to America, 1860–1914." *IJMES* 17, no. 2 (May 1985): 175–209.

Kelley, Robin D. G. *Race Rebels: Culture, Politics, and the Black Working Class.* New York: The Free Press, 1994.

Kerr, Malcolm. *The Arab Cold War, 1958–1964.* London: Oxford University Press, 1965.

Koch, Howard. *The Panic Broadcast.* Boston: Little, Brown, and Co., 1970.

Laclau, Ernesto. "Universalism, Particularism, and the Question of Identity." In *The Politics of Difference,* edited by Edwin N. Wilmensen and Patrick McAllister, 45–58. Chicago: University of Chicago Press, 1996.

Lapidus, Ira M. *A History of Islamic Societies.* Cambridge: Cambridge University Press, 1988.

Lee, Martha F. *The Nation of Islam: An American Millenarian Movement.* Lewiston, NY: Edwin Mellen, 1988.

Leuchtenburg, William E. *The Perils of Prosperity, 1914–32.* Chicago: University of Chicago Press, 1993.

Lewis, Bernard. *Race and Slavery in the Middle East: An Historical Enquiry.* New York: Oxford, 1990.

Lincoln, C. Eric. *The Black Muslims in America.* 3rd ed. Grand Rapids, MI: William B. Eerdmans, 1994.

Lincoln, C. Eric and Lawrence H. Mamiya. *The Black Church in the African American Experience.* Durham, NC: Duke University Press, 1990.

Livingston, Thomas W. *Education and Race: A Biography of Edward Wilmot Blyden.* San Francisco: Glendessary Press, 1975.

Lynch, Hollis. *Edward Wilmot Blyden: Pan-Negro Patriot, 1832–1912.* London: Oxford University Press, 1967.

MacIntyre, Alisdair C. *After Virtue: A Study in Moral Theory.* Notre Dame, IN: University of Notre Dame Press, 1984.

Mamiya, Lawrence H. "From Black Muslim to Bilalian: The Evolution of a Movement." *Journal for the Scientific Study of Religion* 21, no. 2 (June 1982): 138–52.

————. "Minister Louis Farrakhan and the Final Call: Schism in the Muslim Movement." In *The Muslim Community in North America,* edited by Earle Waugh et al. Edmonton: University of Alberta Press, 1983.

Marlow, Louise. *Hierarchy and Egalitarianism in Islamic Thought.* Cambridge: Cambridge University Press, 1997.

Marsh, Clifton E. *From Black Muslims to Muslims: The Transition from Separatism to Islam, 1930–1980.* Metuchen, NJ: Pathfinder, 1984.

Martin, Tony. *Race First.* Westport, CT: Greenwood Press, 1967.

McCloud, Aminah Beverly. *African American Islam.* New York: Routledge, 1995.

Metcalf, Barbara D., ed. *Making Muslim Space in North America and Europe.* Berkeley: University of California Press, 1996.

Michaels, Walter Benn. *Our America: Nativism, Modernism, and Pluralism.* Durham, NC: Duke University Press, 1995.

Moses, Wilson J. *Black Messiahs and Uncle Toms: Social and Literary Manipulations of a Religious Myth.* University Park, PA: Penn State University Press, 1993.

————. *The Golden Age of Black Nationalism, 1850–1925.* New York: Oxford University Press, 1978.

Moses, Wilson J., ed. *Classical Black Nationalism: From the American Revolution to Marcus Garvey.* New York: New York University Press, 1996.

Mottahedeh, Roy P. "The Shuʻubiyya Controversy and the Social History of Early Islamic Iran." *IJMES 7* (1976): 161–182.

Naff, Alixa. *Becoming American: The Early Arab Immigrant Experience.* Carbondale, IL: Southern Illinois University Press, 1985.

Norris, H. T. "Shuʻubiyyah in Arabic Literature." In *ʻAbbasid Belles-Lettres,* edited by J. Ashtiany et al. Cambridge: Cambridge University Press, 1990.

Patterson, Orlando. *Ethnic Chauvinism: The Reactionary Impulse.* New York: Stein and Day, 1977.

Perry, Bruce. *Malcolm: The Life of a Man Who Changed Black America.* Barrytown, NY: Station Hill, 1991.

Poston, Larry. *Islamic Daʻwah in the West.* New York: Oxford University Press, 1992.

Raboteau, Albert J. *A Fire in the Bones: Reflections of African-American Religious History.* Boston: Beacon Press, 1995.

Redkey, Edwin S. *Black Exodus: Black Nationalist and Back-to-Africa Movements, 1890–1910.* New Haven: Yale, 1969.

Roediger, David R. *The Wages of Whiteness: Race and the Making of the American Working Class.* London: Verso, 1992.

Said, Edward W. *Orientalism.* New York: Vintage Books, 1979.

Saler, Benson, Charles A. Ziegler, and Charles B. Moore, *UFO Crash at Roswell: The Genesis of a Modern Myth.* Washington, DC: Smithsonian Institution Press, 1997.

Satter, Beryl. "Marcus Garvey, Father Divine, and the Gender Politics of Race Difference and Race Neutrality." *American Quarterly* 48, no. 1 (1996): 43–76.

Seraile, William. *Voice of Dissent: Theophilus Gould Steward (1843–1924) and Black America.* Brooklyn, NY: Carlson, 1991.

Shimoni, Yaacov. *Political Dictionary of the Arab World.* New York: Macmillan, 1987.

Slusser, George, and Eric S. Rabkin, eds. *Fights of Fancy: Armed Conflict in Science Fiction and Fantasy.* Athens, GA: University of Georgia Press, 1993.

Smith, Steven T. "An Historical Account of the American Muslim Mission with Specific Reference to North Carolina." Master's thesis, Southeastern Baptist Theological Seminary, 1984.

Sollors, Werner. *Beyond Ethnicity: Consent and Descent in American Culture.* New York: Oxford, 1986.

Stanton, William. *The Leopard's Spots: Scientific Attitudes toward Race in America, 1815–59.* Chicago: University of Chicago Press, 1960.

Stocking, George W. *Victorian Anthropology.* New York: The Free Press, 1987.

Stuckey, Sterling. *The Ideological Origins of Black Nationalism.* Boston: Beacon Press, 1972.

Thomas, Richard W. *Life for Us Is What We Make It: Building Black Community in Detroit, 1915–1945.* Bloomington, IN: Indiana University Press, 1992.

Turner, Richard Brent. *Islam in the African-American Experience.* Bloomington, IN: Indiana University Press, 1997.

Ueda, Reed. *Postwar Immigrant America: A Social History.* Boston: St. Martin's Press, 1994.

Van DeBurg, William L. *New Day in Babylon: The Black Power Movement and American Culture, 1965–1975.* Chicago: University of Chicago Press, 1992.

Von Grunebaum, Gustave E., ed. *Unity and Variety in Muslim Civilization.* Chicago: University of Chicago Press, 1955.

Waugh, Earle H. and Frederick M. Denny, eds. *The Shaping of an American Islamic Discourse: A Memorial to Fazlur Rahman.* Atlanta: Scholars Press, 1998.

Wellhausen, Julius. *The Religio-Political Factions in Early Islam.* Translated by R. C. Ostle and S. M. Walzer. Amsterdam: North Holland Publishing, 1975.

Williams, Delores S. *Sisters in the Wilderness: The Challenge of Womanist God-Talk.* Maryknoll, NY: Orbis, 1994.

Wilson, Peter Lamborn. *Sacred Drift: Essays on the Margins of Islam.* San Francisco: City Lights Books, 1993.

Wolfenstein, Eugene Victor. *The Victims of Democracy: Malcolm X and the Black Revolution.* Berkeley: University of California Press, 1981.

Woodward, C. Vann. *Origins of the New South, 1877–1913.* Baton Rouge, LA: Louisiana State Press, 1951.

Wright, Louis E. "The Political Thought of Elijah Muhammad: Innovation and Continuity in Western Tradition." Ph.D. diss., Howard University, 1987.

Wuthnow, Robert. *Christianity in the Twenty-First Century: Reflections on the Challenges Ahead.* New York: Oxford, 1993.

Yates, Frances A. *The Rosicrucian Enlightenment.* London: Routledge and Kegan Paul, 1972.

INDEX

Abdallah, Muhammad Nur, 120–121,
154n. 17, 155nn. 32, 33
Afro-Descendant Upliftment Society,
111
Ahmad, Ghulam, 71
The Ahmadiya Movement, 70–71, 92
Ali, Muhammad (formerly Cassius Clay),
112
Ali, Noble Drew (formerly Timothy
Drew): 1, 7, 15, 16, 18, 64, 74, 85,
134; ahistorical elements in the
thought of, 135, 137; the ambiguous
particularism of, 61–62, 136–137;
and the Black Shriners, 25;
esotericism in the thought of, 56–61;
and Garveyism, 46; hagiography of,
47; as leader of Moorish Science
Temple, 47–48; moral teachings of,
60; overview of, 17; particularism in
the thought of, 46, 54, 61–62,
136–137; universalism in the thought
of, 46, 61–62, 136–137; use of *The
Aquarian Gospel of Jesus the Christ* by,
58–59; use of Rosicrucian texts by,
59–61; views of, on black identity
and black nationalism, 52–56; views
of, on Islam, 46, 54–56
AMMCOP, 126
Ansari, Samuel, 155 n. 34
The Aquarian Gospel of Jesus the Christ,
58–59, 147n. 27
The Arab Cold War, 92–93
Asad, Talal, 3, 142n. 11
Autobiography of Malcolm X, 86, 94, 111
al-Azhar, University of, 100, 131

Azzam, Abd al-Rahman, 93–95, 104
Azzam, Omar, 94

Baghdadi, Ali, 115
Bilal ibn Rabah: appropriation of, by
Edward W. Blyden, 36; appropriation
of, by Wallace D. Muhammad, 108,
119–121, 137; and classical Islam, 8
The Black Church: deradicalization of,
149n. 8; the importance of, from
1880 to 1920, 14; in the thought of
Elijah Muhammad, 65, 68
black consciousness movement, 117–119
black identity. *See* identity
black liberation. *See* liberation
black messianism. *See* messianism
The Black Muslims in America (Lincoln),
2, 142n. 15
The Black Shriners, 45
Blyden, Edward Wilmot: 1, 15, 17, 18,
61, 74, 85, 134; appropriation of, in
Garvey movement, 50–51; and black
messianism, 22, 33–43; and
civilizationism, 24–5, 29–30, 36, 42;
contact of, with West African
Muslims, 28–29; early career of
23–25; essentialism in the thought of,
136; overview of, 16; particularism in
the thought of, 22–23, 33–43; and
the publication of *Islam, Christianity,
and the Negro Race*, 37–38; trip of, to
the Holy Land, 26–28; universalism
in the thought of, 22–23, 33–43;
views of, regarding Islam, 25–33,
36–37; and Zionism, 40–42

169

Printed in the United States
15896LVS00005B/1-15